THE CRISIS
OF THE
DEMOCRATIC
INTELLECT

THE CRISIS
OF THE
DEMOCRATIC
INTELLECT

THE PROBLEM OF GENERALISM AND SPECIALISATION
IN TWENTIETH-CENTURY SCOTLAND

George Elder Davie D. Litt., F.R.S.E.

POLYGON
Edinburgh

© George Elder Davie 1986
Polygon Books, 48 Pleasance, Edinburgh, EH8 9TJ.

Typeset 10/11 point Garamond at
Edinburgh University Student Publications Board,
48 Pleasance, Edinburgh, EH8 9TJ.

Printed in Great Britain by
Butler and Tanner, Frome, Somerset.

British Library Cataloguing in Publication Data
Davie, George E.
  The crisis of the democratic intellect:
  the problem of generalism and specialism
  in twentieth-century Scotland.
    1. Education — Philosophy — History — 20th century
  I Title
  370.1   LA132

  ISBN 0 948275 18 9
  ISBN 0 948275 20 0 pbk

The Publisher acknowledges subsidy from the
Scottish Arts Council towards the publication of this volume.

PREFACE

A sequel to *The Democratic Intellect: Scotland and her Universities in the Nineteenth Century*, the present book considers the paradoxical fact that at the end of World War I the long continued and deliberate movement away from a university education of a generalist type, peculiar to Scotland, and towards a more specialising system, similar to that in other countries, was suddenly put into reverse. Instead of doing away with the inherited order, so as to put the practical on a level with the theoretical, why did the Scots go out of their way to re-establish the primacy of intellect? Is it true, as some authorities claim, that this cultural reaction of the Scottish twenties indicates a "loss of creative vitality" which, expressing itself in "a grimly authoritarian and narrow approach to education" is responsible for "some of the more depressing aspects of modern Scotland" such as "the fear of what is new"?

Based on a systematic reappraisal of the arguments of the Scottish twenties, the ensuing pages present a different view. Properly understood, this restoration of philosophy to its privileged position as the pivot of a structured course provided the institutional background, as well as the springboard, for the renaissance of the twenties, the intellectual achievements of which, in the way of both poetry and ideas, are increasingly earning for themselves the respect of the rest of the world. No doubt, in Scotland itself, the move to reawakening may seem to have for the time being petered out. But the cause of the present difficulty is that the new wine has broken the old bottles, leaving the Scottish people apparently incapable of appreciating the value of the very considerable contribution made by the country to the intellect of the twentieth century.

The essence of the present book's argument was first formulated in a paper presented to the Royal Society of Edinburgh in 1984, and it is by permission of the Society that I make use of a version of this in the early part of the book. In addition, acknowledgement is due to the Humanities Research Centre of the Australian National University where, as a visiting fellow in 1977, I was privileged to discuss John Anderson with the philosophers of Australia, during the celebrations marking the fiftieth anniversary of his arrival among them. I have also to thank Valda and Michael Grieve for (among other kindnesses) permission to quote from the poetry of Hugh MacDiarmid.

The actual making of the book owes a great deal to four persons who have all, in their time, gone through Edinburgh philosophy. I have in particular to thank Dr Murdo Macdonald of the Department of Psychology, and Mr Richard Gunn of the Department of Politics, not only for their encouragement and criticism, but for their assistance in organising the scattered materials into a whole. With them, I would like to acknowledge the considerable help given by Mr Peter Kravitz, in the midst of his labours to make the relaunched *Edinburgh Review*, of which he is editor, worthy of the great name it has inherited from its two predecessors: the long-lived periodical edited by Francis Jeffrey, and the short-lived, but equally distinguished, journal produced by Adam Smith and his friends. Finally, I have to thank Elspeth Davie for keeping an eye on the evolving argument about first principles, helping me to eliminate confusions and irrelevancies.

George Davie
Edinburgh
June 1986

CONTENTS

PROLOGUE

It used to be noted that visitors to Scotland without a taste for metaphysics were liable to be nonplussed by the questions publicly debated, because of the tendency for arguments about mundane matters to develop into arguments about first principles and for ordinary problems about material things to turn into rarefied problems of the relation of matter to mind. Commenting caustically on this situation, Dr Johnson remarked that Scotland was the only country in the civilised world in which the advance of learning and the diffusion of culture had not been accompanied by a corresponding advance in the material quality of life, while William Cobbett, putting the same thing from a rather different point of view, spoke of the Scots of his time as having the absurd idea that the way to improve the condition of the working man was not to give him "bacon" with a small "b", but "Bacon" with a big "b".

The facts, as thus stated, were not disputed by the Scots, many of whom, indeed, had a certain sympathy with these criticisms; but generation after generation, a core of Scottish orthodoxy composed of persons of the most varied status and points of view, nevertheless held to the opinion that their country had got its priorities right. The opposing course was considered by them to be a distortion of human nature which, though perhaps making things easier in the short-run, would be in the long-run disastrous to the quality of life.

But the features to which Johnson and Cobbett drew attention are now often considered to be no longer characteristic of Scotland. The proverbial phrase "metaphysical Scotland", so far as it ever had any meaning at all, applies only to the country as it was, and has no relevance whatever to the country as it is. I cannot agree here, and my reason for writing about Scotland and her universities in the twentieth century is to show that the outcome of a public debate on education, which took the problem back to philosophy and first principles, had the same sort of influence in determining the social and cultural situation of the Scotland in which we live as the metaphysical debates of the Disruption had in determining the social and cultural situation of the Scotland of the nineteenth century. Like the Church-State crisis of 1833-1843, the twentieth-century struggle

i

between the Scottish universities and the Scottish Education Department not only occupied a frenzied decade (1917-1927) on a complex and difficult problem which in most other countries would have been regarded as academic and left to the metaphysicians, but (what is its most significant feature for us and our time) resulted in the break-up of a fundamental institution which had kept the Scottish people together. Just as the ten-year struggle between Church and State over the democratisation of the Church of Scotland terminated in a spectacular secession, which lost the Church its central place in Scottish society, so the debate in the twenties resulted in a disruption of the Scottish educational system in which the universities turned their backs on the S.E.D. and the Scottish schools in order to join themselves, in due course, with the system of schools and universities in England, under the auspices of the Department of Education and Science. If historians of Scottish society are ever to throw real light on the malaise of modern Scottish education to which they very properly call attention, it is, I would argue, to this twentieth-century break-up of the Scottish educational system that they should turn their attention.

In the course of working critically over my view that the intellectual depth and philosophical seriousness of early twentieth-century Scotland is greatly underestimated, I have sought to check on my memories of the latter stages of the period as well as second-hand accounts of earlier times in the light of a wide-ranging survey of the writings produced contemporaneously, the number and range of which amazed me. There were the very extensive and revealing files in Register House on the subject of Ordinance 70 (1913-1923), there were the remarkably readable volumes of the *Scottish Educational Journal* (the teachers' paper) from 1918 (its foundation year) on to the end of the twenties, there were the books and articles by the Scottish professoriate as well as the often very outspoken letters to (and leaders in) the press on the subject of the educational controversy, and, besides these, the minutes of the senates and general councils of the various universities, and last, but of great importance, the poetry and the criticism produced by the Scottish Renaissance movement which was created against the background of the Ordinance 70 struggles and made use of the *Scottish Educational Journal* as an important vehicle for publicising its views. Remarkable, in my judgement, for its quality as well as its quantity, the very variety of materials available was too great to be read by one person and I have therefore proceeded by critically comparing what I remember with portions of the printed word. Produced in this impressionistic way, my account of Scotland and her universities in the twentieth century seeks to raise questions rather than to definitively answer them. At the same time, there is one central point which I want to get over, namely that the Scotland of our own century is still a metaphysical country and that no one will make sense of what is going on without a modicum of philosophy.

In order to understand the key position of the philosophy classes within Scotland's educational tradition considered as a whole, it is necessary to bear in mind the cultural revolution — the expression is, I hope, not too strong — made possible by the creation of a separate department of education for Scotland in 1885, which, given the means for the implementation of its plan in and around 1900 as a result of Andrew Carnegie's magnificent donation to the land of his birth, was transforming the educational scene out of all recognition. Undoing, in a couple of decades, an independent tradition built up over centuries, the S.E.D. altered the pattern of Scottish education so as to prepare it for the new role of being a subordinate though distinctive part of what was to be an all-British system, controlled from the centre. In a burst of bureaucratic planning which the sister-nation watched interestedly with a view to imitating what was good in it, the S.E.D had, by 1908, completed its renewal of the basic structures. Secondary education had been separated from primary education and a whole series of new schools set up. The age of entry to the university had been upped by two years and a stiffish matriculation examination introduced where there had been no examination before, and finally remodelling of the degree courses had been set in motion which would make the universities centres of specialisation and end their generalist tradition.

In spite of their evident impatience with the inherited system, the functionaries in charge of the transformation of Scottish education were by no means iconoclasts. Their purpose was not so much to destroy the characteristic quality of the traditional system, which, following Walter Elliot, I have called "democratic intellectualism", as to restate its values in terms which would make them appicable to the new all-British system which the twentieth century was bringing into being. The new arrangements were still to be democratic but not in the same wide sense as the arrangements of the old system, which, according to the common criticism, had lowered standards allowing, even encouraging, too many unfit persons to enter the university classrooms. "Qualifying examination", as it was called, was intro-

duced — the ancestor and inspiration of what was until recently the
11-plus — so as to separate out at a very early age those capable of
benefitting from further education from those who in the eyes of the
educational experts of the time were, so to speak, dead-end kids
incapable of any further progress. The foundations of public
standards of culture were still further strengthened by a "Lower
Leaving Certificate" taken at about fifteen — the model of our O-
level — which would make a new separation of the sheep from the
goats according to the standards of academic progress. Finally, two
years later, "Highers" made the decisive distinction between those
who were capable of carrying their education beyond the school to
university and those who could proceed no further. The point of this
rigorous selection was to ensure that no fit person was kept out of the
university by being financially disadvantaged. Put in a position to
make the running because of the generosity of Carnegie, the S.E.D.
had set a pattern of educational progress which was to extend to the
whole of the United Kingdom in the course of a century.

At the same time, the S.E.D. sought to redefine the intellectual
principle of the old Scottish system so as to adapt it to the new Britain
in much the same way as they had done with the democratic principle
inherited from the Scottish past. Not taken seriously by the sister-
nation until the new universities began to be founded in England in
the fifties, the S.E.D. idea here was — roughly stated — to steer a
middle course between specialisation and generalism. But the
Scottish administrators were totally out of sympathy with the
traditional idea in their country that all entrants to university — at
least in the Arts and Science departments, should first go through a
common course study structured around philosophy, Latin and
mathematics — subjects which, the S.E.D. felt, were only of limited
utility and which, if compulsory, would only be kept going, in
modern conditions, by a policy legitimising superficiality and
smattering. The universities were thus to be centres for specialisation, but at the same time the S.E.D., taking its stand on what it
regarded as the valuable side of the Scottish tradition, had its face
firmly against premature specialisation and narrow specialisation.
Most clearly illustrated in the S.E.D. plans for university courses, the
proposal was that whether taking a general (i.e. pass) degree or an
honours degree, the student was to pursue a limited specialisation,
not only in the sense of having to concentrate his attention not on one
single subject but on two allied subjects (e.g. mathematics and
physics or English literature and English language) but also being

iv

obliged to study two or three isolated subjects of his choice, perhaps unconnected with his specialities, in order to ensure the broadening of his mind. Specialisation at the universities, thus involved a combination of "majoring" in a couple of subjects while at the same time "minoring' (if the expression be admitted) in a variety of other subjects. But in the schools specialisation even in this limited sense was forbidden and up to the Leaving Certificate whatever their bias or preferences, students were compelled to give equal time to the main subjects of the curriculum and were forbidden to drop any of them. On the intellectual side therefore the system which emerged as the result of the three Scottish reforms diverged considerably, and I think deliberately, from the system of specialisation of the school level as permitted south of the border, and, for that reason, was admired by the many educationalists in England who were critical of their country's arrangements in this respect.

Influential on both sides of the border, during the twentieth century, the reforms launched by the S.E.D. in 1908 are now widely admired as a bold and practical programme for realising under modern conditions the values distinctive of Scotland's traditional system of democratic intellectualism. In consequence, the storm of protest aroused in Scotland from 1917-1927 by the S.E.D. schemes, the result of which was to restore, in the face of S.E.D. opposition, the compulsion on all pass students to take a generalist course modelled on the old and structured around philosophy, is felt by the present generation — in so far as it is noticed at all — as a retrograde step which destroyed or weakened what was best in the S.E.D. schemes.

But though this interpretation of the struggles of 1917-1927 as being a backlash on the part of reactionaries is not without truth in reference to certain details (e.g. the fuss made over Lower Latin), it should, rather, be seen as a Scottish version of the argument about educational and cultural fundamentals. It soon becomes clear, according to my way of thinking, that the S.E.D. and its critics are engaged in debating the question as to whether the aim of education is to produce people who, in Arnold's words, see life steadily and see it whole, or people who are trained to look at things in detail and who are expert in isolating problems and in propounding observationally testable hypotheses in regard to them and thereby producing obviously socially useful results in the short term.

The former, classicist, idea is that a country should be managed by an elite capable of taking long views and wide views of things, who are, in the Greek manner, generalist and, one might say, amateur in their outlook. This clashes with the modernist idea in which it is proposed to have an elite composed of persons taking close views of things, specialists in one line or another, albeit specialists in the broad sense characteristic of the S.E.D.'s pronouncements on education. In Scotland these opposing positions were both developed in the most uncompromising manner, to the point of making the conflict irreconcilable. It was clear enough to both sides that the S.E.D. meant to demolish the privileged position traditionally given to "useless" subjects like philosophy, literature and pure mathematics, but the rival parties, working in the light of their opposed principles, put entirely different interpretations on this fact. The classicists saw this move as involving a provincialisation of Scotland which would leave a monopoly of the "useless" subjects it considered necessary to the training of an elite in the hands of Oxford and Cambridge and which would thus transform the Scottish universities into centres for the production of efficient under-labourers in the system. By contrast, the modernist party welcomed the changes introduced into the status of the Scottish universities because the levelling introduced by the S.E.D. would not stop with Scotland but would spread over the whole of the educational system of the United Kingdom thereby initiating a great educational experiment which, it was hoped, would be a beacon light for the progress of the whole of mankind. In opposition to the view of some of the classicists that the S.E.D. reforms would result in the Anglicisation of Scotland, the modernists pointed out that the Anglicisation of Scotland would, if properly managed, go hand-in-hand with a Scotticisation of England—a hope which seemed to be borne out by the interest English educationalists had shown in the S.E.D. schemes. The result would be an all-British system of education which would have at last transcended the artificial divisions of nationality, established in more backward ages than our own, and crushed the ambitions of feudal nationalism. The classicists, on the other hand, held that this dream of a transcendence of nationality was, in the last resort, a visionary scheme which was kept alive only by the blindness of their opponents to the limitations of human nature.

Thus developing into an opposition between an optimistic and a pessimistic estimate of the human situation, it is distinctive among other debates of the kind in giving free rein on both sides to an *odium theologicum*, Pelagianism on the one hand and the doctrine of original sin on the other.

PART I

SCOTTISH PHILOSOPHY AND SPECIALISATION

I

DARROCH THE MODERNIST

In order to achieve a much needed long view of the commanding position occupied by philosophy in the traditional curriculum of Scottish education, it is necessary to turn one's attention away from the well-known controversies of the eighteenth and nineteenth centuries, where philosophy was engaged in defending its status as queen of the sciences against this or that challenge to the legitimacy of its role, and to fix one's gaze instead on the great crisis of the twentieth century — the Ordinance 70 Affair (1917-1927). This, precipitated by a temporarily successful attempt on the part of philosophy to reassert its shattered authority, led in the event to a breakdown of the unity of the Scottish system of education, preparing the way for the present state of affairs when philosophy has lost its position as a general subject, that is to say as an educational tool in the sense that the three Rs are educational tools, and has resigned itself to the role of a specialist subject of a somewhat exclusive sort, with little to say to others and of which the value is often questioned.

By contrast with the struggle of the early twentieth century, the eighteenth and nineteenth century controversies about philosophy, though remarkably illuminating in certain regards, are much less valuable for anyone wanting to get an all-in view of the function of philosophy in regard to Scottish life and learning, in the sense that they exhibit philosophy only in one relation at a time. For example the dispute between Dugald Stewart and Francis Jeffrey (1804 and 1810) concerns itself only with the challenge to the utility of philosophy from the point of view of admittedly useful sciences like chemistry, while the Leslian controversy of the same period is fully taken up with the relation of philosophy to theology, or again, *The Philosophy of Consciousness* (1838-1839)[1] by J. F. Ferrier concentrates simply on the relationship of the ethical side of philosophy itself to its intellectual side. By contrast the crisis in the twentieth century obliges those who study it to work towards a

3

comprehensive view, an all-in view, because, being the occasion when the system as a whole began to become unstuck, the episode involves a series of connected arguments which successively exhibit the relation of philosophy not only to the other subjects in the curriculum but also to the chief forms of what could be called extra-. mural culture.

The starting point of this remarkable debate was the fact that in sweeping away the rigid structure of the Arts curriculum in preparation for more extensive reforms, the cultural revolution of 1892 had left it quite undecided as to whether the universities were to continue to be the standard-setters of the Scottish educational system or whether the Scottish Education Department was to regulate the universities in the interests of the newly founded system of secondary schools. The Scottish universities, said the S.E.D., were not private institutions like Oxford and Cambridge, but State universities, and the Arts curriculum therefore should be remodelled on utilitarian lines so as to enable the faculties to perform effectively what was now to be their chief function — the training of teachers for the new schools. Claiming to have been always autonomous in regard to the Scottish state in somewhat the same sense as the Scottish Church claimed to be, the universities, in spite of the reforms, were continuing to give a privileged status to the very subjects which the teachers and the S.E.D. (after 1904) felt to be more appropriate to the old system when the Arts Faculty was a training ground for Ministers of Religion.

The tension began to define itself in terms of philosophy as the indirect result of a series of concessions which the universities made to the S.E.D. in the interests of the would-be teachers. Abolishing the privileged position of philosophy classes as compulsory elements in the curriculum, Edinburgh from 1908 allowed the students to take in place of the philosophy class the class in the theory of education. At once the Professor of Education, a lively man called Alexander Darroch, attracted to himself very large classes by expounding an American pragmatist view of human nature as being much more in accord with the modern programme and practices of education than the view of human nature given in the official classes of philosophy from the standpoint of dualist metaphysics, inherited from the Scottish Philosophy of Common Sense (which, in Edinburgh, at least, lived on until after 1920). In consequence, the logic class and moral philosophy class began to empty in Edinburgh, and by 1916, when the S.E.D. started to put on the pressure for further con-

4

cessions, relaxations in the compulsory Latin and compulsory mathematics, the university professors dug in their heels and, taking advantage of a kind of trade-off with education made possible by the arrangements for the new Bachelor of Education degree, they removed the theory of education from the list of philosophical options and in effect made the old philosophy classes compulsory for all Arts students just as they had been in the nineteenth century. Amongst the teaching profession in Scotland as a whole, this snub to the status of education as a subject was regarded as an insult to their professional dignity, and this resentment at Darroch's demotion was one of the factors which led them to unite their various separate associations, their secondary school teachers, primary teachers, etc. in a new and enlarged Educational Institute of Scotland refounded with a view to pushing their claims both for salary and for professional status.

As seen by the E.I.S. leadership, what made the curriculum of the universities unsuitable for teacher-training was its being based on "the semi-religious impulses of the revival of letters, and unaffected by the advance of physical and mental science in the last fifty years".[2] No doubt the compulsory injection of the traditional trio — logic, Latin, mathematics — might be defended as a liberalising element which checks specialisation, but the teachers' reply, voiced by their champion Darroch, was to call for a new set of general studies appropriate to mankind's advance in self-knowledge as well as to the changed situation of Scottish education. "The modern universities do not exist for turning out a few classical scholars or a few expert mathematicians, but for the education of the many who have neither the aptitude nor the ability to profit by the intensive study of these subjects." The general studies of most importance for the university stage in Arts for the majority are the sciences which deal with the problems of adult life, e.g. economics, history, political philosophy, for which no extensive study of classics or mathematics is necessary.[3]

Darroch's word carried all the more weight with the teaching body in Scotland as a whole, and not just in the Edinburgh area, because his educational proposals were grounded in the Deweyite philosophy of pragmatism which in the years 1912-1921 was having a great vogue in America. According to Darroch's lucid if not very systematic exposition, the kind of philosophy which has something valuable to say to modern education is one which takes as the model of all knowledge, not our study of the world in its abstract static aspects, as in mathematics, but in its concrete dynamic character, as in biology. The theory of knowledge, as developed in the philosophy classes proper, is, he pointed out, an introspective analysis from the standpoint of adults which occupies itself with sorting out somewhat artificial problems, irrelevant to everyday life (e.g. "the nature of the external world") and often in principle insoluble, whereas what teachers want is a genetic experimental study of the passage from the standpoint of the infant to that of the adult which is capable of giving observation-based quantitative information as to the much debated, but little understood question of the value or otherwise of specialisation, of the ages at which it is appropriate to start this subject or that, and as to the possibility of measuring intelligence by defining it in terms of behaviour traits.[4]

These experimental researches into education which Darroch promoted in Edinburgh with the help of pupils like James Drever (Senior), the Lecturer in Psychology, overthrew the ideas on the subject which had been put forward by Darroch's predecessor S. S. Laurie from the *a priori* standpoint of the Scottish school of which Laurie was the last considerable representative. According to Laurie, it was obvious that the proper preparation for science is a humanist grounding in great literature, because the technical language of science is parasitic on, that is to say, presupposes a grasp of, the ordinary language of everyday life which study of literature enables us to master. But for the generation influenced by Darroch's pragmatism, Laurie is here illegitimately trying to prove, by appeal to common sense and intuition, a proposition which could conceivably be refuted by experiment, and would have to be proved by experiment, namely that in some way literary study is very useful to scientific study. Had not the experiments, observations and measurements of the American Thorndike — much discussed in James Drever's textbooks — established conclusively that there is very little carry-over between two subjects as different as science and literature? But the separation of studies which is thus fixed as an unquestionable fact — the necessity of an intellectual division of labour — does not, according to Darroch, lead to narrow specialisation, since, as a matter of empirical fact, in addition to his trade, a person has to perform various other roles, parent, citizen, etc. each of which requires a certain amount of skill and knowledge.

Having attacked as absurd the unique claims made for theoretical subjects like mathematics, metaphysics and classics, which are occupied in contemplating the eternal verities to the neglect of the surging evolutionary aspect of things, Darroch goes on to criticise the privileged position accorded in Scottish education to the "lads of parts", that is the small group whose talents enable them to do well in these abstract static subjects like literature etc. Because of the almost religious aura attaching to this trio of subjects, a great deal of time is wasted in teaching them not only to the gifted, but to the ungifted majority, often in the same class, and schoolmasters regularly neglect the latter in favour of the former. In the Scotland of the future, all this must be changed, the education of the few must be sharply separated from that of the many, and the chief energies of the teachers are to be devoted to educating not the "lads of parts" but the "lads of no parts" who not merely are in the majority, but have plenty of talents, provided one does not restrict the notion of talents narrowly to the subjects in the evaluational and analytic group. If Scottish educators are ever to be really socially useful, they should spend less time educating the head and much more time educating the hands and the heart. In the past, education in Scotland has been far too elitist, to the great social disadvantage of the population as a whole. In the future it must occupy itself with egalitarian principles, and see that its duty lies with the many rather than with the few.

All this sounds strong doctrine, but from the point of view of those who cared for the Scottish universities' tradition, there was nothing so very formidable in Darroch's philosophy since he regularly pointed out the limits of his new utilitarianism, making it clear that in view of the unpredictability of the future, we can never actually know at any given time what is socially useful. Marxism, a position with which he had considerable sympathy, explains the past but not the future in relation to which we have all to take up the position of prophet, not of scientist. Darroch thus, as Kemp Smith said in his exchange of letters with the Baron von Hügel,[5] had, in virtue of being a pupil of Simon Laurie, "sufficient philosophy to recognise the weakness of the popular psychologies and theories of education but hardly sufficient strength of character to stem the tide". In himself, therefore, Darroch was no problem.

Darroch, however, wasn't acting alone, and what was obnoxious to the university professors about the kind of anti-elitism preached by him in his heady prelections, was that it was actually sanctioned by the rationalising policy of Sir John Struthers of the S.E.D. The proponent of organisation almost on a German scale, spurred on by an obsessive fear of overlaps, wastage, etc., Struthers saw the role of the Scottish universities in the future not as being centres of *la grande culture*, but as becoming first-rate training colleges for turning out a very efficient set of schoolteachers for secondary education. The ideal to be worked for was to produce an educational system in which — as in Germany — the general and liberal education was completed by the time school was over, and in which the universities could devote themselves wholly to specialisation. There was to be no elitism, one subject was to be on a level with the others, none of them privileged, and the only criterion was the extent to which in an observable, measurable way each contributed to social utility. Using the resources of the State to implement the ideas which were being canvassed by Darroch, Struthers was finally able to produce a situation in which the students who filled the ordinary classes were becoming more and more utilitarian-minded and less and less ready to sympathise with the metaphysical flights and speculative passages which, going beyond the actual subject matter of the class, had been for long such a notable feature of the professorial lectures.

But whatever be the value of Darroch *sub specie aeterni*, there is no doubt of his significance as the spokesman for a party of discreet State-legitimised revolt against the traditional standards. The teachers and the professors were thus locked in conflict, the nature of which emerges very clearly in the course of a speech by the E.I.S. leader, Duncan McGillivray, in 1923, at the height of the crisis. From McGillivray's point of view, the universities were betraying their duty to Scotland by refusing to adapt their lectures to the needs of people who were to be modern schoolteachers. The universities, he said, ought to be an integral part of Scottish education as "an organic whole". In the past, before the period of reform, that is what they had been, but nowadays they were turning their backs on the schools and had ceased to regard the sources from which they drew their very way of life. Since 1870 the universities had played neither a great nor a generous part. Individual professors had spoken out, but the majority were cold, indifferent, even hostile in the sense of having made great difficulties about co-operating with the S.E.D.'s plan of building up a great system of secondary schools equal to that of any other country.[6]

The universities, however, for their part, thought that they had conceded too much, not too little, to the S.E.D. policy — with disastrous effect on their standing as centres of culture. Elaborating this criticism, an article in the *Nineteenth Century* for 1927 makes the point that the pressure from the S.E.D. for adapting the courses more to the needs of intending teachers had produced a lowering of standards which was making nonsense of the historic roles of the universities. The new admission system — by way of the Leaving Certificate — is affecting standards. Hundreds of students are admitted whom it was never meant to admit to the Scottish M.A. In the old days, mere book knowledge was not enough for entry, but rather a desire for education and a developed intelligence. Nowadays, under the S.E.D. system of highly specialised instruction and the force-feeding of pupils, it is quite possible for second-rate minds to get to the university. The new growth in numbers is coped with by vocational degrees and what this development means is that the Arts faculties are becoming institutions for the training of teachers. In consequence, the cultural element hardly exists in the Scottish universities today. It cannot exist because the majority of students "neither expect, desire or even understand it".[7]

Equally concerned with the problem of the lowering of standards, other commentators, writing a decade earlier when the crisis was in its opening stages, pointed out that the kind of democratisation which had developed as the result of the S.E.D.'s teacher training policy coincided with the failure of the universities to hold the loyalty of the classes which had constituted in the past the core of the Scottish elite:

"England [said an H.M.I. who knew both countries well] has schools for all classes, whereas Scotland does not educate its upper classes. Nobles count less in Scotland than Deans of Guild, and in consequence Scotland is ceasing to train her own leaders. The apex of her educational system is on English soil, the lower slopes only are securely based on Scottish soil. This is an accepted factor, shown not only by the increasing popularity of the English public schools with the well-born and well-to-do, but also by the fact that, in the case of the middle classes, the principal function of an undergraduate degree in the Scottish universities is to prepare clever students for taking a second undergraduate degree at Oxford or Cambridge. . . . It wasn't always so."[8]

But of course, in the eyes of the S.E.D. this failure of the universities to produce an elite of their own more and more constituted an advantage rather than a disadvantage. The important thing for Scotland as the Scots were at last beginning to see was not a preoccupation with pinnacles and peaks, but with the down-to-earth routine of keeping education going:

9

What are prophets and priests and kings,
What's ocht to the people o' Scotland?
Speak and Cruivie'll goam at you,
Gilsanquhar jalouse your dottlin![9]

The ordinary people of Scotland have no time for the higher culture, and the ordinary people of Scotland are right.

2

BURNET AND THE DEFENCE
OF GENERALISM

Professor of Greek at St Andrews from 1891 to 1926, John Burnet
was an active member of the Scottish Classical Association, founded
in 1902 for the purpose of defending the privileged position of Greek
which the S.E.D. was seeking to suppress. The victory of the S.E.D.
in this matter after 1904 did not depress Burnet but stimulated him to
some very original reflections on the nature of education, the result
of which was the dawning insight that what really mattered about
classical culture wasn't so much the study of the Greek language itself
as the keeping alive of the broad-based, intellectually versatile
Renaissance outlook which had developed with the revival of the
classics. The dangerous thing about the S.E.D. policy was not its anti-
classical bias, but its vocationalism. In opposing the S.E.D., the cause
Burnet stood for was not that of classical languages, but of generalism
as expressed and maintained by the privileged position of philosophy
in the curriculum.

In posing anew the problem of Scotland's higher education, John
Burnet raised it from the realm of local and short-term claims to that
of global and permanent values, by directing attention to a topic
which had not been much noticed in Scotland itself — that of the
position of elites. In countries such as Germany, France, the U.S.A.
and Austria, there had been considerable discussion as to the training
required for those who were to be the leaders of the given nation.
What has emerged, Burnet notes, is the interesting fact that in all
these countries the training of the elite occupies itself with the
seventeen to twenty age group and achieves its aim by letting the
gifted or ambitious section of the youth loose on the very group of
subjects — classics, mathematics and philosophy — which are
suspect among the Scottish educationalists on account of their
apparently non-utilitarian character.

We need an elite, said Burnet, turning to the case of Britain, just as
much as the Germans do, but we are inclined to think it will be forth-

coming without our having to trouble ourselves. This idea, he continues, has arisen because in many departments of public life we are supplied with an elite by the public schools and the Universities of Oxford and Cambridge, which do their work by imparting subjects of much the same non-utilitarian group to the same sort of age group as the German, the French and the Austrian systems occupy themselves with. The kind of elite produced for Britain by the Oxford-Cambridge system, Burnet continues, is of course of high quality — better, he thinks, than that produced by Germany. But good as it is, it is not enough for Britain as a whole because the elite it is training is drawn from a limited class and a limited area, namely well-bred people in the southern half of England. The problem thus arises as to the possibility of enriching the British elite by finding a method of recruitment, the catchment area of which will cover the masses of the society and regions of the U.K. at present outwith the range of the Oxbridge system.[1]

One would think, Burnet goes on, that Scottish education furnishes an example to the rest of Britain of how to raise an elite of precisely the sort required. But while traditionally Scotland had provided a means of finding leaders and men of initiative drawn from broader sectors of society and living outside South Britain to whom they gave an appropriately non-utilitarian training in the universities at approximately the proper age, though rather lower than elsewhere, a series of recent changes, made all of them in the wrong direction with a view to increased efficiency through specialisation, has begun to make it impossible for the Scottish universities to produce in the future the kind of elite they had produced in the past. In the first place, a rigid ladder of state examinations, constructed somewhat on the 11-plus, O-Level, A-Level lines, with a view to sharply segregating the training of the "lads of no parts" from that of the "lads of parts" in order to do better justice to both, has closed up the side entrances and back doors which traditionally had been the means of making the universities accessible to ambitious and able students of artisan and even of working-class background, who had missed the bus by leaving school early and who later in life were eager to resume their education. "It would be no less than a national calamity if students of the class I have indicated were to be permanently excluded from the universities, but that is the result to which the Regulations of the Carnegie Trust are undoubtedly tending."[2] Moreover, not only have these rationalising reforms, made in the way of introducing an education ladder, narrowed the class basis of the students from which the Scottish universities might draw the materials for an elite, but another set of State-induced changes, motivated in the same rationalising way, is in danger of extinguishing in the Scottish universities the very possibility of producing an elite at all, by abolishing, in the name of social utility and the division of labour, the general and non-utilitarian studies which all the countries in the West consider as a prerequisite of the training of the elite. Speaking of the importance of the eighteen to twenty-one age group, the period during which the student is assimilating the historical inheritance of humanity and forming a personal view of the world for himself, Burnet points out that some people, who imagine they are "practical", would have this type of education omitted altogether and start special training at seventeen or eighteen as soon as they get to the universities.[3] Instead of continuing to use the universities as a seedbed of an elite, which would offset and compensate for the limitations of the kind of elite produced for Britain by Oxford and Cambridge, the Scottish universities, under the pressure of the S.E.D. policy of specialisation which was imposed by means of the awarding and withholding of government grants, are more and more resigning themselves to letting Oxford and Cambridge monopolise the role of giving the kind of non-utilitarian and general training which is required for producing a leadership class in the country, and are increasingly finding themselves obliged to be content with the function of training up very efficient teachers for the S.E.D.'s system of secondary schools.

If these calamitous trends are allowed to work themselves out in practice and go to their full length, Scotland, Burnet is telling us, will be doomed to have the kind of education system which, organised by the State on wholly specialist utilitarian lines, will reproduce among us, and even out-do, the dismal pattern set by Germany. Burnet was thus already perfectly well aware of what recent researches into sources are disclosing, that the Carnegie Trust and the S.E.D. made no secret of their Germanising aims, and that for example Sir William McCormick, the Secretary of the Carnegie Trust, enjoyed astonishing visitors by pointing out to them that the S.E.D. exercised in reference to the Scottish universities a degree of dictatorship which no German university would ever have tolerated.[4] Understood in the light of facts like this, Burnet's book on *Higher Education and the War* — which, A. E. Taylor in his British Academy obituary points out, is not a war book at all, the discussion of the German educational system being completed and expounded in lectures in 1913[5] — ought therefore to be read as a coded document of intentionally systematic ambiguity in which, under cover of attacking the public enemy, Germany, Burnet is busily engaged in turning his guns on the private enemy of Scotland, the S.E.D. "We must not allow the Carnegie Trust to Prussianise us",[6] that is to say, to turn Scotland into a stratified society, more dismal than that of the Middle Ages, which has forgotten how to be intelligent and for which the only problems that exist are bread and butter ones. What has the appearance of being an attack on German education is thus really covert up-dating of S. S. Laurie's famous slogan: What is good for the S.E.D. is bad for Scottish education; what is good for Scottish education is bad for the S.E.D.

Similar criticisms of the changes introduced into Scotland's higher education under the auspices of the S.E.D. were no doubt voiced by other members of the Scottish Classical Association — especially Professor John Harrower of Aberdeen. What set Burnet completely apart from these others and gave his views incomparably greater weight is that in arguing for his position he went back to first principles in a philosophical analysis of the problem of intellectual specialisation. The development of modern psychology, Burnet saw, had discredited among many of the Scots, especially of the teaching profession, the old idea inherited from the Scottish Enlightenment that specialisation stultifies, in the sense of slowing down learning and liveliness of mind, whereas generalism, that is studying a broad group of different subjects, enlivens the intelligence, and increases the amount learned by comparison with single-subject study, because each discipline throws light on the others. Fixing on Thorndike's attack on the claims of generalism, both because it was the most effective of its kind, and because of the weight it carried among the teaching profession in Scotland, Burnet boldly sought to challenge conclusions arrived at as the result of psychological experiment with the help of purely philosophical arguments, that is to say, arguments that had to do with consistency and inconsistency.

The only convincing evidence against "transfer" from one subject to another which Thorndike offers — Burnet begins — is produced by a set of experiments which establish that learning in the sense of the memorisation of a set of nonsense syllables does not normally make us more efficient at memorising a different set of nonsense syllables unless there are considerable affinities — order, etc. — between the two sets. But once we understand the kind of learning involved in the memorisation Thorndike is speaking about, the facts he establishes go to prove only that transfer occurs in a limited way or not at all in what we call rote-learning, that is to say, the getting off of a book by heart in order to produce the appropriate reactions to a certain series of questions. But of course at the stage we are concerned with — the education of an elite, that is to say, a group capable of making discoveries or of devising ways of coping with unforeseeable situations — the kind of learning which is relevant is not the rote-learning of the backward examinee, but the kind of learning which Thorndike and his fellow scientists are seeking to add to — the making of discoveries, the advancement of knowledge. But this kind of discovery-learning involves not uncritical memorising but a conscious comparison of one thing or field with another altogether different thing or field, which, by noting resemblances and differences, will bring out hidden qualities in the thing we start from. What Burnet is concerned with is the fact now recognised as perfectly normal, namely that the breakthrough of a scientist in his own field, the solution of a problem he has been struggling with, very often depends on his accidental hearing from colleagues about facts in some quite different field outside his province and comparing the latter with the former.

The point Burnet is driving at here may be most effectively explained by drawing attention to the way it enables us to answer the charge made by Scottish disciples of Thorndike — like the Inspector of Schools who wrote the articles in *The Scotsman* in September 1917: "No psychologist of repute would maintain that any one subject develops general ability. The kind of attack which suits Tacitus transfers to Thucydides but not to patent law."[7] But according to Burnet this way of stating the problem — and it is still the common one, not merely outside but inside the Arts faculties of the universities — entirely misses the point. Properly understood, the illumination cast by Tacitus on patent law arises not through a one-sided process but through a double-sided process in which as a result of comparison each study simultaneously throws light upon the other. The most important side of any department of knowledge is the side on which it comes into touch with every other department. To insist on this is the true function of humanism.[8] That is to say, the study of Tacitus and the study of patent law become mutually instructive only when a comparison, both systematic and historical, discovers a middle term between them, in the principle, found in Adam Smith, Dugald Stewart and the older Scottish writers,[9] that the extension of the division of labour which leads to the material enrichment of the country also simultaneously leads to its spiritual impoverishment or, in other words, that the intensification of specialisation on which the advance of civilisation depends tends, by increasingly hindering communication between the persons involved in the various specialised sectors, to dry up the springs of inventiveness in that society. Doing what Burnet did not do for himself — developing his argument in the light of the ideas on the subject advanced by Adam Smith and the others — we can make explicit the link between Tacitus (decline and fall of civilisation or otherwise) on the one hand, and patent law (the increase or decrease of inventiveness in that society) on the other. The Thorndike view of patent law as having nothing to do with Tacitus is thus true only of the limited point of view of those who want to get up the complicated facts of patent law without understanding anything about its connection with the movement of civilisation.

But if Burnet is to discredit the S.E.D.'s infatuation with the advantages of specialisation which entirely neglects its disadvantages, it is essential for him to vindicate against Thorndike the well-foundedness of the principle on which the defence of generalism was traditionally made to rest — that subjects throw light on one another as the result of a mode of study which compares them with one another. This challenge calls for Burnet's boldest stroke. He refers the psychologists to the position promulgated by Plato in the *Theaetetus* 185a-186c that new knowledge, i.e. of hidden aspects of the situation, depends not — strictly speaking — on experience in the singular, but from a comparison of various experiences which brings to light facts not explicitly revealed by each of the experiences taken separately. To take Plato's own example in this passage, the comparison of seeing with hearing, by making us aware of a fact outside the explicit sphere of either — namely, of sound as being different in certain respects from colour — discloses to us by that very fact the existence of a mode of apprehension which, though depending on the senses, isn't sensuous in the sense in which sight and hearing are.

The vital point Burnet is making in his argument against the Scottish infatuation with specialisation would have been greatly clarified and strengthened if, as well as going to Plato, he had availed himself of the discussions of the older Scottish philosophers of the common sense epoch who, in their most remarkable analyses,[10] seek to account for the sensuous basis of the metaphysical or transcendental element in our ordinary knowledge regarding common sense, in the Platonic manner, as arising from the fact that the comparison of our various sense fields, sight, touch, hearing etc., makes explicit these qualities which remain hidden so long as each sense field is considered in isolation. Thus, according to Hume, a series of complicated comparisons, both of different visual experiences of the same thing as well as of visual experience with tactile experience of that thing, constitutes the foundation of our grasp of the metaphysical distinction between the aspects or qualities of the thing which are measurable (e.g. shape), and the aspects or qualities of the thing which are immeasurable (e.g. colour). So too in the beautiful and strong, if excessively neglected, arguments of J. F. Ferrier[11]. The most fundamental of all common sense distinctions, that of our experience of the visual extension of a thing as external to and beyond our organ of sight and of the tangible extendedness of things as also beyond, though in contact with, our organ of touch are revealed to us only in a mutual comparison of sight and touch. It is the former which reveals the distinction and relationship of the objects of touch and organ of touch and the latter which reveals the interrelation of the organ of sight and the object of sight. This principle is also at work in Adam Smith's celebrated analysis of the foundations of conscience as an experience of inwardness.[12]

It is the comparison of our own experience of our behaviour in getting hold of the object before us with our experience of the reactions of the spectators to this behaviour of ours that reveals to us the existence of a dimension of our bodily being, which is situated outside the range of our observation and is capable of being made known to us only indirectly from our observation of the other's attitude to us, that accounts for the fundamental distinction familiar to common sense, but metaphysically puzzling, between aspects of our behaviour experienceable by us and not by others, and the aspects experienceable by others and not by us. In this way, the Platonic discussion of the foundations of common sense used by Burnet to illustrate the principle that different experiences illumine one another by means of mutual comparison was carried forward and defended and deepened in passage after passage of the older philosophy which Struthers of the S.E.D. had been taught by Glasgow-Hegelian Caird, his master, to set aside as negligible, superficial and benighted — namely the great school of the Scottish thinkers of the common sense epoch, more especially the particular line among them (Hume, Smith, Brown and Ferrier) who, instead of accepting, as Reid did, the metaphysical claims made by common sense — the external world, the distinction between inner and outer etc. — as unanalysable and inexplicable, set about illuminating them by analysis.[13]

The second stage of Burnet's argument is made necessary in order to meet the reply which vocationalists like Darroch would be liable to make to the results of the critique of Thorndike. Certainly the kind of multidisciplinary education which Burnet describes as unspecialised or general, exists as a historical fact in certain societies, those where the power is held by what one could call a leisure class. In that case, however, the all-roundedness is socially justified as a means to educating certain members of this leisure class to constitute the ruling elite, and therefore, far from having the unspecialised or general character which Burnet attributes to it, this type of education is just as specialised as the unidisciplinary education which is given to the working class of the same community, to enable them to minister to the bodily and practical needs of the leisured part of the community which is thus able to specialise in the theoretical work and the giving of orders.

But, according to Burnet, historical situations like that described in Hegel's section on master and slave[14] don't destroy the fundamental distinction between specialised and generalised education or interested and disinterested knowledge, but only show that the interrelation between the two types of education which Burnet himself has in view has not been properly understood. All education, Burnet says, and not just that of the elite, should have two inseparable phases, a general one with a specialised follow-up. This union of general and special applies not only to the section of the community who go on from school to university at eighteen, but equally to the section who finish their education at eighteen and then go out to work, as well as those that finish at fifteen or sixteen and do the same thing. The general/special distinction, as well as the allied distinction of disinterested/interested, if it is properly understood (according to what Burnet says), operate differently as applied to each section. The study of Greek is, for the Professor of Greek who is a member of the elite, neither an unspecialised subject nor a disinterested study, and in his case the general and disinterested knowledge will exercise itself in the fields of his amateur acquaintance with things like clock-making and machinery. The situation is of course reversed in the case of the artisan-mechanic, professional and vocational knowledge having to do with watch-making or whatever else it might be, and the general disinterested knowledge consisting in a certain cultural curiosity, perhaps as to Greek civilisation. The important thing for Burnet is that this reciprocity of roles — what is interested knowledge for the one is disinterested knowledge for the other, and vice versa — is a guarantee of the kind of open-textured society, desired by Burnet, in which somebody who has fallen outside the ladder of schooling at the age of sixteen owing to slowness of development, or poverty, will be provided with back doors and irregular paths by which he can go on to university education at a late stage in life, and find there the educational means — catch-up classes or junior classes — which will enable him, with hard work, to make up the leeway. Instead of the rigidly stratified system, long operative in Germany and now being introduced into Scotland by the S.E.D., in which nobody could get to the university except by going up the educational ladder in the ordinary way, and in which anybody who had stepped off the ladder earlier would be permanently excluded, and in a lower class, Burnet wanted to reinstate a modernised version of the flexible system which had enabled Scottish education to draw the members of its elite from the widest possible class basis.

The third stage of Burnet's argument[15] is developed in order to meet the demand for hard evidence made by the Darrochs in regard to the ground already covered. Where do we find the disinterested, useless, non-specialised knowledge which is inseparably involved in the pursuit of the useful, interested, specialised knowledge? The problem, so to speak, is to find a location for this disinterested non-specialised knowledge which does not represent it as parasitic on the specialised knowledge, in the sense in which lay or amateur would seem to be secondary to a professional in any field. Secondly, where do we encounter this humanism of which Burnet makes so much in the passage under review? Let us know, Burnet is asked, why we should bother with it by showing us an actual case.

Burnet supplies a direct answer to both questions. Humanism is for him a movement which burst on the scene at the Renaissance, and has subsequently waned, but is due, he thinks, to make a comeback because the evils it came into the world to combat are, owing to its lapse, in danger of themselves constituting a new orthodoxy, the orthodoxy of S.E.D. vocationalism. As for the disinterested knowledge, Burnet locates it in the sort of things that the humanists cared so greatly for, the making of elegant verses, the writing of Ciceronian prose. Concerned with the form of writing as opposed to the content, it was from the first something which, as the pragmatists are very willing to admit, seems devoid of social utility in any direct way.

19

But now, Burnet goes on, though the humanists of the revival of letters were supremely concerned with the way things were said, with the form of literature, it is a mistake to suppose that this was the only aspect of letters which concerned them. They were also equally concerned with the matter of literature, with literature as a vehicle of science. In fact, the renaissance of versifying in classical Latin went hand in hand with an equal passion for the revival of the lost and forgotten science of antiquity, the value of which had been vaguely remembered without anyone being able to master it. The useless activity of literature was thus valued by men of the Renaissance as the means of making possible the revival of the useful activity of scientific discourse about the exploration of nature.

In the Middle Ages, Burnet points out, it had been different. The medieval scholastics thought that they ought to spend all their time on the useful science inherited from antiquity and not let themselves be sidetracked into the useless field of *literae humaniores*, of ancient poetry. As in the Scotland of Struthers and the S.E.D., vocationalism had been allowed to regulate studies in a very thoroughgoing way; by contrast, the starting-point of the humanists was their perception that science had stagnated among the medieval scholastics as the result of their systematic attempt to separate out the useful from the useless elements in the legacy of the ancients, concentrating on the former to the complete devaluing of the latter. Humanists thus showed, according to Burnet, that if you are to locate disinterested general knowledge anywhere, you are to locate it in poetry, whose mode of discoursing about the world provides a kind of starting point for science. It was impossible, said Burnet, to get the clarity of language required for effective science — science at least on a level with or above that of the ancients — without acquainting oneself in practice with the distinctions illustrated in a classical rhetoric between, for example, showing a statement to be meaningful or generally credible (persuasion) and showing it to be true (proof), or between different ways of saying the same thing, and different things said in the same way (form and content). The rhetoric of the Renaissance humanists had liberated the West from the narrow fixation on logic which was distinctive of the scholastics, and the ensuing cultural revolution enabled poetry to find its place as the inspiration of science. In speaking this way of humanism, Burnet is in effect answering the criticism which the pragmatists of Darroch's generation and since were bringing against the thesis of S. S. Laurie that literature is inseparable from science and that the effective study of the latter presupposes the study of the former. Pragmatists had asked, by way of retort to Laurie, for experimental proof that science would wither or be a feeble growth if cultivated independently of literature. What Burnet was saying was that Laurie's thesis had already been put to the test in the experiment historically conducted by the scholastics when they set about cultivating the scientific part of ancient literature while setting aside, as a contemptible trifle, the poetry.

Burnet has thus shown the significance of the humanist movement from a historical point of view, but he has now to face the question of its relevance to education in the living present. The difficulty, however, can easily be cleared up by a glance at the way in which both the classics and, more recently, the "modern humanities" modelled on them have developed. Briefly, the achievement of the Renaissance was to have restored poetry to a place of honour side by side with science, which it has never lost since. But as soon as the idea of the study of literature in and for itself without enquiring as to its utility was firmly established, the connection with science as established by the Renaissance was forgotten. The study of Greek literature tended to be identified with the study of Greek poets, historians, dramatists, etc., in abstraction from all curiosity about their relation to the Greek contributions to philosophy and science which were being made simultaneously. Much the same thing was happening in reference in the study of French or Italian literature, at any rate in Britain. This omission of the study of philosophy and science from the departments of Greek, French, etc., soon began to be felt as a scandal by the utilitarians who began to ask what social point there could be in language studies which seek to justify their existence solely by reference to esoteric things, uninteresting to the majority, like poetry and fiction. Confused by these utilitarian criticisms, the organisers of education became more and more embarrassed about what to say about the value of the classics. They could defend the study of French on the ground of its imparting to large numbers some kind of working knowledge of the language, and in due course the study of French poetry and fiction began to be excluded or put outside French studies on the ground of their being only a minority interest for the cultivated few. In the event, Greek lost its privileged position in the curriculum altogether, and if modern languages like French to some extent took its place they were studied not for the combination of literature and science which constitutes French civilisation or even for the poetry and fiction itself, but more and more for French considered not as a written language but as a spoken language, which deserved its place in the curriculum only because it enabled non-French speakers to learn what French babies learned in their cradles or at their mothers' knees.

Burnet's criticism of the vocationalists culminates in a brief sketch of how the Scottish curriculum would have to be remodelled in order to make it a preparation ground for the education of an elite. The Arts curriculum, he thinks, ought to consist of a generalist stage followed by a specialist stage as at his own university of St Andrews. The generalist or propaedeutic stage ought to be structured, on the traditional Scottish pattern, of some literature, some philosophy, some science, with changes appropriate to the new situation. The classical languages and mathematics were no longer to have a privileged position in regard to literature and science. The courses were to be on generalist lines adapted consciously for propaedeutic purposes in contradistinction to the specialised treatments of the same subjects in the advanced follow-up classes. In the science subjects for example — the only ones Burnet says anything about — the generalist approach is to take a historical form which would bring out the significance of the scientific revolution that had occurred in physics and astronomy between the nineteenth and the twentieth centuries. Burnet would also like to see the lectures give their due to the Renaissance discovery of Greek science, including mathematics, as well as of the way in which the Hellenic inheritance in science was transformed by seventeenth-century analysis. It would be also desirable to say something about the split between the philosophy and the science of the Greeks, occasioned by Aristotle's undervaluing of mathematics in comparison with biology, which was responsible for the decadence of Greek intellectual culture.

At the same time, nothing was further from Burnet's mind than to see the introductory class on the sciences converted into a dry factual account of the various scientific revolutions. A historical account of science would, according to Burnet, be useless for the purpose of general studies unless it was enlivened by a philosophic outlook which courageously sought to generalise the accounts of the past so as to show their significance for the present day situation in the sciences:

"It seems as if this alternation of the mathematical and the biological interest was fundamental in the development of scientific thought and that the philosophy of different periods takes its colour from it.

The philosophy of the nineteenth century was dominated in the main by biological conceptions, while it seems as if that of the twentieth was to be chiefly mathematical in its outlook on the world. We must not, of course, make too much of such formulas, but it is instructive to study such alternations in the philosophy of the Greeks, where everything is simpler and more easily apprehended."[16]

Burnet thus wanted to see the Scottish Arts faculties resume their traditional task of introducing the students to the sciences, literature, etc., by means of general classes illumined and enlivened by the philosophical spirit. He does not, however, dwell on the details of these proposed courses, because, in his opinion, they couldn't be put into operation in modern Scotland owing to the resistance to philosophy and ideas, as well as the utter scepticism and indeed indifference to the value of such things, which in the earlier twentieth century seemed to be in some ways the basic characteristic of the cultural outlook of the Scots. Like other writers in the third decade of this century, especially Dr C. M. Grieve, Burnet felt strongly that "Scotland hated and feared ideas as no other country does", but, unlike Grieve (or, at least, the Grieve of that decade), Burnet also knew that "it hadn't been always so". Far from having "contributed nocht to human thocht" as Grieve at that time thought, Burnet knew perfectly well that Scotland had in its time made a remarkable contribution. What made the resistance of the Scots to his plans for making their educational system the centre of philosophical move-ment so difficult to overcome was the fact that their forcibly expressed apathy to this type of culture wasn't the apathy of an intellectually unawakened nation but rather the apathy of a nation which for some reason had a revulsion against the intellectual interests formerly distinguishing it, and which refused any longer to have anything to do with them. From Burnet's point of view, there was no point in calling for an intellectual renaissance in Scotland until one had carefully investigated the causes of the cultural blight which had come upon the country. At a time when Grieve was fulminating against the hatred of ideas which he could not account for, Burnet with his more intimate knowledge — as a man of the Scottish establishment — of what had really been going on, was drawing attention to the necessity of investigating the sinister role of the S.E.D. in killing off the country's characteristic culture ever since it had got independent control of the educational system.

Expounded in the chapter challengingly entitled "Scotland and

Prussia", Burnet's charge against the S.E.D. is that its Leaving Certificate, which the secondary courses lead up to, and which effectively prescribes their content and goal, kills off the philosophical spirit before ever the students have seen the inside of a philosophy class. Confronting the sixteen-year-old student with a string of unseens drawn from authors he has never read, papers in Latin and other languages, ancient and modern, are so constructed as to prevent the students from seeing that the chief problem set by literary study is the comprehension and assessment of poems and literary works as wholes. The aspect of literature in which it raises philosophical problems is thus suppressed and abstracted from, so as to leave the scholar with the impression that the end of literary study is the acquisition of linguistic skills of a useful kind. Intellectual quality, instead of being allowed to express itself in a philosophical search for the meaning of life, becomes identified with a kind of crossword-puzzle mentality, which isn't interested in grasping the relation of the thing it studies to a wider context and to other things, and for which the high point of mental activity consists of making a series of ingenious guesses about a limited thing, so as to get a coherent picture of it in isolation. Nor is the mental training supplied by the mathematical papers any better, for the whole activity is there reduced to the solving of isolated problems without considering their connection with one another in a system or systems of geometry, and without raising any wider questions of the application of geometry to the physical world it is supposed to be describing.

The situation is made still worse, according to Burnet, because the S.E.D., in the interests of showing itself to be maintaining the highest standards, chooses passages for translation which are normally much too difficult. "The fact is that we ask for too much, and in consequence we get very little. No one would say it was fair to set a French or German boy of sixteen or seventeen a passage of Tennyson or Browning and plough him if he could make no sense of it, but that is just the sort of thing we do in our classical examinations."[17] Obliterating the sense of the whole, the S.E.D. has brought about a situation in which the philosophical content of literature is regarded by increasing numbers of the Scottish students as mystifying and irrelevant.

As a follow-up and clarification of these criticisms of the Leaving Certificate, Burnet, in letters preserved in the S.E.D. files,[18] proposed an alternative approach to secondary education which, instead of suppressing, would awaken and prepare the philosophical interest essential to elites while the scholars were already at school, and before they ever studied philosophy systematically. The idea was that subjects should not be studied singly, but should be grouped with an interrelated partner subject, e.g. French and English, German and English, British history and English, which had a good deal of common ground with one another in the sense that the traditional pairs of Latin and Greek or mathematics and physics had this common ground. Cognates were not to be taught — as they so often are — side by side and simultaneously with one another as if they had no connection whatever, but were to be put over to the classes by the comparative method favoured by Burnet and which, by noting the resemblances and differences, would bring prominently forward into the consciousness of the students the philosophical problems implicit in their interrelationship. Both teachers and pupils should be encouraged to raise, instead of suppressing, the kind of difficult questions which arise over the apparent irreconcilability of a poem studied as a whole from a literary point of view and the same poem from the point of view of historians who explain it as a social product. No doubt this new scheme would seem difficult on account of its unfamiliarity, but the opening up of this long-forbidden field of larger questions and speculative problems would, Burnet hoped, have the exhilarating effect of revivifying Scottish education at all levels.

To carry through this new scheme it would be necessary to have a different sort of examination. The system of external papers set and marked by the S.E.D. in which the schools and schoolmasters had no direct part would be replaced by an internal examination in which the Inspectors would come to the school for a day or two, and fix the grading of pupils in close discussion with the schoolmasters — a scheme which Sir Frederick Dainton has lately been recommending for modern Britain. Liberated from the atomising outlook which regarded poems as merely quarries for unseens, geometry as consisting in a series of isolated and therefore pointless conundrums, new courses which searched by the comparative method for the systematic connection of things might well create the conditions for a renaissance of Scottish learning.

Burnet's proposals were very ill-received by Struthers and his henchmen at the S.E.D. when they were first mooted in 1916-17. Burnet's proposal to reinstitute junior classes, in order to open up the possibility of university attendance to students who for some reason or other had not succeeded in getting into the university by the regular ladder of the S.E.D., was particularly resented by officials who had encouraged and pressed for the abolition of these junior classes, on the ground that the regular method of assessing students was getting so near to perfection that no intellectually fit student could possibly escape the notice of the examiners, unless indeed he were a delinquent. Feeling as they did that educational standards in Scotland had continuously risen since the Highers were instituted at the beginning of the last decade of the nineteenth century, the S.E.D. didn't take very kindly to Burnet's claim that, in the humanities subjects at least, standards had fallen year by year, ever since his appointment to his St Andrews Chair in 1891.

From the point of view of the S.E.D. Burnet was simply being perverse. His criticisms and plans no doubt made a certain sense on the assumption that the Scottish universities should be the breeding ground of an elite in the old sense. The vocationalism of Struthers, however, had given them a different role. They were not so well fitted as Oxford and Cambridge to do the work of elite producing in the style required in the twentieth century, but they were admirably fitted to provide the core of teachers required by Scotland's splendid system of secondary schools.

Much respected in his own time both in the universities and in the E.I.S. as the protagonist of a cultural revolution which would, by restoring shattered unity, make it possible for Scotland once again to figure on the map as the centre of a distinctive educational culture, Burnet might be expected to be of equal interest to our own time for the light his writings throw on the social sources of the great problem which contemporaneously was being incisively and passionately raised by the poet C. M. Grieve — that of Scotland's falling intellectual standards. Burnet's exposition of the new type of mind produced in Scotland as a result of the operations of the S.E.D.'s new education take us at once into the world of *A Drunk Man Looks at the Thistle* (1926) and of *To Circumjack Cencrastus* (1930). Historians of modern Scotland, however, have so far not noticed this aspect of Burnet. For example R. D. Anderson sees him very much in the same way as Struthers saw him, namely as a nostalgic critic of the S.E.D. who is out of touch with the "economic forces" operative in the twentieth century.[19] It is to be hoped that what I write here will enable his position to be better understood in the future.

3

WHITTAKER, GIBSON AND ORDINANCE 70

Leaving aside the rest of Burnet's valuable theory with some reluctance, let me prepare the way for the second round in the debate about the curriculum by a summary of the course of the Ordinance 70 struggle, which will bring out the importance of Burnet as a practical statesman. Its effective starting point was 1916 when the S.E.D. got the Privy Council to veto the four universities' new proposals for entrance on the grounds of their extending the privileged position of Latin and mathematics instead of — as the S.E.D. had hoped and pressed — decreasing it. Elated by the S.E.D.'s check to what they saw as the universities' irrational refusal to change with the times, the three organisations of the Scottish teachers reunited in September 1917 with unusual ceremony and with the blessing of the S.E.D. and the government — under the old and famous title of the E.I.S. — with a view to ending once and for all the universities' Latin/mathematics bottleneck, and as a follow-up proceeded in 1919 to found the *Scottish Educational Journal* to publicise their case and establish their professional dignity. About the same time and with much the same end, the S.E.D. founded a committee under the chairmanship of Lord Haldane which was composed of university leaders sympathetic to the teachers' cause, including Burnet as well as representatives of the teaching profession, and which was given the difficult task of framing regulations acceptable to all parties.

On the basis of the committee's work, a blueprint called Ordinance 70 was promulgated, and from 1919 onwards a newly founded Entrance Board, chaired by Burnet, argued over the contentious question of preparing acceptable draft regulations. Burnet's proposals for a philosophical education, as outlined above, were soon rejected out of hand as insufficiently utilitarian, but, after briefly resigning, he took up the work of chairman again, and after long struggles, a provisional set of entrance-rules which, prepared under Burnet's guidance, abolished the straitjacket of Latin and mathematics, were put in circulation early in 1921. At once a storm arose, the universities refused outright to comply, Burnet resigned in disgust, this time for good, and a new leadership of the Entrance Board, taking its cue this time from the universities, reimposed the requirement of Higher mathematics for all science students, and Lower Latin for all Arts students. The E.I.S., backed by the S.E.D., at once raised objections; Glasgow University, deserting its sister institutions, began to join in on their side, and in due course Draft 2 was suppressed in favour of Draft 3 which put Latin and mathematics back on an equality with the other subjects, destroying their pre-eminence in the entrance system. As before, the universities, that is to say St Andrews, Aberdeen and Edinburgh — the latter taking the lead — were able to put pressure on the Entrance Board and thus organised the issue, in the summer of 1922, of a fourth set of regulations which reinstated the requirement of Latin and mathematics as laid down in the second set. The obtuseness of the three sister universities was too much for Glasgow which, with the private backing of the S.E.D. and the public support of the E.I.S., took Counsel's opinion and availed itself of its right of appeal to the Court of the Privy Council which met at Whitehall on December 12th 1923, under the presidency of Lord Haldane, to decide upon the meaning and value of the Ordinance 70 which he himself had some four or five years before been chiefly responsible for drawing up. In the event, Haldane's adjudication published in the spring of 1924 intensified Scotland's culture crisis instead of resolving it, by means of a built-in and probably intentional set of ambiguities in his judgment which in the first place upheld the appeal by Glasgow University, obliging the universities as a whole to allow students to matriculate without Lower Latin or Higher mathematics, and which went on in the succeeding passage to reinstate the universities' veto, abolished at the beginning of the regulations, by allowing the Arts faculties to impose Lower Latin on all would-be entrants and the Science faculties to do the same with Higher mathematics. As was said at the time, Haldane's adjudication would seem to admit students to the quadrangle but to exclude them from the classrooms and the work for the degrees. It was a complete deadlock.

Instead of being able to get on with the job of teaching, the schools and the universities, as the result of Haldane's decision, found themselves entangled in another year of self-uncertainty and argument, in which the whole story of Scottish education since 1889 was sifted through by the general councils in the hope of finding out what had gone wrong. The universities might have got out of their difficulty by abolishing entrance regulations altogether and going back to the pre-1892 system of open entry, as indeed a considerable party of elder statesmen still urged, or they might have agreed to go their own ways, Glasgow instituting less onerous entrance requirements than Edinburgh. However, in the end, a conference of the representatives of the general councils of the four universities, convened at Perth round about the beginning of 1925, recommended going forward with the scheme for uniform entrance for all four universities based on the kind of regulations sponsored by Glasgow University, in disregard of the possibility that Edinburgh even now might still make objections. More and more the press and the public (for which in a sense the general councils of graduates spoke) were becoming impatient of the resistance to change, especially as the resistance was made in the name of what seemed to be the nonsensical claim that Scottish culture would collapse if it weren't propped up by a university entrance qualification equivalent to our O-Level Latin.

In the summer of 1925 the hope was rising, encouraged by a certain war-weariness, that Edinburgh University would come off its high horse when suddenly, about the beginning of November, three long violent letters published in *The Scotsman*[1] under the signature of E. T. Whittaker (later knighted), the Professor of Mathematics and Dean of the Faculty of Arts in Edinburgh University, made it clear to the public that so far as Edinburgh was concerned, the struggle was by no means over. It was essential to liberal culture, he said, that if he chose to quote a passage from Newton's *Principia* in the original Latin in the course of one of his lectures to the ordinary classes, the students should have some idea of what was meant. An extraordinary performance, full of intellectual arrogance, the letters were read as carrying the dark threat that Edinburgh would disregard the law as laid down by the judgment of Lord Chancellor Haldane. Aroused by Whittaker, his opposite number at Glasgow, George Gibson, Professor of Mathematics and Dean of the Faculty, came out into the open against him. An active participant in the earliest committee work over Ordinance 70, Gibson had withdrawn from the fight in 1921 on the ground of his impatience with the universities for digging in on such a contemptible qualification as Lower Latin, as an eloquent letter preserved in the S.E.D. files for the period shows.[2]

In 1925, however, a month after Whittaker's outburst, Gibson returned to the front, when it was becoming obvious that the "leftist" leaders of the Glasgow teachers (such as Duncan McGillivray) were giving away the game to Whittaker by refusing compromise settlements on the ground that the abolition of the privileged position of Latin and mathematics wasn't enough. What was at stake, Gibson said, was something more than their dignity as professional teachers; it was Scottish education itself. "They were making a new start in Scottish education and it was no time to be halfhearted"; that is to say they must identify wholeheartedly with the compromise settlement.[3]

Gibson's intervention was well timed in the sense that Whittaker's bluster was proving to be a kind of cover-up for a dubious scheme in which Edinburgh University, without actually breaking the law, that is to say, while complying with what seemed to be the intention of the Lord Chancellor's judgment according to the commonest interpretation — abolishing the privileged position of Lower Latin and Higher mathematics — nevertheless virtually restored to mathematics its traditionally elevated place in the science curriculum by giving to physics something like the privileged position which mathematics had lost. A Higher Science which was not backed by an entrance qualification in physics was, the extraordinary regulation ran, to be counted as equivalent to a Lower Science.

The effect of this draft regulation which gave a privileged position to physics seemed to put an obstacle in the way of the development of the new observational sciences like botany, physiology or geography, hindering their development and denying them students. This sort of thing was too much for Gibson. There is something not straight about it, he said, at the October 1925 Court meeting. The elitist pretension of certain subjects as against the others which had bedevilled the Arts Faculty was now threatening to cause similar conflicts in the Faculty of Science.

The concerted attack on the proposal to give physics a privileged position resulted in a well-argued and well-attended meeting of the General Council of Glasgow University on the 7th January 1927. One schoolteacher after another denounced the rights given to physics as unfair in themselves and likely to discourage the development of the observational sciences. In a joint letter submitted to the meeting by one of their number, the professors of these sciences in Glasgow University signified their solidarity with the teachers. Orchestrating the objection to the Edinburgh ideas, Gibson said that the regulations were an attempt to force physics on all the higher students of science, and this was the source of the trouble. For the first time in the history of university entrance, natural science was to get a chance to show its quality, and it would be disastrous if the subject were allowed to perish.[4]

The next move was an appeal to Edinburgh which was at first rebuffed. Physics was to stay on top. In a polite reply, the Glasgow General Council requested their opposite numbers in Edinburgh to meet them for a conference — doubtless in the Station Hotel at Perth, which must have done pretty well out of the Ordinance 70 struggles — and as a sweetener they offered to make common cause with Edinburgh in redressing some wrong suffered by the Scottish universities as a result of the refusal of the English redbrick universities to offer them some sort of reciprocity.

In the event, the conference never took place, Edinburgh having second thoughts. Physics was demoted from its elevation. At last the Ordinance 70 struggle was over.

Looking at the outcome of this struggle in the light of its origins it might seem as if the honours were divided. The S.E.D. got its way in the sense of abolishing the privileged position of Latin and mathematics for faculty entrance. On the other hand, it did not get its way in the sense of carrying through its aim of weakening or destroying the liberal Arts element in the faculty. Burnet's ideas had some influence on the outcome in the sense that Edinburgh and Aberdeen followed Glasgow in making philosophy a literary and a scientific subject compulsory for the Ordinary M.A., an arrangement which also obtained in a more systematic form in Burnet's own university of St Andrews. As for Darroch's idea that history, political economy and political philosophy could reasonably claim the privileged status of general subjects in the Arts curriculum, that possibility was decisively defeated when, in an earlier stage of the proceedings, Sir Richard Lodge, taking advantage of his elevation to the chairmanship of the Entrance Board through the resignation of Burnet, got its members to consent temporarily to his plan of giving special rights to his own subject of history. Lodge's move met with no sympathy whatever in a Scotland in which history still figured as a very secondary subject and Darroch's idea was for the moment dead.

At the same time, although things seemed to go on as before, they were in fact never to be the same again. The great casualty of Ordinance 70 was the plan of the S.E.D. to unite the universities and schools in a unified system of education dominated by its own vocational ideas. At the beginning of the conflict in 1916-17 and later, the universities had had to listen, somewhat impatiently, to the S.E.D. but by the time of the crucial year of conflict, 1922-23, Struthers' successor was complaining that the universities and their Entrance Board were not communicating with him at all as to what they were doing. The break apparently was never repaired, and increasingly the universities turned away not merely from the S.E.D. but from the Scottish schools, and in order to defend their standards from the vocationalism of the S.E.D., began to speak of themselves as British institutions which had more in common with the universities of England than with the institutions of Scotland, and which tended to see their future development as depending on forging links with the schools of England rather than with those of Scotland.

Because R. D. Anderson uncritically identifies with Struthers' view of the university revolt against the S.E.D. policy as motivated by nothing better than nostalgic sentimentalism, in his book *Education and Opportunity in Victorian Scotland* he takes a very different view of the twentieth-century crisis in Scottish education from the one I put forward here. What we have to explain, he says, perceptively enough, is why the Scottish universities in 1954 no longer spoke of themselves as public institutions which had traditionally enjoyed the same sort of independence of the State as the older universities of England. But whereas the present book explains the change of attitude as due to the breakdown of Scottish education which occurred in the twenties as the result of the universities' resistance to the S.E.D.'s narrow-minded dictatorship, Anderson's *dirigiste* predilection for the S.E.D. leads him to explain the universities' new way of speaking about their position as due, in the first instance, partly to the personal peculiarities of Sir Hector Hetherington and partly to the capacity of institutions to create myths about themselves which bear little relation to reality.[5] The result is, to my way of thinking, a complete trivialisation of twentieth-century Scottish cultural history.

The Ordinance 70 affair cannot be properly understood until we see that the constitutional and legalistic issue of who should control the system, the S.E.D. or the universities, rests on a metaphysical argument as to the relative importance in knowledge of the non-utility and *a priori* studies of philosophy, mathematics and literature (in the sense of rhetoric) by comparison with the utility-oriented sciences of observation. Just as the breakdown of the Scottish religious system in the nineteenth century was the result of differences over the relation of faith and reason, so too the breakdown of the Scottish educational system in the twentieth century was the result of differences over the relations of *a priori* and empirical knowledge. Not merely is a philosophical issue evidently present in the initial stages of the Ordinance 70 affair, as defined by the conflicting positions of Darroch and of Burnet, but also, in the later stages, what gives the struggle between Edinburgh and Glasgow a continuing interest for us, and a permanent independent meaning, is that the mathematicians who spoke for their respective faculties were putting forward rival views of the function of their subject, both in relation to the rest of learning and to life. Whittaker and Edinburgh on the one hand took their stand, so to speak, on the intellectual elitism of the new physics, while Gibson and Glasgow should, I think, be understood as putting forward the anti-elitist case of mathematics for the million which would be required by a truly democratic education. Once again, Ordinance 70 had produced a discussion of relations between specialism and generalism; more limited than that between Burnet and Darroch, but not less illuminating.

Appointed in 1912, Whittaker, according to the five obituary articles in the *Edinburgh Mathematical Proceedings* for 1957, set out to revolutionise mathematical teaching in Scotland, and soon put the university on the map by attracting to it a succession of research students from outside Edinburgh who produced in the early days articles and dissertations, D.Sc.s and Ph.D.s by the dozen, in reference to the new themes produced by the revolution in mathematical physics. The students were brought in by setting up a research laboratory and advertising research facilities in the press. By contrast, Gibson, who was appointed to the Glasgow Chair about the same time, occupied himself with carrying on the two-fold aim of his teacher, George Chrystal, Whittaker's predecessor. The first part of the programme was to advance the cause of Scottish education by bringing together the universities and the schools in the line of reform promoted by the S.E.D. Chrystal's views on this subject — more choices and more modern subjects — were somewhat similar to those of Darroch, whose mentor he had been, according to the latter's obituary in the Edinburgh Senatus minutes,[6] and who worked with him on various co-ordinating committees, aimed at bringing the schools and universities together in fulfilling the S.E.D. plan. Chrystal's second aim was to advance the higher algebra among the Scots by expounding it in a form which made it acceptable at once to their commonsense realism and to their utilitarian idea of mathematics as a kind of tool for engineers. The commonsense realism of Chrystal's approach is illustrated by the fact that his *Elementary Algebra*, a book of 400 pages, is notable for containing some fifty pages of graphs, the object of which is to give the various forms of equations a visible, palpable meaning, thus appealling to students brought up in a tradition suspicious of symbols, and accustomed to regard the significance of words (and mathematical formulae) to lie in their reference to observable things, to non-verbal realities.

As for Gibson, he usually followed the same sort of method as Chrystal of making mathematics intelligible by giving the symbols an observable graphical meaning, as is shown by the title and preface of his chief textbook, *The Calculus Graphically Illustrated*, but he also draws inspiration for his exposition from the history of mathematics, especially the work of the Scottish and English geometers of the eighteenth century. It isn't that he is unappreciative of the work of continental analysis, but his two long review-articles on Cantor[7] written at the outset of his career — though welcoming the new light on the nature of the infinite — go out of the way to criticise the Germans for making too much of symbols in their own right, and he backs up his criticism by making a fresh examination of the *Analyst* controversy in the eighteenth century, his object being to show that Cantor in his obsession with symbols does too little justice to the geometrical method of research as carried through by Robins and Colin Maclaurin. So too in regard to his practical aims, Gibson's affinity with Chrystal is shown by the fact that he found his associates and allies among the mathematics masters of the Scottish schools — Peter Pinkerton, with whom he collaborated in a textbook, and John Mackay of Edinburgh Academy, with whom he shared an interest in the history of Scottish mathematics.

All this was very different from what we find in Whittaker, who is interested, so to speak, in the growing end of the subject, and not in the grass roots, who had a hierarchical view of the place of mathematics in regard to other sciences, and whose chief book — *The History of Electricity Theories* — was occupied with the kind of algebraic researches, the meaning of which could not perhaps so easily be "graphically illustrated". The Edinburgh Mathematical Society had been founded by Chrystal with a view to keeping the mathematical teachers in the Scottish schools in touch with the advances of the subject, and Gibson no doubt kept faith with the founder's intention. It is therefore no wonder there seem to have been tensions when Whittaker saw the Society not as a means of communicating to others advances made elsewhere, but as a centre of creative researches which might make a contribution to the worldwide advance. The difference between the two men can be well expressed by reference to their diverse attitudes to the Ordinance 70 problem. With Gibson, the important thing seems to have been to reunite the schools and universities in a forward movement, which would be worthy of Scotland's past achievement in the mathematics and the sciences as he understood it, whereas with Whittaker, one might feel that the breakdown of the Scottish tradition in mathematics was felt as a blessing in disguise in so far as it had been an impediment to the ambition of putting Edinburgh back on the map of international learning, irrespective of what happened to the sister universities or to the Scottish intellectual heritage.

As to Whittaker's belief in the power of symbolism, of which Gibson had been suspicious, it is not possible for a non-mathematician like myself to venture anything. However, it isn't so difficult to give an insight into their rival philosophies of the place of mathematics in the sciences if we look at their respective attitudes to the thing that interested Gibson most, the Scottish contribution to the subject. In two interesting articles,[8] contributed to the *Proceedings of the Edinburgh Mathematical Society* in 1927 and intended as a kind of conscious farewell to the past, Gibson writes very appreciatively, even perhaps nostalgically, of Maclaurin, Simson and the other great Scottish mathematicians, without raising any questions as to whether they have any relevance to the mathematics of the present day which Whittaker was introducing. By contrast, at the first of the annual mathematical colloquia, instituted by Whittaker on his appointment in order to spread the light,[9] D. M. Y. Sommerville, in a series of lectures which was published the next year in a textbook on non-Euclidean geometry,[10] and more recently reprinted in Dover Books, not only shows himself aware that the Scottish philosopher Thomas Reid — fifty years before Riemann — had worked out a version of non-Euclidean geometry accurately enough and discussed its relation to common sense, but in addition, more interested in the living science than in history, Sommerville made use of the fact of Reid's clear-headed if limited anticipations of modern geometry as a means of breaking down the resistance of his hearers, the Scottish teachers of mathematics and science, to the role claimed for spherical geometry by modern physics as a description of actual space. Did his audience object to the applicability of spherical geometry to space on the ground of its flouting common sense?

Sommerville met the difficulty by drawing attention to the fact that the great champion of common sense, the originator of the Common Sense Philosophy, Thomas Reid, not merely didn't find anything absurd in the notion of spherical geometry, but even considered that it might in certain circumstances be reconcilable with common sense.

In Gibson's articles on Scottish geometry, on the other hand, there seems to be no trace of this idea put forward by the mathematicians working on Whittaker's side, that the geometry of the Scottish Enlightenment might, in certain places, have reached out towards the modern movement and even in some slight way have something to offer our century. In an interesting reference to the Ordinance 70 arguments, which were now almost over, he suggests that Scottish geometry is worth looking at only for what it has to offer us about the problem of how to teach mathematics, how to lead people up from the graphical triangle to the symbols. But the verdict on the past he wants to put over is that for all their excellence — and he admired them very much, clearly — the classical Scottish geometers like Simson, because of their lack of enthusiasm about algebra, have nothing to offer the present day. This hard and fast, take it or leave it, attitude to the Scottish tradition is very characteristic of the products, like Gibson, of the Scottish universities in the Ordinance 70 struggle, and contrasts somewhat unfavourably with the subtlety and flexibility of their opponents who are willing to pick and choose in reference to the Scottish tradition.

Gibson himself, however, seems not to have been an extreme man, and in writing this farewell to Scottish geometry, he is no doubt concerned to check the excesses of pupils who still want to uphold the truth of Euclid and Greek geometry against the illogicality as they see it of the very different kind of geometries required by the new physics. For example, a former student of Gibson's, John Anderson of Sydney, who is likely to rank as the most distinguished philosopher produced by Scotland in our century, not only shows himself hostile to the non-Euclidean geometry, but also exhibits a studied coolness to the passages in Thomas Reid which Sommerville had commended to the modern generation of Scottish mathematical teachers. Seeking to check a revulsion on the part of his students against the new mathematics, Gibson then is arguing that the day of the Greek geometry is done, and that the ideas which have come in with Whittaker must henceforth be accepted and used, whatever one might think of their philosophical consistency — a position very different from that of John Anderson, who had no sympathy whatever with the pragmatic tendency to disembarrass oneself from the difficult problems of the relation of logic and modern physics by enunciating, so to speak, a doctrine of the double truth.

Thus there was a philosophical dimension to the arguments between the Edinburgh and Glasgow mathematicians. As to its exact nature, in dealing with mathematicians, one must, as a layman, be cautious in one's comments, but at any rate the passionate disagreement between Whittaker and Gibson as to the place of mathematics in the syllabus seems in itself sufficient evidence that some question of first principles, that is to say of philosophy, lies behind their argument, and gives it its bitterness. In the event, as John Eaton[11] told me, no Glasgow mathematician set foot in Edinburgh between the wars. The pity of it is that this estrangement happened and that the two sides did not meet to carry forward their philosophical argument about the foundations of their subject. But this tantalising cut-out, this sudden silence which damps down the excitements of an incipient argument about first principles, is all too characteristic of the Scotland of Ordinance 70. The intellectual enthusiasms rise up and are then suddenly chilled, the ideas force themselves forward only to be frozen out. It is a world where the soaring lyricism of the *Drunk Man* topples over into sudden bathos, or where Burnet speaks out, and nobody listens.

4

GRIERSON AND GRIEVE: LITERATURE
AND ITS RELATION TO SCIENCE

At the start of the Ordinance 70 affair the entrance regulations for the Ordinary Arts Degree gave a privileged position to four subjects — mathematics, Latin, philosophy, and English literature. By the end, the former two had lost their place as the result of the illuminating controversies I have touched upon, that between Gibson and Whittaker about Scottish geometry, and that between Burnet and Darroch. By contrast, English literature emerged from the years of ordeal with its privileged position intact, though badly shaken by certain controversies which arose regarding it. Leaving aside the situation of philosophy for subsequent discussion, let us confine ourselves to the questions brought to light by the Ordinance 70 struggle, as to the relation of English literature to science, philosophy, etc., on the one side, and to French literature, German literature, world literature, British literature, etc., on the other.

The chief man in the subject in Scotland, H. J. C. Grierson (later knighted) made no secret of his enmity to the S.E.D., attacking their policies in letters to the newspapers as long and as hard-hitting as those of Whittaker.[1] His experience as Professor of English Literature in Aberdeen since the early nineties, and in Edinburgh after 1915, had left him with a conviction as strong as John Burnet's about the continuous fall in standards. Summing up the situation as Grierson saw it, Kennedy Stewart in his *Nineteenth Century* article[2] of 1927 set down a "vivid recollection" of an English literature class where a professor, one of the most eminent figures in English literature of the day, was trying to overcome the handicap of having students for whom the facts were to be learned off by heart, and the theories to be disregarded, by seeking discursively, almost conversationally, to bring home to them the beauty of a certain passage in Shakespeare. Three-quarters of his students sat crouched over their notebooks, feverishly striving to get every word down on paper, without the slightest comprehension of what he was driving at. Later they would read over their confused notes and wonder what it was all about.

Throughout the whole course, the limitation of this preponderant element tends to turn classes like Grierson's into mere opportunities for fact-grabbing. But — Kennedy Stewart continues — the unfortunate effects do not stop there. The great part of the value of a university training in Scotland is traditionally gained outside the classroom in intellectual communion of developing minds in conversation and debate. Ever since the ideas of Darroch had begun to catch on and the student-teachers had become convinced that the facts established statistically or by measurement in a psychological laboratory were our only source of reliable knowledge about human nature, the ideas of the metaphysical poets, as expounded by Grierson, began to seem more and more like a waste of time. The extra-curricular communion of developing minds began to die out because of a growing fear that philosophical argument was totally fruitless. Like Burnet, Grierson ascribed this turn of events to the S.E.D.'s vocationalist policy of using government grants to suppress the universities as the education centres of an elite; after this preliminary agreement the decisions of the two men radically differed over the basic question of how to safeguard the educational interest of the elites they both wanted to recreate. Whereas Burnet went back to the idea of the Renaissance humanists that the discipline of poetry, by reason of its combining clarity of language with boldness of imagination, provided a foundation for science which would desiccate and die out in its absence, Grierson, for his part, stuck to the post-humanist idea (denounced by Burnet) that the special beauty and intellectual quality of poetry and literature could be kept alive only by segregating it from science. Expressly combatting Burnet's idea that the university education of a modern elite would have to include a certain amount of science, Grierson urged that it is a waste of time to make the study of science compulsory for literary students. Physical science in some form should doubtless be studied at school as Struthers' system, however inadequate otherwise, has sensibly ordained, but it should be dropped by students of English literature when coming to the university, for the fundamental reason, Grierson tells us in his *Rhetoric*, that scientific writing is essentially devoid of literary value.[3]

Grierson's position here is not merely at variance with the tradition of Scottish rhetoric, as kept alive by his predecessors in the Chair, but what is more to the point, his idea of the necessity of a divorce between literature and science was being challenged by the Glasgow-trained Scottish philosopher who drew much of his inspiration from Burnet, whom we have previously met in connection with his comments on Reid's mathematics, and who as lecturer in Edinburgh from 1920-1927 had been able to witness, from a vantage point, the Ordinance 70 arguments between the professoriate, the teachers and the S.E.D. Matthew Arnold, John Anderson was to say, was wrong in asserting that the business of literary criticism was to assess novels and poems, but that it had no business to assess science, which was the special province of the scientists. But just as the literary critic's right to assess poetry does not depend on his being a poet but simply on his being well read in poetry, so too the fact that a man of letters is not a scientist does not unfit him for criticising the writing and even the logic of science provided his culture has a scientific as well as a literary foundation.

The point made by Anderson in a general way was formulated with specific reference to Grierson by the late Principal Tom Cottrell of Stirling University, some decades later, when Burnet's inter-disciplinary ideas had come into fashion again as the result of the influence in the organisation of the new universities of A. D. Lindsay of Keele, along with his pupil John Fulton of the University of Sussex. Mediating between Leavis and Snow, Cottrell carefully compares three or four ways of stating the second law of thermodynamics in order to distinguish between what is literary (the form) from what is non-literary and scientific (the content). Illustrating from actual cases how the same truth can be stated — without detriment to its truth — in numerous different ways according as it is aimed at getting across to this or that kind of audience, he thereby makes explicit the kind of criticism, latent in Burnet, of the Grierson position that the writing of science, just because it aims at clearcutness and straightforwardness, does not involve the complexity of structure associated with literary style, with which it has therefore no connection.[4]

Though Burnet and Grierson both therefore saw the 1889-1892 reforms as precipitating a fall in standards, they nevertheless differed very sharply as regards the question of how to save the situation and prevent further cultural collapse. The solution for Burnet was to undo Struthers' work, ending the vocationalism and the Leaving Certificate in order to create a Scottish renaissance which would recover in a modern form the standards which had gone before. Distinguishing sharply between the S.E.D. and the teachers, Burnet had good relations with the latter, who honoured him at their conference in 1920 by making him a Fellow of the E.I.S., paying tribute to his services to Scottish education.[5] "He has shown to a sceptical world that the humanities are still of importance to humanity." By contrast, Grierson, like the majority of professors, was prepared to accept the Leaving Certificate; the mark of falling standards consisted for him in the presence in his classroom of note-taking student teachers who were incapable of appreciating the finer points in his lectures. The kind of elite he wanted could not be created so long as there were these intending teachers in his class. The Faculty, he said at the final settlement of the Ordinance 70 crisis in 1926, was not going to make English compulsory. If students were going to be teachers they would get compulsion from another source.

Far sharper than might at first sight appear, the difference between Grierson and Burnet is at its starkest in the contrast between the contribution of the Chair Grierson held, that of Rhetoric and English Literature, to the Scottish version of the Western cultural inheritance, as compared with the function in regard to it of the other Scottish Chairs, in philosophy, in classics, in the exact sciences. Whereas the function of the latter Chairs — the ones Burnet speaks for — was to keep the Scots abreast of the movement of ideas in philosophy, the sciences, etc., so as to enable the Scottish universities to contribute if possible to the advance, the chief role of the English Chair, as defined by David Masson, Professor from the mid-sixties to the early nineties, was to encourage the Scots to present themselves to the world as contributors to, and part creators of, something they had never actually created, namely the great and varied poetic literature produced by the sister nation. Adam Smith, a century before, was aware of the ambiguity of the project, but to the generation for which Masson and Grierson spoke the whole thing seems a straightforward operation of good sense. Scots, Masson said, must internalise their Scotticism and cease henceforth to weary the world by parading the external facts all too frequently publicised since the success of the Waverley novels. That is, they must, according to Masson, hold on to their distinctive values — those of the thistle and not the rose — but take care to give them a public meaning in terms of appropriate events in English history and keep silent about their actual significance in the Scottish past. Thus whereas Burnet wants the Scottish universities in their dealings with philosophy and the sciences to communicate directly with the international movement of ideas, giving to it and taking from it, the Professors of English Literature in Scotland want the Scots to make contact with world literature in a much more indirect and roundabout manner, identifying themselves with the rich poetic heritage of the sister nation and dissociating themselves from the relatively meagre contribution made in the same line by their countrymen in the days of their independence.

Of course, Masson and Grierson felt themselves obliged to take up this peculiar position because of the altered situation of their class; owing to its having ceased to be a philosophical subject, rhetoric, had become transformed into a language and literature subject like French or German, the object of which was to give a kind of a *Kultur-geschichte* based on English poetry and prose. The problem was to find a way of fitting into their courses on English literature a Scottish contribution in which writers who depended on the Scottish past like Burns and Walter Scott were being succeeded by a new generation — Thomas Carlyle, Alexander Smith, John Davidson — who, though in some sense Scottish in their *internalised* values, seemed to have entirely broken away from the *externalised* Scotticism to which they hardly ever referred at all. Living in a Britain whose leading thinkers, such as T. H. Green, were sanctioning the view that the history of the world had to be regarded as the history of a few great nations in that it was to be understood in a progressive sense, the smaller nations simply being satellites which were dragged along, often unwillingly, in their wake, it is reasonable enough that the pioneer professors of English literature in Scotland would regard the example of Carlyle or Davidson as decisive for the future form literature in Scotland would take. At the same time one cannot be so happy at the way in which they discharged their intellectual obligations to the older tradition of Scottish writing by pushing it into a corner in a sort of embarrassed manner as if it lacked all significance because it did not fit in to what they took to be the mainstream. By contrast, Burnet's remarks on language and literature studies at St Andrews in his *Essays and Addresses* provide a remarkable example of an attempt to give Scotland's independent contribution its due place in world literature without either exaggerating its value or depreciating it in a embarrassed way.

In the light of this illness-at-ease of Scotland's professors of English literature with respect to this dilemma of the two kinds of contribution to literature produced in Scotland, or rather, to be precise, the plurality of Scotland's scattered achievement in this line, one cannot help wondering if the unresponsiveness Grierson complains of on the part of the student teachers crowding his classrooms, was not only due to a fact-obsessed mentality which could make no sense of his metaphysical ideas, but was also in part the result of his giving them the impression of poetry and literary culture as something altogether exotic as far as the Scots were concerned. Grierson perhaps saw them as nothing but teachers, but the facts of the case seem to me to put it beyond doubt that they were on occasion Scots first and teachers second. The point is that at the very climax of the cultural struggle in the autumn of 1925, just when Whittaker was putting his letters in *The Scotsman*, and the second round was about to begin, an unforgettable challenge against the claims of Grierson on behalf of English literature which had turned its back on science and washed its hands of Scotland, exploded on the pages of the teachers' organ of struggle, *The Scottish Educational Journal*, and continued to reverberate for eighteen months.[6] Sensing the imminent breakdown of the educational system in the fresh outbreak of fighting just when all had seemed settled, the editors set about serialising C. M. Grieve's *Contemporary Scottish Studies* with the idea that the poet's programme for a Scottish renaissance was not only newsworthy in a Scotland at odds with itself over the question of cultural change, but might even draw the attention of the schools, the universities and the S.E.D. to the possibility of an entirely novel and unexplored solution to their dilemma.

Published in the very same numbers of the journal as contained comments on Whittaker's outrageous letters, and announcements of Gibson's forthcoming lectures on Scotland's geometrical tradition, Grieve's articles outlined a view of literature's place in the curriculum which, contradicting Grierson's line, not only reaffirmed the tie-up of literature with philosophy and science but declared the first responsibility of literary teaching in Scotland to be not the diffusion of a taste for the poetry produced by the sister-nation, great though that might be, but the critical assessment and collecting together of Scotland's own variegated contribution to world literature as expressed through the whole range of languages, living and dead, which the nation's writers had used — Latin, lowland Scots, Gaelic, as well as English. In sharp contrast to the inherited state of affairs, where pride of place went to English literature as something set apart from all other literatures as well as from all of science, the literature of Scotland was now to include the country's contribution to philosophy, to economics, to science, and in addition was to be studied not by itself alone but in fruitful cross-reference to the literature of comparable countries. Confronted by the crack-up of the educational and cultural structures which had sustained post-

Union Scotland, the poet called on his countrymen to burn what they had adored, and adore what they had burned, overcoming their differences in the construction of a new edifice whose cornerstone would be the stone the builders rejected.

Up to a point, the poet's critique of Scottish culture as seen from outside the universities was in principle similar to that of John Burnet. Both were concerned to put Scotland back on the map, both are full of comparisons of its education and culture with those of other Western countries. Both also identify the problems of Scotland in the same way — the disappearance of a nationally based elite who would exercise a distinctive role in the world comparable to the elites in other countries. But though the similarities exist, the poet's attack on Scotland's so-called cultural institutions is far more radical than the professor's, starting where the latter's leaves off and making explicit — although some would say exaggerating — conclusions which in Burnet are only latent. According to Burnet, the disappearance of the distinctive elite is due to the mechanical, external character of the S.E.D.'s Leaving Certificate examinations, which by obliging the students to concentrate on details rather than on the whole have destroyed the breadth of mind associated with the old tradition of a philosophical education and made it more and more difficult for the universities to produce the comprehensive type of mind characteristic of the older type of leaders of society. But in a critique of Scottish institutional culture which went deeper, the poet drew attention to the fact that the type of instruction developed in the university with the conscious view of correcting the narrowing of outlook imposed by the S.E.D., namely the classes of appreciation of English literature as taught by the Massons, the Saintsburys, the Griersons, the Raleighs, were having the opposite effect of what was intended, as the result of certain inherent limitations. In a way, the values put over in these classes — the sense of poems as wholes, the idea of literature as a critique of life — produced in the students a genuine awareness of the necessary role of imagination and invention as essential to the elites. At the same time, the English classes effectively discouraged any idea of themselves as a sort of distinctively Scottish elite because of their being organised around the principle that the history of literature in a progressive sense was the history of a few great languages. For the poet, on the other hand, this policy of keeping literature alive as an exotic import is necessarily self-defeating:

> Oor four Universities
> Are Scots but in name;

They wadna be here
If ither folk did the same
— Paid heed tae a' lear
Exceptin' their ain,
For they'd cancel oot syne
And leave us wi' nane.[7]

If all countries acted on the principle of importing their culture from abroad with a view to employing their population in nothing but productive activities, there would be no culture to import.

Classics of the cultural conflict of the Scottish twenties which succeed in distinguishing the essentials from the accidents in a remarkably illuminating way, Grieve's poems and criticisms draw attention to a vital aspect of the problem of the society and the curriculum which is neglected in Burnet's otherwise masterly analysis. Read in this light, Grieve's chief contribution to Scottish education consists of drawing attention to the fact that Masson's principle of the internalisation of Scotticism as being the best way of preserving the intellectual values associated with the country is not appropriate to its new situation in the twentieth century. Scotticism must be in some way re-externalised, or it is going to recede so far into the background of the British consciousness as to cease to matter. Hammered out in the course of Grieve's questioning of the standards supported by the English departments, this novel way of looking at the country's cultural problem is the chief legacy of the otherwise forgotten Ordinance 70 struggles to the present generation. Although perhaps the majority have so far refused to side with Grieve's solution, it still remains a fact that the either-or sharply posed by him has replaced Masson's principle of the internalisation of Scotticism as the right way to look at the problem.

5

KEMP SMITH AND THE METAPHYSICS
OF ORIGINAL SIN

Philosophy was in a very different position from English literature, the only other subject to survive the Ordinance 70 struggles with its monopoly intact. The conflict between the principles of elitism and of anti-elitism which, as we have shown, caused so much trouble in the English departments, were coped with much more effectively by the philosophers who as a result managed to regain something of their lost prestige. Indeed, the immediate effect on philosophy of the Ordinance 70 affair was a kind of renaissance which at first in the twenties had considerable promise. But after having established once again their position as a kind of central subject in the Arts curriculum, the philosophy departments of Scotland did not know what to do with their advantage, and turned in on themselves in a self-defeating manner without giving the lead which the universities might have expected of them. Instead of taking the initiative, the philosophy departments for a generation marked time in an unconfident way, jealously upholding traditional standards which they certainly believed in, but for which they were not prepared to do battle. In the years after World War II the Scottish Arts faculties found them-selves faced once again with a new set of challenges from the kind of neo-utilitarian forces of which in the old days Darroch had been the spokesman.

The important thing from the point of view of the story, as I understand it, is that under pressure from the teachers, as we have already noticed, the special place of philosophy in the curriculum had been successfully challenged in the first decade of the century. Losing its monopoly, philosophy had been converted into an option for which Darroch's class on education might be substituted. During the war, however, philosophy had once again been made compulsory in Edinburgh, the leading university and the model for the others, as the result of the Senatus' decision to assert liberal values in the face of the S.E.D.'s pressure towards vocationalism. Among the teachers, this

46

demotion of education was felt as a kind of deliberate snub to their professional pride, and protests were made at the great gathering in the autumn of 1917 when the E.I.S. was refounded in preparation for the struggle with the universities.

However, in the event, the teachers did not sustain their protests against philosophy's comeback. For one thing, Edinburgh University, setting an example in appointment which was followed by the others, filled the Philosophy Chair vacancy in 1919 with a Scot who, because he had encountered Deweyitism in the United States in a dozen years' teaching, was able to check the rising tide of educational optimism among the Scottish teachers without hurting their feelings too much. Taking advantage of the fact that not all the teachers were agreed about the value of the new psychology, he was able to stop them arguing with the university and to start them arguing with one another. The result was that the teachers didn't keep up their protest against the reintroduction of pure philosophy as a compulsion — a fact puzzling to modern historians of education for whom philosophy exists only as an entry in the university calendar, but intelligible enough to those who know something about what happens in philosophy classes. In fact, the silence of the teachers on the subject of the "unfairness" to education and allied subjects like psychology of the new privileges granted to philosophy is not too difficult to explain if we bear in mind that numbers of the teachers still knew enough about philosophy to be able to see the limitations of the subjects which were supposed to replace it. Dr William Boyd's *History of Western Education* (1921) in a passage quoted in a review in the *S.E.J.* by George Pratt Insh (a friend of C. M. Grieve) exhibits very clearly the reservations of Scottish educationalists — including even Darroch himself — in regard to the American claims about the value of the new pedagogy. "The reaction against philosophy," Insh says, quoting from Boyd, "which is a feature of contemporary thought about education, will have its day and pass, and it will be seen that science is not the supplanter, but the ally of philosophy in the development of education."[1]

There were no doubt some leaders of the teaching profession like McGillivray who were enthusiastic about the new developments which wanted to give psychology a pre-eminence over philosophy, but the language in which they made their claim was all the more likely to excite the scepticism of colleagues because it was the language of the philosophy classroom, not of the psychological laboratory. The *S.E.J.* reported: "Mr McGillivray was well inspired to allude to the great difference made to our view of education by the application of measurement to its various activities. In proportion as quantitative measurement is applicable to a field of enquiry it becomes scientific. England, the U.S.A., is ahead of us in this regard."[2]

These accusations about Scotland as laggard in education, still too much preoccupied with the rival philosophies of pedagogy as put forward on the one hand by S. S. Laurie, the defender of the primacy of literature over science, and on the other hand by Alexander Bain,[3] the defender of science, and too little interested in the concrete psychological results of educational experiment as carried through by Thorndike, etc., had been a familiar feature of the Scottish educational scene from the beginning of the century. At last, however, in the mid-twenties things were beginning to move, and in 1924 the new ideas were put to the practical test by the appointment to the chair, as successor of the suddenly deceased Darroch, of Godfrey Thomson, who was to make Edinburgh a well-known centre of intelligence tests, and who sought to give respectability to his new departure by getting the rising star of English education, one Cyril Burt, to act as his external examiner from 1928. But this systematic application of measurement to education — profitable to Edinburgh University because of the intelligence tests formulated and published by Thomson's department — didn't diminish the scepticism of ordinary teachers. The effect of introducing all this technology of pedagogy was to cut the education classes off from the universities, uniting them more to the training colleges, and the general debate about knowledge and education, so far as there was one, was once again left in the hands of the professors of philosophy.

What saved the restored privileges of philosophy from the continuing attacks of the teachers was thus, in large part, due to the fact that Darroch's old department was now full of technicians of intelligence measurement, who, believing themselves to have converted pedagogy into a positive science, were no longer interested, as Darroch had been, in joining issue with the traditional philosophers as to whether the "new utilitarianism" shed more light on the subject than the ancient metaphysics. At the same time, we must not forget what is perhaps the most important of the facts, that the universities on their side sought to make the compulsion to take philosophy more acceptable to the intending teachers because in the contests for the philosophical chairs (which were pretty frequent in the early twenties), the appointing bodies tended to avoid men like

J. B. Baillie — still remembered as a translator of Hegel's *Phenomenology* and the runner-up for the Edinburgh Logic Chair in 1919 — whose occupation of the professorial chairs would have been provocative to the teachers. Not only because Baillie, as Professor at Aberdeen, had publicly associated himself with the clamour for making Latin a compulsory requisite for university entrance, but also because, as nominee of the retiring Edinburgh incumbent, Pringle-Pattison, he seemed to stand for a continuation of the sectarian tradition which for over sixty years (that is, ever since the Free Church lobby's scandalous defeat of Ferrier's applications in 1852 and 1856) had made Edinburgh's Philosophy Department a kind of rallying centre of academic conservatism. Here modern ideas were rejected in the name of the Scottish tradition of the Philosophy of Common Sense and particular hostility was accorded to the ideas of State control of education as put forward by the Hegelians of Glasgow. By contrast, Baillie's successful rival, Norman Kemp Smith, over and above the fact that twelve years at Princeton had brought his outlook up to date and made it difficult for him to take seriously defences of Lower Latin on the ground of its being the essential prop of Scottish culture, was anxious for Scottish philosophy to break away from the acrimonious disputes about the relation of State to Church or the universities, as well as of faith and belief to reason, which he himself regarded as long having outlived their usefulness, and which were, besides, so unrestrained in their language as to be painful to read. Scotland, he felt, had dwelt too long in the disputes of the past, and the task of the universities now was, putting behind them the disputes of Ordinance 70 along with the memory of the earlier disputes about Free Church and Established Church, to show what philosophy could do in the way of providing a reasonable guidance through the pitfalls and complications of the modern world.

The foundation of the authority which Kemp Smith was to establish over his classes was in part due to the fact that he sympathised with their general post-war desire to make amends for the traditional tangle of controversies, religious and educational, inherited from the Scottish nineteenth century, and to give the country a fresh start on the basis of the kind of twentieth-century ideas which were circulating in the rest of the world. The original feature of Kemp Smith which marked him off as quite different from other representatives of his generation was his deeply felt conviction that the new ideas deriving from men like Freud and Nietzsche, when they were properly understood, assimilated and developed, pointed forward not to the kind of brave new world of liberated happiness expected by men like A. S. Neill, but rather to the necessity for a critical revaluation of the kind of ideas associated with Calvin so as to bring out what they had of value, separating it from what was out of date. In short, the new idea behind Kemp Smith's philosophy which made it surprising and interesting was a sort of secularised version of the doctrine of original sin. Taken up also by Kemp Smith's lecturer, John Anderson, who carried it to Australia, where it was later to be expounded by Anderson's disciple John Passmore in his book *The Perfectibility of Man*, this reassertion of the limitations of human nature as opposed to the doctrine held by the apostles of progress and perfectibility has to be regarded as the chief distinguishing feature of philosophy in twentieth-century Scotland, as opposed to the form modern philosophy took in other Western countries.

In Kemp Smith's case the doctrine was put over to his large ordinary classes in terms of a discussion of the theory of knowledge without any mention whatever of its theological origins. According to Kemp Smith, the growth of human knowledge does not start from blank ignorance and then develop through the piecemeal accumulation of one fact after another. Rather knowledge begins in a sort of illusion, and develops in the course of a critical struggle against illusions which at every turn reassert themselves in new forms after they have been conquered. In his lectures Kemp Smith took care to say nothing about the relevance of the theory of knowledge he was expounding to the hopes of the educational optimists who were carrying on from where Darroch left off. At the same time, it was not difficult for the intending teachers in the class to see the relevance of what Kemp Smith was saying to the pedagogical movement which was still going ahead in Scotland. Persuasively presented, this secularised version of original sin, in the epistemological form he gave it, was well enough understood by many in his classes to be a timely check on the libertarianism and over-optimism which were being sponsored by the most vocal members of the teachers' movement in Scotland such as A. S. Neill. Put over with Kemp Smith's characteristic tact, his implied criticism of the modernist ideas of education provided a kind of rallying point for those in the teaching world who were sceptical of the educational ideas which were being promulgated by Darroch's successors.

All the same, the problem remains as to how Kemp Smith in 1919 succeeded in putting over this discreet philosophy of intellectual fallenness as a forward-looking and fertile movement of ideas to a student body whose war experience predisposed them to sympathise rather with the ideas of Bertrand Russell. "One recalls (from the autumn of 1919) the crowded classroom of nearly 300 students, most of them ex-servicemen, restless and expectant, ready to show their impatience of teaching which seemed to be merely a carry-over of pre-war days."[4] What was it about the lecturing which made so many of the audience feel that "they were in the presence of a great teacher and a personality of commanding force?".

The nature of the intellectual ascendancy which Kemp Smith established over his large classes can be conveniently confirmed and illumined by looking to the parallel of the remarkable intervention which he made into what one could call the extra-mural sector of Scotland's ongoing educational struggles — those connected with the Workers' Educational Association. The activity of the W.E.A. was increasing, alive with hopes that the Russian Revolution was spreading eastwards from the Red Clyde, where classes had been organised with a certain amount of cautious encouragement from Glasgow University (appropriate to its left-of-centre stand in Scottish affairs). Much more conservative than its western sister-institution, Edinburgh University was at a loss to know what to do about the contagious passion for organised education which seemed to be gripping the working classes, when Kemp Smith, very recently arrived, suddenly took the lead. The lately published volume of letters to and from his friend, the Baron von Hügel, offers us glimpses into Kemp Smith's resourcefulness and boldness in his efforts to stem the encroaching tide of Marxism as it came eastwards.

In these letters we see Kemp Smith organising a syllabus of sets of lectures to be given to the working men by advocates and professors. The Astronomer Royal consented to give a course, as well as the head of the Edinburgh School of Art, and the Marxist threat is highlighted by the fact that three or four out of the fifteen or so courses were concerned with economics. Again, we get glimpses of Kemp Smith's arguing with the representatives of John Maclean's labour colleges at trade union committee meetings, with a view to getting the working men to take their social education from professors rather than from agitators. The idea evidently was to counter the rival claims of the independently organised labour colleges by ensuring that lecture courses for working men which the university sponsored were of the highest quality. "Next year [i.e. 1921] we co-operate with the British Association, which visits

SCOTTISH PHILOSOPHY AND SPECIALISATION

Edinburgh in September in arranging three public lectures to working men — probably on the general theme of science and education."[5] Occupied though he was with his university class in this his opening year of 1919 Kemp Smith nevertheless evidently considered the work of organising these workers' lectures to be just as important as his university teaching. We even get a sight of him going down to lunch break meetings at Nelson's Printing Works or again at a factory in order to rally the enthusiasm of the workers for these university-organised lectures.

Kemp Smith himself taught the philosophy class of the Edinburgh W.E.A. — a demanding task of one two-hour meeting every week for twenty weeks. The experience however gave him real satisfaction, not only because his class rose in numbers during the year from 66 to 99, but even more perhaps because the face-to-face argument with the working men obliged him to speak his mind freely on the subject about which he felt very strongly, but about which he generally preserved, in speaking to middle-class audiences, a cautious silence: the tendency of the twentieth century to be far too optimistic about the possibilities of human achievement. "I have undertaken to give a public lecture to the Edinburgh W.E.A. at the beginning of May,"[6] he writes on February 12th 1920, "and am choosing as my subject: 'Traditional Views of Human Nature'." In his opening letter to the Baron von Hügel in 1919, before there was any question of his being appointed to a chair in Edinburgh, Kemp Smith had written: "For some years I have been ambitious to write upon what I should describe as 'traditional views of human nature' — meaning the Christian doctrine of original sin and the Enlightenment (or Pelagian) doctrine of human perfectibility — on the lines of a plea for a better understanding of the former view."[7] What made the taking of the W.E.A. class a source of such pleasure to Kemp Smith was that his audience of workers was ready to take seriously his warnings about the liability of socialist plans to defeat themselves because of their over-optimistic views of human nature. There was, in Kemp Smith's view, nothing wrong in principle about the idea of State-centred planning — twentieth-century conditions demanded an increase of *dirigiste* policies — but if socialism understood in this sense was to work, it must, Kemp Smith thought, rely on a conception of human nature which owed more to Calvin or Augustine than to Pelagius. The distinctive feature of Kemp Smith's adult teaching therefore is that he spoke frankly on controversial topics on which elsewhere he preserved a discreet silence. In 1921 he talked to them on the subject of education and propaganda, in 1922 he took up with them the subject of democracy, and in 1924 he challenged the fashionable idea — just at the very time when Godfrey Thomson was establishing it as Edinburgh orthodoxy — that people are endowed by nature with varying quantities of intelligence. "Tomorrow night I am speaking to the Discussion Club of the W.E.A. on the thesis: 'That all men are equal in intellect, and differ only in character' — in favour of which much can, I think, be said."[8] Kemp Smith's own story, as told in the *Letters*, of his involvement with the W.E.A. confirms what I had myself heard before the war from a colleague who, prior to coming to Edinburgh to teach, had been warned by Tawney of the kind of man who was Professor of Philosophy there. Naturally, Tawney evaluated the affair from his point of view, but what is not in dispute is Kemp Smith's remarkable achievement in breaking the influence of the Glasgow Marxist groups as the result of personal face-to-face arguments with the workers.

Kemp Smith's influence on the W.E.A. reached its climax in the autumn of 1924 at a well-attended meeting in Edinburgh's Usher Hall at which, under his chairmanship, the Secretary for Scotland, the Rt. Hon. William Adamson, and William Graham, a Junior Minister, addressed the predominantly working-class audience on the importance, for the Labour Movement, of the work being done by the Edinburgh University classes in the W.E.A. field. Thereafter, Kemp Smith's personal involvement as a lecturer to the W.E.A. conferences seems to have stopped, although he retained the chairmanship for a very long time subsequently. This favourable attitude to Adamson in 1924 was paralleled by the interest which he took in Ernest Bevin some fifteen years later when, somewhat to our surprise, Kemp Smith sat in on a session of a Trades Union Congress at its Edinburgh meeting just before the war. Thus without being properly speaking a socialist — I remember him deploring very much the singing of the Red Flag at the T.U.C. Congress — one of Kemp Smith's leading ideas certainly seems to have been that the cause of organised culture in Scotland in the twentieth century depended upon promoting a union between the Scottish universities and the moderate element in the Labour Party.

The events of the autumn of 1924 as recounted in the *Letters*, considerably clears, to my way of thinking, the puzzle as to why the outspokenness characterising Kemp Smith's discussions of education and knowledge before the W.E.A. classes is put aside in favour of the almost excessive tact and reticence which led him, in his university lectures on the problem of knowledge, to suppress completely the public and pedagogical implications of what he was saying. For one thing, the death of Darroch in the autumn of 1924 seems to have destroyed the conditions which had made for the continuing debate about the role of philosophy in regard to the new theories of education. Darroch's successor, Godfrey Thomson, primarily interested in technicalities of intelligence measurement, instituted the policy of turning education into an empirically based science. Kemp Smith may not have approved but so far as Edinburgh was concerned the philosophical debate had been ended because education had been, it was hoped, at last put beyond the reach of speculative argument.

But the most important event in the autumn of 1924 was the retirement from the Deanship of Sir Richard Lodge, who had been associated with a moderate policy and who had tried to make common cause with Glasgow in promoting the S.E.D. schemes. In the contest for the Deanship Kemp Smith had been supported by the group of professors, headed by Lodge himself, who wanted the moderate policies to continue. In the event, the opposite point of view prevailed, and Whittaker, as we have seen, was appointed to the Deanship with a view to circumventing or defeating the Glasgow/S.E.D. schemes for abolishing the privileged position of Lower Latin and Higher mathematics. Kemp Smith acquiesced in the result uncomplainingly, glad that he would be free to concentrate on his teaching and his classes, but, reading between the lines of what he tells the Baron,[9] Kemp Smith would not have refused the Deanship if it had been offered him, and he was deeply interested in the critical problems for deciding the future of Scottish education raised by the Ordinance 70 controversy.

The changes which came over the Ordinance 70 argument as the result of the appointment of Whittaker to the Deanship, and of Godfrey Thomson to the Professorship of Education, seems to have induced Kemp Smith to withdraw from the public debate, and to concentrate his attentions on the programme outlined in his Inaugural Lecture for teaching philosophy in a Scottish university. The teacher of philosophy stands to his students in a relation of greater delicacy than does the teacher of any other subject in the university curriculum. The Scottish student, he goes on, is not, indeed, entirely at the mercy of his teachers in any subject, and certainly not in a class of philosophy. Nonetheless, he continues, in what is perhaps an allusion to the kind of teaching given by Sir Henry Jones in Glasgow, if a teacher selects his material and does not press his conclusions until he has prepared the ground beforehand, he can prejudice the issues before they have been squarely faced. If however the teacher of philosophy enables the students to appreciate the conclusions they will in consistency stand committed, according as they adopt a philosophy of one or another type — idealistic, sceptical or naturalistic:

"and if further he can interpret to them the great historical traditions within which those conflicting philosophies appear, then the Scottish student may generally be relied upon, sooner or later, to acquire a philosophy for himself. What that philosophy will be is determined, as is only fitting, by wider and more representative influence than can or should be brought to bear in the classroom."[10]

Kemp Smith goes on to clarify his position when he comes to discuss scepticism:

"Professor Paterson has recently said that the Scots — and we always like to hear ourselves praised — have the most complex character of any people in the world. Is not David Hume one of the greatest figures in the history of philosophy, and does he not represent a national trait? For though we are theologically inclined and endowed with a Celtic fervour in the convictions we adopt, are we not hard-heartedly sceptical in equal degree? To what is the admitted Scottish capacity for philosophy due, if not to this happy combination of caution and tenacity, of circumspection when we are invited to accept a statement and, of readiness to fight for it once we have made it our own?"[11]

What we have to notice here is the absence of the elitist appeal — the *odi profanum vulgus et arceo* — which was characteristic of philosophy teaching at Edinburgh as given by his two predecessors, Campbell Fraser and Pringle-Pattison. "I do not think that Fraser," said Pringle-Pattison, speaking for himself as well as for his forerunner in the Chair, "made much impression on the average undergraduate, apt to be indifferent to philosophy."[12] This approach contrasts sharply with that of Kemp Smith, who without expecting to turn the mass of his captive students into philosophers nevertheless had some confidence in his power of holding their interest, and in giving them a certain respect for philosophy and its problems. Understood in this way, Kemp Smith's hold over his classes as a whole is summed up in the last sentence of the Senatus' minute about him at the time of his retirement in 1945. "His balanced humanity symbolised, as it expressed, what is most valuable in our academic tradition" — where "our" refers to Edinburgh's role as Scotland's metropolitan university which sets the standard for the others. The point is that Kemp Smith succeeded very well in renewing the intellectual tradition which was broad and not exclusive, by showing how, properly managed, the restoration of compulsory philosophy could supply the generalist liberalising element to counter-balance the largely utilitarian specialist character of the rest of the Ordinary Degree.

Considered in reference to their contents, the lectures on theory of knowledge by which Kemp Smith drew and held the attention of such large numbers of students — often over 200 — were concerned not, as one might expect from his *Inaugural*, with expounding the metaphysical issues involved in deciding between a secularist or a religious or a sceptical view of man's place in the universe, but rather with the pedagogical problems, at present agitating all the Scottish universities as to the relations of philosophy and the special disciplines, whether the former ought to have a certain precedence. The high point or centrepiece of the lectures was a difficult discussion in which, without prejudicing the issues and while being pretty fair to both sides, he discussed the question of the relationship of our knowledge of the singular proposition "the Prime Minister is a human being" to our knowledge of the universal proposition "all human beings are mortal". The contrast was stimulatingly brought out between the position of the positivists (including what we would now call Popperians) that we know the truth of experience of the singular proposition independently of that of the universal proposition, and on the other hand the position of those like Kemp Smith himself, who maintained that we cannot know the truth of a singular proposition without in some sense knowing out of experience the truth of the general proposition in the form that "it is of the nature of the organism to die" or that the experience of living is inseparable from that of an alternation between exhaustion and self-recuperation. The first view commits one to the fashionable doctrine that our knowledge progresses by the piecemeal accumulation of one fact after another, but its disadvantage is that it leads to various paradoxes which in Mill's case was that of a circularity and which in Russell's case lead to another, and more complicated, set of contradictions. The alternative view which was clearly that of Kemp Smith, though he did not make propaganda over the point, was that the growth of knowledge was a perpetual battle against the illusions of experience, and this chimed in with the semi-secularist view of original sin which he entertained, but which carried with it the difficulty of explaining how experience enabled us to know the necessary connection between being an organism and wearing out, that is, how living connects with dying. Without, therefore, putting too much bias into his statement of the problem, and without perhaps himself being able to solve it, Kemp Smith left his classes with the view that the traditional ideas about the advance of knowledge which represented it as being complicated, precarious and liable to go wrong, were just as well founded as the view of knowledge's advance which is held by modern education as being a fairly straightforward accumulation of separate facts. The letters to von Hügel show what great satisfaction Kemp Smith got out of his success in giving new life to the traditional role of the philosophy lectures in Scotland as a prime source of "light and leading":

"The past term has been a very busy — *over*-busy — one. My teaching has gone really well in all my classes, and that is cheering. For the past two years I have given my best energies to making a really good start in this respect, and feel that I have succeeded. And in a University where traditions among the students regarding classes and teachers counts for much, this is a great gain. I shall hereafter feel more at freedom to think of my own work."[13]

The meaning of these values of balanced humanity which Kemp Smith so successfully put over from the Philosophy Chair with a view to liberalising an increasingly narrow curriculum cannot, however, be properly appreciated without understanding the sharply conscious opposition between the kind of humanism he stood for and the very different kind of Scottish humanism which was being fought for at the same time by his old teacher, John Burnet. According to Kemp Smith the privileged position restored to philosophy at Edinburgh in 1919 would be sufficient in itself, if tactfully used, to enable the Scottish universities to ride out the storm of Ordinance 70 in the sense of offsetting the anti-elitist spirit which was being introduced through the co-operation of the teaching profession and the S.E.D. For Kemp Smith there was no need to institute the radical outspoken self-criticism of what had happened to the Scottish intellectual inheritance, and the path which for Burnet represented the way of advance — the attacks on Thorndike, Darroch, and the values of modern education — seemed to Kemp

Smith far more likely to inflict lasting damage on the standards of the university by provoking a continuation of the bitter arguments with the teachers and the S.E.D.

Kept in the background with his usual tact, the importance for Kemp Smith's general views of his rejection of Burnet's position, despite his admiration for Burnet in other ways, did not become evident to me until very late in Kemp Smith's life when I heard him comment on the Burnet chapter which I had included in the original draft of my book *The Democratic Intellect*. Raising himself on the pillows of the bed on which he was soon to die, he left me in no doubt of his reservations about Burnet as an educational theorist. "I had," he said in emphatic tones, "a *considerable* respect for Burnet, but..."

Well received when read at Belfast University to a group of colleagues which included Professor W. B. Gallie, who found it stimulating from the point of view of the work then engaging his attention — his *Lindsay and Keele* — the Burnet chapter had been written as one of the high points of the book, but in view of Kemp Smith's objections, I kept it out of the published work in order to check on its veracity. Subsequent researches, however, served only to confirm my previous conviction as to the value of Burnet's critique of the modern development of Scottish education, making me aware of certain limitations in Kemp Smith's point of view which I had not before noticed. I began to feel that the chief difference between the judgment of Burnet and that of Kemp Smith on the fate of the Scottish academic tradition is in large part due to the fact that the former takes his standard from his experiences at Oxford, whereas the latter looks at things in the light of his years of teaching in the United States. From Burnet's point of view, the innovations introduced by the S.E.D. — the tendency towards specialisation as well as the peculiarly mechanical nature of the Leaving Certificate — greatly damaged the Scottish university tradition in the sense of making it impossible for it to produce the kind of elite which might in its rather different way complement and rival the elites produced by Oxford and Cambridge. But confirmed, by his American experience, in the view that the function of universities was to provide a professional training rather than to produce an elite on the Oxbridge pattern, Kemp Smith seems to have taken a much more favourable view than did Burnet of the changes which the S.E.D. had introduced into the Scottish universities. Judged by American standards both the Leaving Certificate and the narrowing of the university curriculum made for the kind of accuracy which the modern world required, and in that sense the reforms of the S.E.D. were hardly deserving of the bitter criticisms which were being directed against them. No doubt the modernisation of education could be really socially and intellectually dangerous if as elsewhere it drew its inspiration from the pragmatist ideas which were so prevalent in American education. But, as Kemp Smith well knew, in the Scotland of the twenties, this kind of superficial philosophy with which Darroch had been associated was beginning to lose its influence, and in the philosophy classes which were compulsory for wide ranges of the students a more cautious theory of knowledge was being put forward which stressed the intellectual limitations of man, and thus provided a check on the unthinking optimism which hoped for so much from the the accumulation of knowledge about this or that field. Burnet was, therefore, from Kemp Smith's point of view, probably wrong in saying that the Scottish tradition had been destroyed. On the contrary, it was being renewed in terms suitable to the twentieth century.

Considered as rival ways of restoring the Scottish Arts tradition, there is no question but that Kemp Smith's procedures were, in their immediate effect on the post-war situation, remarkably successful, and seemed to point the way forward for Scottish academic development, whereas Burnet's ideas on the other hand were a complete failure. During the years of World War I and for two or three years after, Burnet no doubt had been a man of affairs with a responsible position in the centre of Scottish educational reorganisation, but when it became clear that his proposals for restoring the intellectual quality of the Scottish Arts curriculum depended upon a radical rejection of nearly everything the S.E.D. had done in the way of instituting Leaving Certificates and of specialising the curriculum, nobody took him very seriously from a practical point of view, however much they might respect him as a theorist. By contrast, Kemp Smith's quite remarkable success in interesting his ordinary classes in a certain kind of traditional and non-optimistic view of knowledge, seems to have discovered a formula for reconciling the modernisation policies supported by the teachers as well as by the S.E.D. with a reassertion of traditional intellectual values, and the role of the philosophy classes in all the Scottish universities was greatly influenced by Kemp Smith's success, not merely in the post-war years, but for a couple of generations, that is, down to 1960. As I understand his work, what Kemp Smith had done was to show how the Glasgow idea of co-operation between the Scottish universities and the specialising proposals of the S.E.D. could be made to work without damage to the intellectual tradition of the Scottish Arts faculties, which could assert their original sin values in a form appropriate to the twentieth century. In reference to his own time and for all the Scottish universities, Kemp Smith thus seemed to have resolved the contradiction between the rival claims of the open door, on the one hand, and intellectual standards on the other, which had been responsible for the Ordinance 70 controversy. By contrast Burnet might seem quite an impractical idealist, some would even say a sentimentalist.

But if we extend our horizons beyond the fifties so as to take in the next three decades of the twentieth century, it becomes obvious that we have to revise this estimate of the comparative value of Kemp Smith's and Burnet's ideas in such a way as to do more justice to the latter. Kemp Smith no doubt had shown effectively enough how the values of "metaphysical Scotland" could be re-established in such a way as would balance the anti-elitist ideas of the teachers and the S.E.D. without prejudice to the practical values they represented. But in order to keep the metaphysical flag flying it would have been necessary at the same time to keep up a kind of polemic against the utilitarian values which, though dead in Scotland in the somewhat crude forms associated with Darroch, were nevertheless very much alive in intellectual and educational developments south of the border in the formulation of them given first by logical positivism and then by linguistic philosophy. In view of this threat to their metaphysical values it might have been expected that the teachers in the Scottish philosophy departments would have remembered about Burnet and gone back to his carefully worked out critique of the superficiality of pragmatist ideas and some of their psychological applications by comparison with the values asserted by traditional philosophy. But instead of doing anything like that, the Scottish philosophy departments continued to expound the problems in the manner modelled on Kemp Smith, and though strongly disapproving of the philosophy of Bertrand Russell, as well as of the various schools including the logical positivists which derived their inspiration from him, were very careful to avoid entangling themselves in public controversies in defence of their metaphysical positions. Instead of taking their example from Burnet and making a stand in defence of their distinctive philosophical tradition, the philosophers in Scotland steered clear of the kind of polemics which might have been liable to bring back the infighting between the S.E.D., the teachers and the universities of the earlier decades of the century. In the event, when the crisis came later in the century with the reorganisation consequent upon the Robbins Commission, the Scottish philosophy departments, one might say, surrendered their values without fighting for them. The distinctive metaphysical tradition seemed to die out in Scotland without anyone, academic or non-academic, raising a voice of protest.

But of course it would be very surprising if an intellectual tradition which was so conscious of its distinctiveness as that of the Scottish universities and which had been so full of life up to the second or third decade of the twentieth century should suddenly consent to suppress itself and disappear altogether without trace. Burnet's educational ideas might seem to be dead and forgotten so far as Scotland itself was concerned, but they remained very much alive in Australia whither they had been taken by John Anderson, who went out to be Professor at Sydney in 1927 just when the Ordinance 70 struggle was ending. Unlike the Scottish philosophers who remained in Britain, Anderson was profoundly conscious of the incompatibility between the intellectual values embodied in the traditional Scottish curriculum, and the neo-utilitarian reorganisation of education which in the years after World War II was increasingly undertaken by the various governments of the English-speaking world. Starting from where Burnet left off, Anderson devoted his later years to a systematic discussion of the problems inherited from the Ordinance 70 affair — elitism versus anti-elitism, liberalism versus utilitarianism, vocationalism versus generalism.

6

JOHN ANDERSON AND THE DEWEYITES

The politically and philosophically perceptive son of one of those socialist schoolmasters who in the early years of the century had pushed the S.E.D. towards a policy of egalitarianism and modernisation, John Anderson had the unique experience of witnessing the Ordinance 70 struggle not only from the anti-elitist standpoint of the new schools, but also from the elitist standpoint of the universities. Throughout the whole length of the ten-year conflict — from his graduation year at Glasgow in 1917 to his departure for the Sydney Chair in 1927 — Anderson had, by a fortunate coincidence, been personally associated as student, as lecturer, and as creative thinker with three of the professors most deeply involved in the Scottish educational conflict: George Gibson of Glasgow, under whom he had got a First in mathematics with philosophy, Norman Kemp Smith of Edinburgh whose department he joined in 1920, and John Burnet of St Andrews whose work in Greek philosophy was to be a major influence in his intellectual formation. Pushed into the background of his consciousness during his first sixteen years in Australia when he was engaged in forging his philosophy and in creating the beginnings of a distinguished school — Passmore, Mackie, Kamenka, Armstrong — Anderson's interests in the issues raised by the Ordinance 70 affair surfaced in his writing with the appearance in Sydney in 1944 of the blueprint for the post-war reorganisation of education in both Australia and Britain from the pen of his Sydney colleague Eric Ashby (later knighted). Then in the process of incubating the ideas which were given to the world in 1958 in his *Technology and the Academics*, Ashby did much to prepare British public opinion for accepting the State-centred reorganisation of the universities as carried out under the auspices of the Grants Commission in the sixties.

In particular, the thing which made Anderson seriously rethink the problem of education was Ashby's idea (derived, as he acknowledges, from Lyon Playfair of the nineteenth century) that the universities would have to turn their backs on the values associated with useless subjects like philosophy and literary study if they were to be equal to the great task of the modern world — the redefinition of academic standards so as to make them serviceable for the new technology. In the light of Anderson's Scottish experience, Ashby's plans represented a resurrection, so to speak, of Struthers' and Darroch's bureaucratic anti-elitism which in the new and more extreme form it was assuming after World War II was likely to be all the more dangerous to the values of civilisation, because the conditioning of the war years, leading to an acquiescence to regimentation, had broken down the British people's resistance to centralised State control. Appalled by the prospect of victory for an educational policy which saw a utilitarian-minded levelling of all the subjects as the passport to a materialist Utopia managed by functionaries, Anderson did not waste time in nostalgically regretting the lost privileges of the values of intellect, but at once sought to rouse philosophy and literature to their new role as the spearhead of a high quality counter-culture, engaged in actively fighting against the degradation of critical standards liable to occur in a planners' paradise. Reformulating ideas like those of Burnet, so as to adapt them to the culture-crisis of the later twentieth century, Anderson's educational writings make both the elitism of the Scottish universities and the issues of the Ordinance 70 affair come alive for our own age in terms which we can understand.

Confining ourselves to Anderson's recently published (and remarkable) 'Lectures on Spencer and Dewey',[1] in which, reverting to the pedagogical problems of his student days, he compares Matthew Arnold's principles with those of American pragmatism and Victorian utilitarianism, let us concentrate especially on the grand climax of his course, in which he makes a very thorough critical anlysis of the favourite textbook of Darroch's Scotland — John Dewey's *Democracy and Education*. The dualism of self-development and service, Dewey claimed, "is too deeply established to be easily overthrown; for that reason, it is the particular task of education at the present time to struggle on behalf of an aim in which social efficiency and personal culture are synonymous instead of antagonists".[2] But Dewey, Anderson retorts, with regard to this claim, is making the assumption of voluntarism — "that if you want . . . two things they cannot be incompatible".[3] If the claims of self-development and the claim of social service are opposed in any given situation this opposition must be regarded as an accident, something not in the facts but capable of being eliminated. But how does Dewey know that? What method does he prescribe to us for bridging the gap? Bringing out into the open positions which are already implicit in Kemp Smith's cautious critique of Marxism, Anderson proceeds to attack the idea which has meant so much to the Scots since Burns first formulated it — that the day is coming when "man to man, the world o'er shall brothers be for a' that".

From Dewey's point of view, however, the conflicting aims which Anderson has declared to be unreconcilable are already in a fair way to being reconciled, thanks to the scientific revolution which is the distinctive feature of the post-Renaissance world. The dualism between personal culture on the one hand and service to society on the other applies in its hard and fast form only to the civilisation of Greece and to a certain extent that of the Middle Ages. Personal culture consisted, among the Greeks, in a spiritual activity exclusively indulged in by a leisure class who contemplated nature without interfering experimentally and manually with what it saw, and who went on to speculate in a non-verifiable way as to the hidden causes of the ambiguities and puzzles presented by the observation of nature. The contrasted term of service to society consisted, on its side, in the routine of unreflective manipulations of matter — the hewing of wood and the drawing of water — which were performed by a class without sufficient leisure to interest itself in the purely contemplative activities of scientific self-culture. But now, in the modern world, the relation between the classes has been completely altered, as the result of the fact that instead of being contemplative merely, science has become experimental.

The turning-point came, according to Dewey, when the ideas suggested by contemplation were no longer evaluated by a merely speculative reflection according "to their aesthetic consistence or agreeable quality or prestige of their authors"[4] but were capable of having their worth tested practically in experiments which might be repeated by others and which, when they provided a recipe for controlling the movements of matter in the interests of man, could be systematically reproduced in factories as manufactures. In the case of what had been the leisure class, the experience of the utility of this co-operative interference with nature in enabling mankind to become masters of parts of it, taught its members that the scientific self-culture, in addition to involving the spiritual activities of contemplating nature and of playing about speculatively with the hypotheses thus suggested — that is to say the activities which had seemed to set them apart from the rest of society — also essentially involved, in the novel development of experimental testing, a physical acting on nature similar in principle to the kind of work done by the hewers of wood and the drawers of water who had previously been looked down upon. The latter, for their part, were made to realise as the result of their participating in the practical follow-up of the experiments that the systematic manipulative interference with nature in which their work lay was not the unreflective uncontemplative routine of a merely physical character, which it had hitherto been regarded as being, but by reason of its involving the experimental confirmation and practical realisation of ideas originating in reflection and contemplation, enabled them, in some indirect way, to share in the spiritual activity which had before been supposed to be a monopoly of the other class. The dualistic separation of the two classes which had obtained among the Greeks was thus from the Renaissance onwards beginning to be dissolved by a revolution in which the opposites, self-culture and service to society, were becoming in Dewey's words to some extent "synonymous".

The transformation of class-relations brought about by the scientific-technological revolution has, Dewey admits, by no means abolished the division of society into a class which labours with its muscles for the material sustenance of everybody else and a class which relieved from economic pressure devotes itself to the arts of experience (i.e. contemplation) and of social direction. But he is nevertheless confident that an extension from nature to man of the experimental procedures which have produced the modern world of natural science and of industry will produce a truly democratic society in which "all share in useful service and all enjoy a worthy leisure devoted to personal culture, hopefully of an intellectual kind". Dewey is thus quite untroubled by the doubts voiced by Anderson as to the possibility of doing away with the antagonism between the non-productive labour which occupies itself in "culture" and the labour which produces food, clothing, shelter, etc. How then are we to overcome whatever remains of the dualism? Admitting that the antagonism cannot finally be abolished without "changes in industrial and political conditions" which he does not discuss, Dewey points to the crucial role of the schools in preparing countries for the advent of the classless society. The political and economic emancipation of the masses, says Dewey, has shown itself in education in the development of the common school, public and free, which has destroyed the idea of learning as a monopoly of the few who are predestined by nature to govern social affairs. But the revolution, he continues, "is still incomplete and the (Greek-derived) idea still prevails as a truly liberal or cultural system cannot have anything in common, directly at least, with industrial affairs, and that the education which is fit for the masses is a practical or useful education in the sense which opposes practical and useful to the nature of the appreciation of art and the liberation of thought".[5]

The way round the difficulty, according to Dewey, is for these common schools to become the focus of a pedagogical experiment which will show that, far from there being an antagonism between education for thinking and education for doing and physically acting, neither side can be fully and effectively cultivated and taught apart from the other. To this end we must, Dewey says, put behind us the one-sided style of communication in which cultural ideas are handed over in textbooks by the teacher to the class without the latter's being able to test them experimentally just as we must also get away from the equally one-sided communication in trade education where the apprentice learns by physically imitating the master in a rule of thumb way as if reflection, thought and ideas did not enter into the business. The ultimate inspiration of Dewey's philosophy of education is thus the vision of the classroom as the scene of a two-way communication between the teacher and the pupils, who, on both sides are engaged on the same level in the same experimental project, and whose exchanges about how to sort out the difficulties are mutually illuminating in the sense of enabling both sides to participate in the various kinds of communal discovery, intellectual and practical. The abstract unfamiliar ideas connected with culture are given life and brought down to earth by the necessity of devising ways of experimentally testing them, while the concrete, all too familiar, activities of a physical kind are intellectualised and made problematic by the necessity of looking on them as crystallisations of discoveries made about itself in the child's exploration of the world. These experimental projects look forward to a society from which dualism has been abolished. "Consensus," says Dewey, "demands communication"[6] — meaning by that the sort of communication which is educative because it is vitally social or vitally shared, and not the sort of communication which has hardened into a mould and become a mere routine. The experimental consensus of the classroom thus constitutes for Dewey the cradle of the classless society of the future.

John Anderson, for his part, is sharply critical of Dewey's ideas. Granted that there is no consensus without communication, it doesn't follow that communication necessarily leads to consensus. For Dewey — as also for Herbert Spencer — communication produces consensus or agreement, only because he takes it for granted that the disagreement which expresses itself in a failure to co-operate, is due to the lack of some clear-cut piece of information — which can in the long run be discovered and communicated — as to how to overcome the block. But according to Anderson, what Dewey and Spencer fail to see is that the inability to achieve co-operation may be due to the fact of there being no clear-cut recipe for resolving the difficulty.

But let us cite a passage in which Anderson puts his side of the case in his own very distinctive way. "The point is that communication is limited, that there will always be forces opposed to it, that there will always be social conflict — conflict in particular between an objective and critical attitude to things and a subjective and uncritical attitude. This is something which the humanitarian and progressivist outlook cannot admit." [7] In these words, Anderson spotlights what he regards as the central defects not only of Dewey but of the whole modern school from Russell to Ryle. In order to bring out the power and originality of Anderson's contribution to philosophy, it will therefore be necessary to look very carefully into the meaning of this conflict between an objective and critical attitude and a subjective and uncritical attitude to things.

To clarify the Andersonian doctrine sufficiently to bring out its force and novelty as well as its relevance to the issues raised by Ordinance 70, let us contrast it with the Deweyite position as just explained, starting from what these two thinkers, otherwise so different, have in common, a concern for the problems raised by the tension between on the one hand the tradition of intellectual culture inherited from Greece as essentially contemplative, that is to say, developing its theories quite independently of practice, and on the other hand the modern movement of intellectual culture which connects its theories and practice and which is interested in theorising only in so far as its ideas can be tested by manipulation of nature and reproduced in manufacture. The tension between these two diverse traditions of doing science provides a starting-point for Anderson's thought as well as that of Dewey. Where they fall apart is that for Dewey the modern experimental method of doing science has completely displaced from its central position the Greek method of a purely contemplative science occupied in speculating with hypotheses, and has transformed it into something which has to be got rid of altogether or assigned a purely peripheral role. By contrast, for Anderson, the rise and progress of the modern movement for a socially useful science, technically as well as experimentally oriented, far from preparing the conditions for the extermination of the Greek-derived tradition of intellectual culture as theoretical and disinterested, has given it new work to do. It has a new lease of life in the form of an independent movement of ideas which is antagonistic to the modern, experimental science, not in the sense of repudiating it and getting back to societies on the model of the Greek city-states, where experimental science as we know it does not flourish, but in the sense of calling attention to, of bringing to light, the aberrations and blind spots afflicting our experimental science, when, as the result of being over-preoccupied with researches subordinate to the general aims of economic growth, it, as so often happens, loses its grip on reality. Exhibited in a succession of cultural and educational crises over the years, from the time of the "battle of the books" about 1700 to the Ordinance 70 Affair in Scotland of 1917-1927, a great argument unfolds in which the proponents of Greek-derived classical values criticise and attack the pragmatism of the modern sciences for their excessive pursuit of material values of the kind Dewey defends, as liable to be counter-productive because of the tendency of the scientist to take for granted superficial views of the philosophical and logical problems raised by his own subject. Far from disappearing, the purely contemplative and free play of mind which we associate with the Greeks reappears in modern civilisation in the form of literature and literary criticism insofar as they direct attention to the kind of problem which the scientists, the practical men, the State etc. neglect on account of their very familiarity.

Identifying with the tradition of Arnoldian criticism, Anderson at the same time draws attention to a limitation in Arnold's point of view which the critical movement must transcend if it is to make its mark on our times. In *Literature and Dogma* Arnold stated that the business of criticism is not with scientific matters but with literary, social and religious matters because in regard to the former we have a quite clear grasp of the conceptions we work with, whereas in regard to the latter we are still groping in the midst of a fog, involved with conceptions the unclarity of which sets a task for the critic. According to Anderson, however, Arnold is seriously wrong here. He is not entitled to assume that there is any subject matter which is clear cut and definite, and in regard to which we do not have to recognise the tentativeness of our conceptions and the need for a constant criticism of them. The exactness of those sciences, especially modern mechanical science which is assumed to be quite clear and definite, is a spurious exactness, which aims at paring away any difficulties and ignoring the inconvenient characters of things — inconvenient, that is, from the standpoint of the researcher's special interest of socially useful science. In an interesting note on the subject of scientific revolutions, Anderson goes on to say in the same passage[8] that their periodic occurrence proved not so much their inevitability as the need for the sciences to be subject to constant critical scrutiny.

It is important to understand that in calling for a criticism of science, Anderson is not calling for the establishment of a special kind of criticism parallel to literary criticism but quite separate. What he means is that the literary critic of the Arnold or Leavis type ought to keep an eye on scientific writing as well as on pure literature. In order to train the judgment of those who are to exercise this high calling, their education, Anderson lets us know, must follow the same broad line of training which Anderson gave himself in Glasgow University in the second decade of the present century, at the very time when the generalist tradition was under attack from the specialist pedagogy of the S.E.D. No doubt his extensive programme, which calls for a philosophical education based on logic but comprehending literature, the natural sciences, the study of industrial society and history, will be objected to as being quite beyond the capacity of modern man. But as against this, it is well to point out that, as is shown by the articles, addresses and reviews which Anderson produced as Professor of Philosophy at Sydney, he himself made a courageous attempt to fulfil his own programme, and in that way set an example which others can follow.

Instead of repeating Anderson's position in more or less his own words, let me explain more carefully its distinctive point by continuing and sharpening up my comparison of his philosophy with that of Dewey. "Every advance in experimental matters," says Dewey, with a view to dismissing the efforts at a renaissance of classicism, "is sure to aid in outlawing the literary, dialectical and authoritative methods of forming beliefs which governed the schools of the past."[9] In the reconstruction of culture which Dewey looks forward to, we must relegate purely literary methods — including textbooks and dialectical methods — to the position of necessary auxiliary tools in a movement of education which seeks to turn out pupils worthy of the coming age of socialised science. But, according to the way Anderson sees things, Dewey is able to dethrone (relegate, outlaw, i.e. deny authority to) the classical tradition, only because he has broken the connection of logic and literature characteristic of classicism in order to let experimental science monopolise logic, and thus acquire the authority which goes with logic, and which is thus lost to literature. Divorced from logic, literature is reduced by Dewey to a set of presentational techniques, the object of which is to give life to, in the sense of rendering readable, the exposition of a set of experimentally-based propositions which are already logically impeccable but which, because of their technicalities, are, humanly speaking, somewhat unpalatable. Literature, as the result of this Deweyite reduction, becomes in Anderson's words, an "ornament of study rather than its substance".[10]

In speaking of literature as the substance of study, Anderson is not merely asserting that logic is just as much an essential part of literature as it is of experimental science. Rather, his point is the more far-reaching one, that the prior task of logic expresses itself through literature, the prime concern of which is to face society, or rather the readers in it, with the possibility that the preoccupation of the contemporary generation with the experimental verification of certain hypotheses, which are being explored with a view to their social applicability, is liable to result in a defective sense of reality which will turn a blind eye to areas of experience irrelevant to the practical aims of the experimentation. Just as the literature of Greece — philosophy, drama, history, etc. — kept the Greeks intellectually awake by a disinterested contemplation of life and nature which, by drawing attention to certain apparent contradictions between different views of things, kept alive the idea that the world must really be somewhat different from its appearances as comprehended in the fashionable hypotheses, so too in modern times, critics of the Matthew Arnold type may perform the role of the Socratic gadfly in regard to their fellow citizens by drawing attention to the sharp contrast between the scientific and social orthodoxy of the day, and the way the poets, both present and past, look at things. Following in Arnold's footsteps, Anderson carries further the criticism of life, in the view he puts forward that Dewey's philistine attitude to literature, which subordinates it to science, is bound up with his confused belief in the reconcilability of all social tendencies as if there was only one type of social organisation and as if assisting one social tendency did not mean hindering the others.[11]

In order to carry further our contrast of Anderson and Dewey, let us look at the crucial fact which in Anderson's estimation explains the public activity of literature as being, in his own words, a movement which exists *"to disengage some character of things which is obscured or ignored in customary activities"* (italics mine).[12] We get to the nature of the thing, Anderson says, by way of a phrase from the visual arts — "restoring the innocent eye" — that is, he explains, "restoring the power of seeing things objectively", by criticising certain assumptions common to the "sight" of society and originally present in the writer himself as a member of it, which, by the working of the familiarity-breeds-neglect principle, have made everyone blind to the existence of certain characteristics present in the environment but not actually noticed.

Now different as is Dewey's philosophy from Anderson's, and contemptuous as Dewey would be about Anderson's view of the role of art and literature, Dewey nevertheless is as aware as Anderson is of the existence in society of these cultural blind spots which, by becoming habitual, deaden the cultural process and produce a state of affairs in which the communication system of society *"becomes cast in a mould and runs in a routine way, losing its educative power"* (italics mine).[13] A fact of which Anderson makes so much — intellectual blindness, unconsciousness of what is there — also has a place in Dewey's educational philosophy.

The theory advanced here, says Dewey in a comment on his argument as a whole, "assumes *continuity*"; the other theories — among which Dewey would from his own point of view justifiably include Anderson's — "imply certain divisions, separations or antitheses technically called dualisms".[14] Consistently with his general theory, Dewey interprets the fact of cultural deadening as due to the continuing influences of the dualism, which by keeping alive the Greek-derived tradition of the sharp separation between the education of leisure class and that of the working classes, has slowed down the social advance as a whole by cutting off intercommunication between them in this very important field. The problem, Dewey makes clear, is a serious one, but it is not for him insoluble, and in a way contains its remedy in itself. It arises from our inability to transcend the Greek philosophy of education and life and blocks the path to the development of a purely democratic society where "all will share in useful service and all enjoy a worthy leisure".[15] As regards the question of how to break through the blockage, we already know in a general way that the remedy lies outside education in the increased political and economic emancipation of the masses. Some kind of a socio-political revolution, according to Dewey, by breaking down the barrier between the two traditions of education, is one day going to put an end to the cultural blight and habitual blind spots by promoting a two-sided complete form of communication, of which Dewey gives an exciting account in his first chapter. Communication, he says, is essentially educative:

"Try the experiment of communicating, with fullness and accuracy some experience to another, especially if it be somewhat complicated, and you will find your own attitude to your experience changing; the experience has to be formulated in order to be communicated. To formulate requires getting outside of it, seeing it as another would see it, considering what points of contact I have with the life of another, so that it may be got into such a form that he can appreciate its meaning."[16]

In short, one has to assimilate imaginatively something of another's experience in order to tell him intelligently of one's own experience. Communication in the full sense is therefore not a mere process of passing over a piece of cut and dried information; it is a vital sharing in which book-knowledge is revitalised, deepened, opened up, so as to make it raise fresh questions and become the starting point of a new inquiry. Understood in this way, communication gives a foretaste of what life will be like when the class barriers have disappeared in the future. But Anderson is going to take a quite different line from Dewey in regard to the problem of how a group can overcome a habitual blind spot, or in other words how there can arise in a group a consciousness of something about itself of which hitherto the members of the group have been unconscious. For Dewey, as we have just noticed, physical causes — in this case the tradition-laden separation of the group into a leisure class and a labouring class — have first to be dissolved in some kind of political change which, establishing the communication between the sub-groups, enables each to learn from the other and the whole can then move steadily forward in a mutually supportive unison.

By contrast with Dewey's monism (i.e. what he calls the *continuity* of his system) Anderson's answer depends very much on what he, for his part, speaks of as the *pluralism* of his philosophy. Conditions for a group's overcoming its habit-bred blind spots and clearing its eyes, so to speak, of motes, are present only when it is aware of itself as surrounded by foreign groups of a comparable type, and would be absent if the group were alone in the world — e.g. in the form of a smoothly-organised world state — and had nothing with which its members could compare it. The abolishing of the blind spot actually gets going when some gifted member of the group, as the result of travel, etc., is able to compare the way his own group conducts its life with the way foreign groups go about their business. In Burnet's account of the origins of Greek philosophy[17] — that is to say in a text which Anderson certainly studied with care — the moment of illumination comes when the traveller notes a foreign group to be very different in one particular department of its life (which afterwards would be called a religious or spiritual department) as compared with his own group, though in other departments of life (what we would come to call the economics etc.) it might be very similar. Before making this discovery, the traveller did not, indeed could not, make this distinction in regard to his own group. Now, however, comparison suggests that the one side, i.e. the religious, involves speculations about things which are not properly observable, whereas the other side (economic behaviour etc.) involves thought which is practicably testable in the sense of being concerned with things which are empirically given.

Now, of course, it is possible that this new knowledge of the dualism of the life of his group may not be communicated at all by the traveller. But suppose him to be a sort of Matthew Arnold who has cultivated a talent for putting over the problems raised by the dualistic aspect of a society in language capable of interesting the fellow-members of his group. How, for example, are the untestable beliefs about these completely unobservable objects of religion related to the more or less unanswerable questions raised by astronomy which, though not concerned with the unobservable, is concerned with what may be seen, but not touched or manipulated? How, secondly, is this sphere of merely speculative ideas, whether they are about unobservables as in religion, or about the merely visible as in astronomy, to be related to the practically testable ideas which have to do with the group's economic life? In this case, the critical-minded traveller's new consciousness of the division of his own society into two parts, a transcendental part and an empirical part, becomes the starting point of something very important to Anderson's philosophy — a movement of ideas in which more and more people get caught up. As the result of the movement started by the critic, the custom-bred blind spot in the tribe's knowledge of its nature disappears without there being any need for the kind of external social transformation of class relations which Dewey has in mind.

In the light of this sketch of the genesis of a movement for criticism and philosophy which Anderson regards as essential to the existence of a free society — "the servile state is the unopposed state",[18] i.e. the state without critics — it is not difficult to get the point of his account of how intellectuals like Matthew Arnold (and Anderson himself), by an extensive comparison of the local and the present with the past, managed to discover the principles which are essential to training the judgment, and to fixing consistent standards in reference to literature in its criticism of life. The crucial moment is a follow-up of the initial stage just mentioned, in which comparison of our society and other societies draws attention to this sharp and problematic division between the spiritual side of the community's life and the material side, concerned as they are respectively with questions imponderable and ponderable which had remained hidden by their very familiarity in the days when the routine of the group's activities was not disturbed by the tales of the intellectual traveller. The supreme moment of truth comes for Anderson when, as happened in the Roman world as well as in the modern world, men suddenly became impressed by the unique value of the contribution of the Greeks — especially the Athenians — as compared with that of other peoples, ancient and modern. The Greeks in their philosophy and their literature develop, with the utmost thoroughness and consistency, the various sides of the complicated debate as to whether the unverifiable speculations starting with the problem raised by religion should be set aside altogether, except insofar as they can indirectly aid the practical-minded verifiable speculations concerned with the sciences useful to life and society, or whether this stratum of so-called useless, unverifiable speculations, far from being subordinated to the useful sciences, is essential for overseeing the matter critically in order to check the tendency to fall into error through an excessively one-sided concentration on the achievement of material goals, or in other words on the subordination of science to economic aims. But the greatest achievement of Greek literature is for Anderson — following Burnet — the discussions arising out of the trial and death of Socrates, who was executed by the Athenian democracy for sharply criticising its utilitarian ideas from the point of view of a philosophy which took its stand on transcendental principles. The distinction drawn in the dialogues which Plato — in explicit reference to the execution of his master — wrote to point out the limitations of utilitarianism, empiricism etc. have not, according to Anderson, gone out of date, and still have a great deal to teach.

The value of Greek culture to the critic is, according to Anderson, that by comparing it to the culture of other countries, he is able to bring to light the reductivism, the solidarism, the voluntarism, which are the chief defects of modern theorising. The fact that Greece could produce culture of this outstanding quality on the basis of a backward economy, which depended in large part on slavery, sufficiently refutes the reductive idea favoured by Dewey and so many of the moderns that the intellectual progress of a community depends on its material progress in a one-sided way. So too, the subtle argument in which the Greeks bring out the nature of happiness as complex and in many respects unrealisable (e.g. in Plato's *Philebus*) provides the starting point for the critique both of the solidarist idea — so much in vogue in modern times — that the interests of each is reconcilable with the interests of all, as well as of the closely allied voluntarism which holds that if the interests of sections in a society conflict, there must surely be some way of reconciling them.

It is, of course, impossible, from Anderson's point of view, to understand properly and apply the standards of classicism without carefully comparing the various works of the Greeks in order to distinguish the first-rate from the others. What makes Burnet's contribution so very valuable is his carefully worked out assessment of culture which gives reasons for preferring Plato's philosophy to Aristotle's, and which, within the corpus of the Platonic writings, distinguishes carefully between the intellectually outstanding dialogues and the others, setting aside for example the *Republic* in favour of the later, and much more self-critical, *Theaetetus*. Other classical scholars are, for Anderson, by no means up to this level. Our hide-bound uncritical traditionalists and — worse still — others are so caught up in the modern movement of utilitarianism, socialism, etc., that the result of their researches is to discredit the Greek classical philosophers in favour of the ideas of Dewey and such like.

However, it is impossible to uphold classicist standards by a study of Greek and nothing but Greek, and the critic would not be up to his job unless he was able to pass from Greek to modern literature, from modern literature to physics, from physics to economics, with a view to fixing accurately the philosophical foundations of all these studies, and of exposing the errors of the modern school which crop up in every subject and which as fast as they are expelled from one field reappear in another. The critic thus, as Anderson puts it, quoting Croce, leads "a perilous and a fighting life",[19] engaged as he is in a perpetual struggle against the one-sidedness of scientists and administrators, ignorant, ever contemptuous of philosophy and literature, who by seeking to subordinate intellectual standards to economic growth or by discouraging basic science in favour of the useful science which seems likely to produce the materialist Utopia of the solidarists are actually, Anderson assures us, imperilling the whole existence of civilisation. No doubt the Deweys and the Darrochs have the upper hand in the twentieth century, in the sense that government policy has turned against classicist standards. However, classicism, for Anderson, is not likely to die out. The ordeal of dethronement has reawakened it, giving it a new vigour. It can therefore look forward to a lively future in which it will play a leading part in the intellectual opposition to the consumer society.

The question of Greek culture is thus agreed by both sides — the Deweyites and their opponents — to be the key to the war between classicism and modernism. For Anderson, the emergence in Greece of philosophy and mathematics made an epoch in the history of man because, in giving birth to logic, they made possible a new sort of relationship between theory and practice in which the intellectuals come into their own. However, the establishment of logic in a central place in the curriculum did not ensure the maintenance of civilised standards because logic was no sooner consolidated in institutionalised ways than it lost touch with life, detaching itself from literature, from natural science, etc. Culture thus went into one of those declines from which it is periodically rescued by a renaissance of Greek studies. From the point of view of the Deweyites, however, Anderson makes far too much of the contribution of the Greeks because he had forgotten that methods of enquiry, like everything else, can progress. Greek geometry no doubt was an epoch-making invention but it was superseded at the Renaissance by the Cartesian analysis which greatly facilitated research, and today computerisation is going to extend further our powers of mathematical understanding, replacing the old algebra. So in the same way the Greek logic, of which Anderson has so high an opinion, has, Dewey points out, given way to a modern logic which has provided us with intellectual tools of very much improved quality. The fact is, according to Dewey, that cultural "development" has taken place by the entrance of shortcuts and alterations in the prior scheme, and these are the things which made possible scientific growth. On the modernist view, "the aim of education is to facilitate such short-circuited growth",[20] substituting for ancestral methods a direct method and emancipating the young from the methods of the outgrown past to which men like Anderson would have us return. No doubt, there have, in the past, been periods of cultural decline, but Dewey does not say much about them, because of regarding the chief obstacle to culture as being something outside culture — the untimely survival of the division of society into a leisure class and working class which has come down from the Greeks. Once this unfortunate state of affairs is remedied, progress will be irreversible.

Anderson himself does not deny the possibility that education and culture can progress as well as decline. However, the key to the achievement of the real advance which will take us beyond the Greeks lies, for him, in consistently adapting Greek principles to situations which the Greeks themselves did not encounter. Accepting as the core of culture the classic discussions between Socrates and his auditors which began with both sides being on equal terms but which ended in his establishing his intellectual authority over the others as the philosopher who relied on logic and nothing but logic, Anderson takes up the question as to what happens when the special sciences are broken off from philosophy as they were already beginning to do in Aristotle. The problem here, of course, is that raised by Burnet and Thorndike about specialisation, generalism and the possibility of "transfer", and Anderson's discussion of it exhibits his sharpness of mind in the sense that it enables us to distinguish the valuable parts of Burnet's treatment of the subject from the incidental parts where he leads us astray.

Burnet, for Anderson, is very sound insofar as he seeks to get beyond narrow specialisation by recommending the study of a normally specialised subject side by side with some other specialism with which it is comparable and has relations with a view to letting each shed light on the other. The greatness of Burnet for Anderson consists in the fact that Burnet did not just theorise about the possibility of pairing off cognate subjects against one another, but in his book on *Early Greek Philosophy* as well as in in his *Greek Philosophy: Thales to Plato* he actually employs his comparative method to excellent effect. "The work of Burnet . . . with its striking combination of philosophical and historical insight," Anderson says in the 1958 lecture on 'Classicism', brings home to us "the way in which knowledge of philosophy can help us to determine the course of philosophical thought and the views of individual thinkers, while knowledge of the doctrines of individual thinkers and their historical connection can help us to arrive at philosophical truths (to learn philosophy)."[21]

That is to say, Burnet starts by making the point that Hegel, in two important respects, got the order of Greek philosophy wrong — he supposed Heraclitus to have succeeded Parmenides whereas in fact the former came first and is referred to by the latter, and later a similar mistake is made in regard to the dating of the group of Platonic dialogues which begins with the *Theaetetus,* which is taken to be one of the early and immature group of dialogues whereas in fact it belongs to Plato's later and more mature period. The kind of modern scholarship which believes itself to be "scientific" might regard Burnet's preoccupation with this historical point as irrelevant to the study of Greek philosophy, and a mark of Burnet's weakness. For Anderson, on the other hand, Burnet's strength lies in the fact that he was able to show these Hegelian mistakes in dating to be responsible for serious misunderstanding of very remarkable philosophical texts, which Anderson shows us how to use in reference to our own age.

While it is clear enough[22] that Anderson agrees with Burnet's view of philosophy as being a corrective to the narrowing effects of specialisation, it is by no means clear at first sight whether Anderson also accepts Burnet's further claim that this critical generalism which occupies the time of the intellectual elite, gains effectiveness if it is broadly based class-wise, that is to say, if it is what Walter Elliot (followed by myself) called in a certain special sense "the democratic intellect". "We either have an education," says Anderson, "which is 'universal' in the sense of developing general standards of judgment, but it is not 'universal' in the sense of being for everyone, or else we have a general education in which standards are lost." Anderson therefore in the full sense repudiated a democratic education in the sense of an education purveyed on the basis of equality all round, but it does not follow from this that he repudiated the "democratic" or popular element in education as understood by Burnet.

The solution is this. Anderson took very seriously the problem of the possibility of a democratic intellect. He speaks of "the question as one he has frequently mentioned" — whether there is a universal aptitude for criticism or whether criticism is really embraced by the so-called "democratic" views.[24] Let us therefore look carefully at Anderson's discussion of the point in order to show that his final opinion depends upon distinguishing sharply between Burnet on the one hand and Dewey, and others like him, on the other. The democratic basis understood as Burnet understands it, can be, according to Anderson, a source of strength to the work of criticism and philosophy, but understood as Dewey understands it, it ruinously weakens criticism.

First let us consider, with Anderson, Dewey's view that criticism and philosophy can find a place in the democratic system of education (understood in a Deweyite way) provided it accepts the role of a vocation on a level with other vocations, occupying itself in supplying them with constructive criticism when they call for it, and does not claim that it should be put on a pedestal in order to look down on all other studies, pointing out their blind spots. Thus for Dewey philosophy and criticism have their place in a democratic education as auxiliary subjects merely, coming to the aid of psychiatry, physics, etc., in order to clear up some metaphysical confusion in their theories which prevents them from being experimentally testable or put to practical use. From Anderson's point of view, on the other hand, this subordination of criticism and philosophy to the needs of the special sciences and their production of practical results, inevitably, as we have seen, weakens critical standards.[25]

But, even if we do distinguish sharply between philosophy on the one hand and the special sciences on the other, the latter each being confined to a field of its own, the former surveying the inter-relation of the fields, and rendering the special sciences aware of their underlying unity, it is still open to the Deweyites to argue that criticism and philosophy in this Andersonian sense are just as much vocations as are the special sciences, because like them they are the responsibility of professional scholars. Now it may be — Anderson replies — that "culture will not persist unless there be professional scholars of this kind",[26] but that does not mean that the training in criticism that they give is training for a job. The training the criticism gives — whether by books or by lectures — interests people, according to Anderson, not because it is useful in a definite way to their professional activities, but because it wakens them up intellectually in much the same way as poetry does.[27]

It is by way of this non-vocational aspect of a culture, kept alive by criticism, that Anderson seeks to draw attention to what is found in Burnet's claim that the intellectual elite can draw strength from their breadth of social basis. Most of the time, Anderson says, the intellectuals engage in a battle with the rest of the community, economic-minded as it is, in order to prevent a lowering of standards. But at certain times, in certain societies, the culture and scholarship enjoy a respect from the majority. These circumstances obtained on the occasion of the classic efflorescences of intellectual culture, like that of Scotland in the eighteenth century.[28]

The view that the culture in the classic periods has nourished itself by drawing on popular roots is traced by Anderson to Matthew Arnold, who, of course, had a considerable influence on Burnet, and with whom Anderson himself is largely in agreement:

"Arnold's position suggests that education cannot be a universal thing, that we cannot have education for everybody, though we might have a certain participation in education (an approach to judgement) on the part of people who do not go the whole way, that is, do not become thoroughly critically-minded. If we use the special term 'scholarship', it could be argued that it was favourable to the flourishing of scholarship in a community if people who did not become scholars at least went far enough to have an appreciation of scholarship. In that case scholarship would have a certain social standing and would not be confined to a few struggling against the social stream, though I should say there would always be something of this character, something of a struggle against commercial and other narrow interests in the existence of scholarship anywhere."[29]

Because of the widespread tendency of what I call Deweyites to claim that the notion of "democratic intellectualism" either means absolute egalitarianism or means nothing,[30] it would be as well to cite a passage from David Hume's essay on 'The Rise and Progress of the Arts and Sciences'[31] (in the eighth paragraph from the beginning) which shows what the considered version of the notion — the version held to by Anderson and Burnet — really means:

"Though the persons, who cultivate the sciences with such astonishing success, as to attract the admiration of posterity, be always few, in all nations and all ages; it is impossible but a share of the same spirit and genius must be antecedently diffused through the people among whom they arise, in order to produce, form, and cultivate, from their earliest infancy, the taste and judgement of those eminent writers. The mass cannot be altogether insipid, from which such refined spirits are extracted."

As to those who eloquently claim that Hume's notions of democracy and education are hollow and insincere as compared with those of Cobbett, it is as well to point out that Cobbett's ideas of democratic or mass education seem to have been drawn from his experiences in the army. The model of mass education is for him the N.C.O. explaining the "naming of parts" to the recruits. Understood in this sense the issue between Hume, Anderson etc. and Cobbett depends upon Burnet's distinction between rote-learning and judgemental learning. Once again, therefore, the Deweyites, if I understand them aright, have simplified the whole question unduly in order to make their point. Anderson, it may thus be said, perhaps goes along with Burnet in the thesis that the culture of the few is not altogether cut off from the culture of the many, but it has been queried — especially among Anderson's Australian pupils — as to whether he would have accepted Burnet's belief in the value of the tradition which counts philosophy as a compulsory subject. The answer, however, seems to me to be that whatever Anderson thought about the position of philosophy in regard to the Australian curriculum, he was in sympathy with what Burnet said about the theoretical desirability of its retaining its status in the Scottish curriculum. The work of the intellectual producer, Anderson says, resides not in "social levelling" or any other "practical" undertaking, but simply in making discoveries — rejecting conventional or customary associations like that of "benefitting" from all social activities. The philosopher therefore would be "following an intellectual tradition within an intellectual institution. It is the custody of such traditions and institutions which requires privileges or 'charters', and the work of egalitarianism in breaking these down is one of the major causes of injury to intellectual activity in our present period."[32] In this quotation from the posthumously published article on 'Empiricism and Logic' which belongs to the same group as the lecture on 'Classicism' which contains the acknowledgements to Burnet — that is to say in writings produced at the very end of his life — Anderson, as I understand him, seems to be taking up a stand in defence of the same kind of notions of the curriculum as Burnet wanted to apply to Scotland.

So far Burnet is first class from Anderson's viewpoint but he goes astray when, in his book *Higher Education and the War*, he seeks to strengthen his interdisciplinary approach by putting forward the idea — already being canvassed by Dewey and later popularised by Sir Eric Ashby — that subjects can be taken out of their isolation and brought into fruitful connection with one another, not only by the internal philosophical approach (Burnet's real contribution) in which comparison enables each subject to throw light on the others, but also by an external, practical approach in which their bond of unity is the fact of their all being useful for promoting some technical or manufacturing profession, in the sense in which Ashby claims that the proper education of a brewer would involve not only the chemistry related to beer and the principle of the machines involved in its production as well as the economics of its marketing, but also the ethical study of the problems of drunkenness as well as the aesthetics of public houses. The two lines of approach which Burnet speaks of as complementary or mutually supportive — on the one hand the practical utility as a means of grouping together isolated subjects, and on the other, the intellectualism which explores and brings to light the defects of each subject from a philosophical point of view by setting it side by side with the others — are for Anderson really irreconcilable and hinder one another's advance if taken together. If the practical approach is preferred, a distinction has to be made between the useful and the useless, purely academic part of the various subsidiary studies, and the former aspect has to be favoured over the latter, with the effect of lowering standards, and producing a superficial, not to say erroneous treatment of the aesthetics, ethics, economics, even chemistry of brewing or whatever it may be. If on the other hand the theoretical approach is taken, the argument over the problem of the interrelation of the various subjects has to be followed out wheresoever it leads by the logic of the situation, irrespective of what the result is going to mean in the way of hindering the practical efforts to produce results. Watching the way in which the careers of his former students developed between 1914-1918, when they joined the army, Burnet did not accept that the practical versatility encouraged by the participation in the war effort was a totally different kind of versatility than the intellectual comparison of subjects he had encouraged in his own classroom.

Far from promoting the philosophical breadth of mind, the efforts of the twentieth-century State to make science serve human needs have, Anderson pointed out, the effect of lowering cultural standards and of making science itself less useful to society than it would have been if it had been left to its own traditions of disinterested research. The scientific advance which has given us "the Bomb" has — Anderson thought — been bound up with this decline in the standards of enquiry. Science has been practicalised, "it has been concerned with 'getting things done', with facilitating transformations and translations, not with just finding out what is the case and with the 'criticisms of categories' that that involves".[33] That is to say it has, under pressure of the State, sought to make practical use of certain results of its subatomic researches before it has known properly what it was doing in the sense of having cleared up certain contradictions between the various points of view opened by its discoveries — a drastic step which seems to have broken with the intellectual tradition in which it has developed.

But apart from this silent correction of the practicalism into which Burnet was led by his enthusiastic participation in the war effort, Anderson's positions read as if they had been arrived at by a development of Burnet which, abstracting from the Scottish references, generalises and sharpens the attack on specialisation, giving it the form of systematic philosophy. The clarification of Burnet's insights which results from this follow-up can be best illustrated by a comparison of what both say on the topic so central to each — of the close connection between philosophy and science on the one hand, and literature on the other. The scholars of the Middle Ages, Burnet had said, were just as aware as those of the Renaissance of the superiority of Greek science to what they had in their own textbooks. The latter, however, were incomparably more successful than the former in recovering Greek science and assimilating its lessons because, according to Burnet, the medievals, in their practically-minded way, tried to study the science of the Greeks in abstraction from the labours the study of Greek literature would require, whereas at the revival of learning, the study of Greek science was treated as inseparable from the study of Greek literature, and it was this perception of the close connection between the study of poetry and the study of science which made possible the Renaissance.

But having asserted in a striking manner the close connection between the field of philosophy and the field of poetry, Burnet omits to explain in what this connection consisted. By contrast, Anderson sees the importance of filling the gap, and his elucidation of the interrelationship of literature and science forms one of the most valuable as well as one of the most central parts of his contribution to philosophy. Literature, philosophy and science, he says, are all concerned with the intellectual task of criticising the ordinary point of view of the community to which they belong, with a view to calling attention to the things which are taken for granted. All of them, in fact, are criticism in the sense of being aimed at the disclosure and destruction of what is illusory in our point of view. Where they differ, according to Anderson, is roughly speaking, that literature so to speak asks the questions or draws attention to unnoticed contradictions in parts of our habitual point of view, while science and philosophy go on to attend to the facts in the light of which they seek to remove the contradictions by altering our way of looking at things. Or alternatively, literature in some sense is concerned with criticising our existing hypotheses and propounding alternative hypotheses, whereas science and philosophy are concerned in their different ways with following up the hypotheses which may have been suggested by literature in order to determine how far they are true, and what has to be changed in our inherited point of view. In this way, Anderson performs the very important service of producing a view of the things which intimately connects literature with intellectual activities and connects both of them with life.

In this way, Burnet enables Anderson to correct certain defects in Matthew Arnold's views of criticism, broadening its scope and making it more relevant to the problems of the modern world. The result is a most notable attack upon the new philistinism which arose in the teaching world, in Scotland and out of it, as the result of Dewey's influence.

From the fact that the papers on Burnet and against specialisation come in the last years of Anderson's life, 1958-1962, I permit myself the surmise that the welfare state reconstruction of education after 1945 on Deweyite lines was an appalling prospect for Anderson, prompting him to restate in a more considered as well as a sharper form, the classical values which had been upheld by the Scottish professoriate of his student days against the new utilitarianism of Darroch. Diagnosing the slide into pragmatism as end-result of the subjectivism which entered into modern philosophy with Descartes' epistemological doubts, Anderson sought to recapture the Greek directness advocated by some of his teachers, and the texts they used, as the only way to restore elitist standards. "For an answer to Hegel and his subjectivism we have to drop epistemology — the intrusion of mind into logic and of a false logic into psychology — and return to the Greek consideration of *things*, as Burnet, no less by the English realists, assists us to do."[34]

The call for a return to Greek realism which was to be found in Burnet in reference to philosophy was paralleled for Anderson in the defence of the value of geometry which was put forward by his mathematical teacher in Glasgow, Gibson. The invasion of the exact sciences by the anti-realist subjectivism was, as Anderson seemed to have seen things, the result of the widely advocated view then coming into Scotland that the new non-Euclidean geometry provided just as good a metric as did the Euclidean geometry for a space of experience, the nature of which was now regarded as determinable subjectively by our choice of principles. If we are to block the subjective view of physics which provides a welfare state with a kind of justification for its practicalism and its utility view of science, it is necessary, Anderson thinks, to return to the Greek realism of Euclid, and with this aim he thrusts aside the attempts being made in Scotland by Sommerville of St Andrews to reinstate Thomas Reid's pioneering defence of a limited form of the non-Euclidean idea of a curved space which Riemann was to carry forward after Reid's time. Reviving the distinctive traditions of Scottish Hellenism, as represented on the one hand by the work of the three St Andrews historians of philosophy — Ferrier, Lewis Campbell and Burnet himself — in setting aside Hegel's perversions of Greek thought so as to restore the credit of Heraclitus and of Plato in the eyes of the modern world, and on the other hand, in the current of Scottish mathematics from Robert Simson through Playfair to Gibson himself, all of them in their various ways busying themselves with the criticism of Descartes' reductivism and subjectivism in geometry so as to get back to the objectivity of Euclid, Anderson set himself to make a major contribution to the field of logic. His aim was to check the cultural decline which had set in with Hegel's subordination of the laws of logic to history so as to make them developmental, and which had been carried further by the efforts of Hegel's critics, the symbolic or mathematical logicians like Russell, to reform logic by treating its principles as being dependent on the arbitrary facts of language. From Anderson's point of view, the first condition for strengthening the hands of the critics in their struggles against the false hopes animating the forces of modern anti-intellectualism was the reinstatement of the principles of Aristotle's logic, at which he energetically worked for the whole of his career.

But what of the standpoint, in regard to all this, of the Deweyites, who, unlike Anderson, see civilisation, not as a halting advance by turns falling away from its intellectual foundations among the Greeks and by turns recovering them in a Hellenic renaissance, but as a perpetual progress effected by shortcuts and by the invention of precision tools to replace the clumsy machinery inherited from the Athenians? At first sight, Anderson's distinctive line of philosophy seems liable to be written off as a Quixotic provincialism which refuses to give up the old things and which, tongue-tied in the face of the whirl of modern progress, blames its failure to organise its materials into a book on logic on Kemp Smith's refusals to do the same sort of service for Anderson as Anderson did for him in 1922-23, when he sorted out the confused notes of the second draft of the *Prolegomena to an Idealist Theory of Knowledge*. But the Deweyites are stopped short in their dismissal of Anderson as a thinker out of touch with the becoming tendencies of his time, and are forced to hedge and qualify, as soon as they encounter the trenchant analysis by which Anderson, by the courageous application of the principles of logic, uncovers the quietistic roots of the noisy ideas, anti-elitist and libertarian, which had been a continuing inspiration of the teachers' movement in the Scotland of his youth. Sharpened up in the light of Anderson's logic, Kemp Smith's Calvinist critique of Marxist ideas is rescued from its obscurity and developed with redoubtable force and unforgettable originality.

We will get a better grasp of the argument between Anderson and Dewey about the significance of the contribution which the movement for literature and literary criticism (taken in a broad sense) makes to the modern world if we start by taking note of their fundamental disagreement on the significance of the Marxist doctrines which, in some sense, formed one of the chief starting points of both thinkers. "The doctrine of history as struggle," Anderson says, "is at once the liberal and the scientific part of Marxism; the doctrine of socialism as something to be realised ('classless society') [i.e. the part Dewey develops] is its servile part. The point is not merely the drabness that might result from attempts to eliminate social struggles, but the impossibility of eliminating them — and therewith, the loss of independence and vigour which can result from the spreading of the *belief* that they can be eliminated."[35] The valuable side of Marx for Anderson was thus his vision of society, not as a movement towards "this kiss of the whole world" as Schiller calls it in the *Ode to Joy*, but as a developing conflict in which the working classes find themselves in alliance with intellectuals and artists in a common opposition to the consumer society which, coming into being under bourgeois auspices, is interested only in a rise of the material standards of living, and not in making discoveries and establishing truths for their own sake. The course of the present century has, however, Anderson claims, disproved the Marxist expectations about the working classes, which have more and more adopted the consumer values propagated by the bourgeoisie. At the present day, therefore, the central struggle is between the largely victorious consumer movement supported by the working class, as well as by the possessing class, on the one hand, and the counter movement of intellectuals and artists which occupies itself with attacking the illusions fostered by the materialism of the state planners etc.

From Anderson's point of view, Dewey is right when he points out that the post-Renaissance link-up between science and industry, experiment and manufacture, has begun to break down the old barriers between the leisure class and the labouring class, uniting them in a common aim. But what Dewey has failed to see is that the society produced by the unification of these two classes is a consumer society which is interested in science only for its material fruits, and which has neither patience with, nor understanding of, the spiritual activity responsible in the last resort for the thing which gives rise to the useful inventions, i.e. the disinterested research and the detached play of mind which criticises ideas. We have to recognise that what is good in culture "has had to fight, and still has to fight for its existence; that science is faced not merely by open obscurantism but with obscurantism and scepticism masquerading as science"[36] which is less interested in seeing things as they are, than in following up lines of inquiry sanctioned by the unfulfillable but officially accepted dreams of realising universal happiness. This draws attention once more to the difficult cultural problem of how science can lose its way by reason of its working with a set of ideas so closely sedimented by habit as to escape notice — to borrow the term employed by Husserl in his valuable and somewhat similar discussion of the same subject in the *Krisis*.

Anderson, different as he is from Dewey, sees the problem in much the same light; because we all up to a point have to consider utilities, we thus inevitably have routine activities, thus we all have a tendency to fall into custom and uncritical living, in the sense that we take for granted the means to an end, concentrating consciously on the latter to the neglect and forgetfulness of the former. Anderson's very general description of the problem[37] is clarified considerably in the light of the examples given by Dewey of how knowledge can go dead in the classroom:

"The cheapening of devices, like printing, for recording and distributing information — genuine and alleged — has created an immense bulk of communicated subject matter. . . . All too frequently it forms another strange world which overlies the world of personal acquaintance. The sole problem of the student is to learn for . . . purposes of recitations . . . the constituent parts of this strange world."[38]

That is to say, the student, by means of what is mostly rote-learning, masters and applies the results of scientific achievements — e.g. Log tables — without understanding the nature of the argumentation and evidence which led to the discovery of logarithms by John Napier. For the student and the teacher, mathematics thus becomes the sort of short-sighted problem solving condemned by John Burnet, in which the general context of the problem in its relation to the rest of knowledge is lost sight of because taken for granted.

When we compare the account given by Anderson and Dewey of the causes of the blind spots which thus come into being as well as the remedies for them, we find that, for the latter, the way to bring to life the subject-matter of dead textbooks is to lay bare their social roots in classroom "projects" in which teacher and pupil co-operate — e.g. in showing how mathematics arises out of land measurement. Seen in the light of Dewey's general philosophy, this socialisation of science which restores meaning to the desiccated texts is a carry-over into the classroom of a revolution in social behaviour which in the wider world is — it is to be hoped — putting an end to the segregation of the leisure class and the labouring class. The blight on science, the freezing of communication into a routine, is thus for Dewey a sort of secondary effect of the dualism which affects the behaviour of human groups and effectively blocks their progress. Science, for Dewey, will never take wings until the division characteristic of the modern world between the advanced countries as the standard-bearers of scientific culture and the underdeveloped countries as the providers of primary commodities — that is to say the leisure-class/labouring-class separation in one of its twentieth-century manifestations — has been completely overcome and until everywhere on earth shall share in the work of the world and all enjoy the leisure for culture.

By contrast, for Anderson, the continued existence of the struggle and of sharp differences between the various nations is what supplies the conditions in which it is possible for an individual nation to become aware of its knowledge as desiccated, routinised and sedimented in important respects as well as to keep before itself the cultural standards which guide its judgement. Freud, Anderson says, "can make nothing of the social facts from which the argument began ('why the national units should disdain, detest, abhor one another, even when they are at peace, is indeed a mystery'). The mystery might have been reduced," Anderson comments drily, "if he had considered the ways of living, the 'causes', in which men are caught up."[39] Each social unit is a complex movement and counter-movement of the most varied sort, and this struggle within each unit gives rise to the differences and competition between all of them, taken as an interrelated group, and accounts for the general struggle. If we want to understand the foundation of cultural standards, if we want to understand how there can arise in a group an awareness of that towards which it has an habitual blind spot, we must, according to Anderson, hold fast to the fact of the differentiated and competing developments of groups in relation to one another. A Deweyite world from which conflict and class antagonism had vanished, far from being a world in which cultural communication would flourish as never before, would be a world in which culture would wither and die.

To get Anderson's meaning here, we have to see him as engaged in discussing a question which he does not explicitly raise, i.e. how do we get round the limitation in our perception of things which results from the operation of the principle "familiarity breeds neglect"? The position emerges clearly if we take the principle to an extreme form, viz. what is unvaryingly present in our perception of anything is not noticed. Stated by Hobbes in the form "always to perceive the same thing is tantamount to not perceiving it"[40] the principle may be illustrated by asking how we would make the ordinary distinction between the foreground and the background of our visual experience if all the objects of the foreground we saw, varying and recurring, were seen against a background which was unvaryingly blue? We could not, that is to say, be aware of the presence of the blue background unless we had also been aware of the foreground objects in the absence of the blue background and had seen them against a background of some other colour.

Without being explicitly stated by Anderson, this Hobbesian principle provides him — in my understanding of his work — with his explanation of routinisation. After some new particular method of doing something (e.g. of painting, or of counting) has been accepted by our community so as to become a part of the inherited customs, it is taken for granted in a non-questioning way, and thereafter acquires the status of a constant background to the foreground results which are achieved by its means, and which henceforth monopolise the interests of the members of our group. As our method of counting (say, it is by an abacus) is not, and cannot, be singled out for consideration independently of the results achieved by its means so long as we do not have experience of the fact that the same results can be achieved — perhaps more expeditiously — by a different method, for the same reason, we cannot notice the blue background to the things we see moving about (the background does not exist visually for us) until it so happens that we see the same sort of things, the same sort of movements suddenly happening against a background of a different colour. Then when the blue background recurs, we recognise it in its independence and are able to attend to it.

To do justice to what Anderson says about the way the means-end relationship can become routinised, it is important to note that the complications of the argument are due not to its having got sidetracked into accidental particularities, but to its being concerned with a relationship which is itself pervasive and familiar, and which, on that account, has been neglected by many philosophers, namely the relationship of the distinguishable but inseparable. Roughly speaking, the relationship is neither internal nor external, but something between the two, and on that account, hard to explicate. In order to distinguish between colour and shape, we require the experience of same colour/different shape, same shape/different colour, and just as in order to distinguish between foreground and background it is necessary to have the experience of same fore-ground/different background, same background/different fore-ground, so too with regard to the relationship of method and result, or means and end. In this case too the drawing of the distinction is a complicated thing which proceeds on the principle: same method/different results, same results/different methods. For example, Greek geometry can be produced as the result of using either traditional Greek methods or Descartes' analytic method, while the same traditional methods can alternatively result in a non-Euclidean, modern geometry.

Now, in the light of these principles which Anderson uses but does not mention — which, by the way, Kemp Smith does, in a paper read a few months after Anderson went to Australia, 'The Fruitfulness of the Abstract'[41] — let us look at the two ways in which, in Anderson's account, the neglect of the familiar can be overcome, in the kind of situation we have been discussing. The first way of getting round the difficulty as to how we can notice the familiar does not require us to look beyond our community to other communities because it depends on the fact that there will always be in our own community misfits and exceptions who cannot manage the standard method and work out methods for themselves — counting on their fingers etc. But while the observation of the way of counting done by this minority enables us to do what we could not do before, attend to the method in independence of the results, the critical appraisal of its value in the proper sense will not take place until we look to other countries, comparing their way of counting with ours, and paying attention to the comments made on our country's method of counting by members of the foreign group who are acquainted with what we do.

Thus the starting point of the problem is that if our group does not look outside of itself to others, it has what Anderson calls an inferior perspective on its contemporary activities, or, as I might put it, it cannot single out for attention what is unfailingly present in its experience. The detached view, which comes into being when we compare our own group's way of experiencing its relations to the rest of the world with what we learn to be the point of view of other groups to this same fact of our relation to the world, is what overcomes — to quote Anderson — "the limitation which taking things to be means to certain ends imposes on anyone's powers of apprehension".[42]

To illustrate in detail the kind of thing Anderson is driving at in these very general principles, we need do no more than revert to John Burnet's criticisms of the S.E.D. In the first place, it was by taking the trouble to contrast what happened examination-wise in the Scotland of his time with the equivalent arrangements in Germany, France and England, that he uncovered the accepted and unattended-to routines of the Scots sufficiently to make the still surprising discovery that the distinctive policy of the S.E.D. Leaving Certificate was that of encouraging a merely problem-solving mentality. Looking at Scottish education in the light of the classical past as well as of the most advanced countries of Europe, he saw it as equipping its best students simply for carrying out assignments belonging to some wider field which remains outside their ken, and for which those responsible are trained elsewhere and otherwise. Take away, however, the possibility of this comparison with the kind of training prescribed in Germany, France, England, as well as ancient Greece, and the deliberately limited scope of the S.E.D.'s aims escapes notice, because we now lack the means to discriminate it and make it an object of our critical attention. In the second place, a closer study of

Burnet's critique of Scottish education enables us to give body to Anderson's abstract but penetrating observation that the judgement of a critic expresses itself not only in drawing distinctions which have been overlooked, but also in making explicit unnoticed structures or connections.[43] That is to say, as well as pointing out that the psychologists' argument against general education, which was so acceptable to the S.E.D. of Burnet's time, depended for its persuasiveness in obliterating the distinction between rote-learning of a subject and learning it by comparing it with other subjects, Burnet goes on to argue that the programme of producing a merely problem-solving mentality is not so to speak an isolated decision, but is part of a structure which is organised with a view to limiting the Scottish universities to the production of "subaltern talents" (i.e. factors for the rulers, and not rulers).

Moreover, one does not need to go to Burnet to show what Anderson is driving at. C. M. Grieve's work in poetry and Lawrence Saunders in his very original book *Scottish Democracy* would do equally well. The starting-point of the discoveries (one might call them) made by this latter pair in their respective fields, was a looking beyond Scotland to other countries. Why stick to the convention — Saunders asks — of considering the development of the Scottish universities from the eighteenth century onwards in the light of, and in comparison with, the universities of England and nothing but the universities of England? A whole set of interesting properties of the Scottish universities which are hidden when they are regarded in the British context is brought to light if one begins to note their resemblances and differences with what was happening in the American universities throughout the same period. So with Grieve.

The question which led him into his work for a Scottish renaissance arose from his noticing the sharp contrast between the readiness of the Scots to acquiesce in the fading out of their tradition of writing serious poetry in Lowland Scots and in Gaelic with the literary revivals in Norway, in Catalonia and in Ireland, not to mention other countries, of which the inspiration was the will to give a fresh lease of life to their ancient languages, rescuing them from their present-day obscurity. This comparison with the behaviour of these other analogous countries in regard to their national culture was what drew the attention of the Scots (or some of them) to the fact that there was something anomalous about their taking for granted the decline of their culture as if it did not matter to anybody or as if nothing could be done about it. Indeed, further reference to Burnet and to Grieve not only enables us to illustrate Anderson's point, but also to clarify some obscurities he gets into as regards his very interesting and distinctive views as to the relations of science, criticism and poetry. "The poet," Anderson says, "might be said to be making discoveries for himself (whatever man may know)," "breaking the crust of custom" etc.[44] But, he goes on to claim some years later, "if anything could be said to be the theme of literature, it was criticism itself". The clash between human agencies presented in a literary work (he said), involved a clash between men's illusions and realities. Literature is thus, for Anderson, a sort of process of discovering illusions in the routines of the writer's group or country, as the result of his making comparisons with what is happening in comparable circumstances abroad. Of course, the contrast may begin not with a reference to abroad, but with what was happening in his own country in the old days, or with the very great differences in the way in which two specialisms can regard the same thing, e.g. the biological and the historical view of man. It follows, therefore, that there is not much difference for Anderson between what the poet does and what the scientist does and what the social theorist does, at least in their opening moves, a point of view which is certainly borne out by the work both of Burnet and of Grieve in calling in question what was in their time universally taken for granted about Scottish culture.

A cursory reading of Dewey might suggest that for him too, as for Anderson, the work of literature and of art is to reveal to us hidden depths in ourselves which we have been accustomed to neglect. The shock of self-knowledge which the teacher experiences in the process of communicating facts to his pupils resembles, according to Dewey, the effective encounter with art.[45] Literature, he explains, speaking in a voice not very different from Anderson's, reveals a range of depth and meaning in experiences which otherwise might be mediocre or trivial, and neglected on that account.[46] But a due attention to the context of his remark shows that he isn't saying what Anderson said at all. For Dewey, the shock of novelty is given by poetry only insofar as it brings home to us the fact that there lies hidden in our hearts, in experiences often too ordinary to be worth bothering with, a vision of the radiant future similar to that put forward by the pragmatist philosophers. When poetry and the arts "serve as organs of vision", it is because "they arouse discontent with conditions which fall below their measure; they create a demand for surroundings coming up to their own level".[47] That is to say, poetry is good only when it makes us want life to be like a work of art, only when the texture of the poem as written up by the poet wakens us up to the demands of the ideal of organic unity which shows up by contrast the disorganised class-ridden state of industrial society and encourages us to work for a new arrangement of things from which conflict and its self-defeating rivalries have been eliminated.

Without saying much about literature, Dewey lets us see that he values it as a useful weapon for promoting social movement. "Homer was to the Greeks," he says, "a Bible, a textbook of morals, a history and a national inspiration."[48] Modern poetry, if it is of any worth, must serve an analagous purpose in the dominant movement of modern society, the movement to demolish unnecessary unhappiness. Poetry, therefore, is artificial and therefore bad only insofar as "it becomes an asylum of refuge against the hard conditions of life".[49] Good poetry by contrast encourages in us feelings and ideas which, far from being a technique of day-dreams, turned in upon themselves, function as "a method in act which modifies conditions", i.e. industrial and political as the context shows. "We will change forthwith the old conditions, and storm the heavens to win the prize." Without mentioning the Internationale, Dewey's view of poetry echoes its sentiments.

To do justice to the problem of the nature of art, we have, Dewey goes on, "to compare what was said in another chapter about the one-sided meanings which have come to be attached to the ideas of efficiency and of culture".[50] Poetry is bad, therefore, when it identifies self-culture with "an inner play of sentiment and fancies", cut off from the work of the world; poetry is good when it enables us to see beyond this present self-divided world, and to work for a world in which personal development and social efficiency are no longer antagonistic but reconciled with one another.[51]

Anderson, of course, is sharply critical here. Dewey admits that the dualism of self-development and of social efficiency is too deeply established to be easily overthrown. How does he propose to overcome the difficulty? In typically modern style, Dewey refers us to research. But what leads him to suppose that research will show how the antagonism may be eliminated? It may well be that research will show that the antagonism defies elimination, that the price of getting rid of it will be too high in the sense of its leading to the reappearance of the antagonism in some more acute form in some adjacent context. "Do you know the damned? Are you acquainted with the irremediable?" asked Baudelaire in one of his poems. You cannot make personal development and social efficiency synony-

mous instead of antagonistic by a mere demand, by a mere wish.
Dewey, however, behaves as if he thinks this to be so, and in effect
takes up a Pelagian position — to speak in the language of the old
theology — without giving any reasons for it, and as if it was a
position that was so obvious that it did not need to be argued.

Why is Dewey silent here? It is not as if these metaphysical issues
made no practical difference, as can quickly be shown by their application to the classical-modernist controversy which concerns Dewey
very much. "The importance of classics in education is that they are
concerned," according to Anderson, "with the permanent, not in
Spencer's [or Dewey's] sense of the permanently useful but of what
is independent of people's particular purposes at particular times, and
therefore can carry over from one civilisation to another."[52] It is with
the permanent in this sense that Greek tragedies are found to be
concerned, and that is why they make sense and are valued by other
civilisations. But as soon as we look at the problem from Dewey's
point of view, the widespread agreement as to the value of Greek
tragedy between one civilisation and another — a fact not, of course,
denied by Dewey — becomes very difficult to justify. For that
philosophy would apparently exclude from itself, as outdated and
productive of unnecessary unhappiness, the situations which are
described in tragedies like the *Agamemnon* and the *Antigone*.

PART II

POETRY AND THE PROBLEMS
OF PHILOSOPHY

JOHN ANDERSON AND C. M. GRIEVE

The story of Scottish philosophy in the twentieth century illustrates the remark of Professor T. C. Smout that Scotland's distinctive institutions often have remarkable powers of survival. In the twenties, philosophy, as I have been arguing, regained the privileged position in the curriculum it had lost in 1908. What I want to show now is how, in the second half of the century, when the universities were beginning their rapid expansion, the loss of interest in metaphysics on the part of the philosophy departments was compensated for by the fact that the central problem of metaphysics — man's relation to nature — was taken over from philosophy by the sciences of man which sought to resolve it by a mixture of observation and modern logic. Once famous as a centre of *a priori* metaphysics Edinburgh now began to establish a new reputation for itself throughout the world as a place in which the riddle of the universe was going to be answered by the social sciences.

Judged as solid contributions to knowledge, it is doubtless impossible at this stage to get any general agreement as to what, if anything, has been achieved by these ambitious projects of solving, by observational and mathematical methods, problems which formerly were supposed to be the province of metaphysical speculation. But, as with the whole business of Ordinance 70 in the earlier half of the century, the significance of the various moves made becomes much clearer if we turn our attention away from the carrying out of the programmes and attend instead to the preliminary debate over the question of whether the programmes were feasible at all. Just as the title of the Ordinance 70 struggles to claim our serious attention depends far less on their actual outcome than on the unusually high quality of the arguments, of first Burnet and then Anderson, against the Deweyites, as to whether various special sciences would fall apart if they were not organised around the central subject of a speculative philosophy, so the value of the various innovations of the sixties in Scotland such as epistemics and artificial intelligence, cannot begin to be properly assessed until one averts one's eyes from the hardware or software in order to listen in to the long and impassioned argument with himself in which C. M. Grieve ('Hugh MacDiarmid'), both in prose and in verse, struggled with the problem of whether the traditional speculative approach to the great question of the universe and man's place in it had not been rendered out of date and ineffective by new and much more obviously powerful methods of research provided by systematic experimentation backed up by a mathematical logic. Postponing what we have to say about the Scottish universities in the second part of the present century, let us first look into the poet's tortuous journey from metaphysics to positivism in the hope that we will thereby get the same sort of preliminary understanding of the changes that were to come over the relationship of philosophy to the sciences in post-war Scotland as our study of Burnet's and Anderson's discussions of first principles have given us in regard to the changes which came over the Scottish curriculum in the earlier years of the century.

A peculiar enough proceeding in the eyes of some, this achievement of a bird's eye view of the macrocosm by going first to a poet who was especially interested in the idea of a Scottish renaissance, finds additional justification in the fact that, unlike the Scottish universities of the fifties and sixties — i.e. of the decade when the changes actually began to be put through — MacDiarmid was engaged in a constant self-questioning as regards the standards which were to regulate the relations of present to past, of innovation to tradition, in reference to the changes which were coming over philosophy and the sciences as well as the arts. In this matter, his development differed very significantly from that of the universities, in the sense that the rejection of metaphysics in favour of positivism, which both were in their different ways to carry through, took place, in their case, automatically, and one might say unthinkingly, by the brute fact of an alteration of standards — e.g. change of textbooks and course-material — which would bring work done locally into line with what they supposed was done elsewhere, and not, as in his case, by means of a conscious debate within himself, conducted in the light of the best available knowledge. This transition from classicism to modernism, about the value of which the poet had no quarrel with the universities, this story of his self-doubting leap to an affirmation of the future, provides, in my opinion, a far more comprehensive and trustworthy picture of the complex of criticial issues involved in a cultural revolution than does the bland official account, which impatiently rejects the idea of there ever having been a crisis in twentieth-century Scottish education and which speaks of the smooth passage — seen to be necessary by any reasonable citizen — from an antediluvian state of affairs where subjectivity set the standards to one where they are set by statisticians.

The members of COSLA and the Principals of the training colleges — to move no higher up the ladder of power — no doubt see things differently. What has a poet to do with practicalities? But the answer is that this one, at least, was in the midst of things at the two great turning points of the century. In the crisis of the twenties, the E.I.S. opened up to him the pages of its *Scottish Educational Journal*, in which he published, in over fifty instalments, his powerful, original — and deeply divisive — *Contemporary Scottish Studies*. In the crisis of the sixties, Edinburgh University, in a similar way, acknowledged the poet's power. The reforming Vice-Chancellor, Sir Edward Appleton, seems to have found the poet's support for the new sciences a refreshing contrast to the academic conservatism of so many Scots — a state of affairs symbolised by the fact that a painting of the poet has hung for so many years in a very prominent place in the University Staff Club. In a Laureation speech which does the university credit, the poet's special position in Scottish life was publicly acknowledged by comparing him to George Buchanan, to David Hume and to Thomas Carlyle — all of them noteworthy for thinking for themselves about fundamentals and for not being afraid to speak their minds.

The consideration of Grieve's intellectual career will enable us to bring into a sharper, more fruitful focus both the problems and the insights contained in John Anderson's philosophy, because of a significant series of parallelisms between the lives of the two writers. Members of the same generation, the poet (born 1892) and the philosopher (born 1894) were alike, not only in being decisively influenced by A. R. Orage and his journal, famous for intellectual debate, *The New Age*, from about 1910 and again in the early twenties, but also in the way they worked out their respective *weltanschauungen* by applying *New Age* ideas to the culture-crisis in the Scotland of 1912 to 1927 which found its public expression in the Ordinance 70 struggles. What makes the comparison between these two Scots especially illuminating is that their respective efforts to make sense both of the world and of the struggle in Scotland by looking at them from a *New Age* point of view, led each of them, working quite independently, to identify by turns with the two points of view we have been explaining at length — the classicist point of view of Burnet and the modernist point of view of what we could call a Deweyite Marxism — moving, however, from the one to the other — it is most important never to forget — in a reverse order. Accepting in the beginning the aspect of the *New Age* ideas which Anderson at that time rejected, Orage's anti-Marxism, Grieve began where Anderson ended, by formulating a classicist position somewhat comparable to Burnet's, and ended where Anderson had begun, namely with a modernist position, which, influenced by the spirit of Deweyite Marxism, strongly repudiated, in many places, the classicist traditionalism of a Burnet kind. Keeping in view this remarkably sharp contrast between Grieve and Anderson, let us bring out the strengths and the weaknesses of each by first comparing the versions of the classicist position which both worked out — the poet in the twenties, and Anderson from the forties onwards. As for the anti-classicist periods in the work of these two most notable intellectuals of the Scottish twentieth century, I will reserve the topic for consideration in the next chapter where particular attention is paid to the changes which came over the poet's position.

At the outset of his career, Grieve sympathised with what we might call the *New Age* version of Matthew Arnold, with which, as we have seen, Anderson too was to identify. The poet acted on the principle that if his creative work was to be up to standard, in the proper sense of the term, he must not only have acquainted himself with the best that had been thought and written in the rest of the world, but he must use this international range of reading as a means of bringing to life the deficiencies which had arisen in the literary tradition of his own country through habits of insularity. In working to produce a literary movement in Scotland which would, in accordance with Arnold's ideas, avoid provinciality in time and space, Grieve therefore acted on the same kind of principles as Anderson had in view, when in 1937 (see his *Art and Reality*) he told the Australians that the way to create a literature of the Antipodes which was not a mere echo of ideas and styles fashionable in England, was not to try to bring into being there and then a distinctively Australian position in speech and in thought, but to write books in standard English which were nevertheless able to achieve an un-English style of writing and ideas because of their finding inspiration in the culture of France, Germany, Italy, etc. instead of the old country.

Grieve's first book, *Annals of the Five Senses*, was constructed more or less in accordance with the recipe recommended by Anderson to the Australians. That is to say, the launching of a literary movement in Scotland which was to speak with a distinctive voice and not be a mere imitation of what was fashionable in England was achieved by a heavily intellectualised or, as the poet called it, cerebral style of story-writing, which used the English language in order to put over a continental way of looking at things.

In his first attempt to start up a cultural movement in Scotland, the kind of literature Grieve wanted to see arising was in effect to be constructed according to principles which, unknown to the poet himself, had been laid down long before — in the fifties and sixties of the nineteenth century — by David Masson, when he promulgated his principle of the internalisation of Scotticism.[1] It was, Masson held, certainly right that the Scots should seek to put over to the world the distinctive ideas which, as both the eighteenth-century Enlightenment and the nineteenth-century arguments over religion had showed, were liable to arise out of the Scottish experience. But, he went on, if the Scots wanted to get a hearing for their characterisitc points of view in the changed conditions of the later nineteenth century, it would be necessary for them to present their ideas in detachment from the Scottish historical positions, in which they had originated. The Burns-Scott approach to Scottish literature may have been effective enough at one time, but the parade of the peculiarities of the Scottish speech, of Scottish history, of Scottish customs, had been, Masson suggested, overdone by this time, and, if not discarded or cut back, would result in a provincialism which would stifle the very ideas which they wanted to get over.

Using his influential position as Professor of Rhetoric and English Literature at Edinburgh,[2] Masson pressed on the Scots a principle which was to be faithfully followed by a long line of Scottish writers from Robert Louis Stevenson and John Davidson, through Robertson Smith down to John Anderson and the young C. M. Grieve himself — that if Scots' writing was to have a future, the line to be followed was that discovered by Thomas Carlyle, who managed to put over and make saleable the distinctively Scottish point of view before an international public without referring to Scottish facts, background or history at all.

About this time (1922) Grieve, as the result of working for a literary revival in Scotland based on the Massonian principle of the internalisation of Scotticism, came into conflict with the people who still held to the principle condemned by Masson — the externalisation of Scotticism in the limited sense of identifying Scottish literature with the use of the Doric, that is to say, with a somewhat desiccated, impoverished and localised form of lowland Scots. In the course of these disputes, the poet experimented with Scots, putting it to the test of whether, if its range were extended by judicious revivals of words from the vocabulary current in the classic period of the Makars, or contained in *Jamieson's Dictionary of the Scottish Language*, it might constitute an adequate vehicle in which to write a kind of metaphysical poetry which, leaving aside the English example, drew its inspiration from French, German, Russian etc. models. The result was astonishing to the poet himself and to his friends, since in using this new medium of an externalised Scotticism devised by himself, he had managed to produce philosophical poetry of a far higher quality, both in regard to the profundity of its ideas as well as to the graphic precision with which they were put over, than he had ever been able to manage when he was writing in English in the mode of internalised Scotticism. In the light of this experience he extended the range of the Arnoldian formulae which he had so far followed. For the writer who wanted to "make it new", to detect and overcome the tradition-bound limitations of his community's culture, it wasn't enough to seek inspiration in the source recommended by Anderson to the Australians, that is to say, a study on Arnoldian lines of the major literatures of the continent of Europe; it was also essential to study carefully what the Norwegians, the Catalans and the Irish had done by way of reviving a modern literature by taking their cue from the literary achievements of the classic periods in their own country's past, when the language, be it Catalan, Norwegian or Irish, had been in full flower. The way to produce the literature in modern Scotland which measured up to the "becoming tendencies" in the great writings of the last hundred years in the various countries of the West, especially on the continent, was now to be achieved by breaking with Masson's principle of the internalisation of Scotticism, and by starting up a Scottish renaissance similar, it was hoped, in character and effects to the renaissance of Ireland and the other corresponding countries.

To come at once to the evaluation of the books of short poems with which Grieve started the Scots renaissance — *Sangschaw* and *Penny Wheep* — the crucial question of what is achieved in these poems will never in my estimation begin to receive an adequate answer until they, and their composition, are considered as a practical illustration of the theory of literature, no doubt originating in the *New Age*, which was familiar to the poet himself, and which is explicitly worked out by John Anderson. How did it come about that the "Back to Dunbar" movement resulted in a renovation of the provincial and limited canon of Scots as used by the versifiers of the time, which raised its intellectual level to a sufficient extent to constitute it a vehicle for a philosophical poetry of the modern kind, which, though remaining highly distinctive and in some sense Scottish, was in line with what was being done in the philosophical literature of larger countries? As I see the matter, the crust of custom was thereby broken (to speak on Andersonian lines), in the sense that the extended Scots made it possible to restore life to, and make publicly exciting, various philosophical points of view, which, familiar enough among the Scots as the result of being the stock in trade of their philosophy professors and well known to relatively large sections of the population, were, on that account, unthinkingly taken for granted, and were discussable — when they needed to be discussed — only in a heavily technical and traditional vocabulary, which weakened and hid the life in the ideas. Understood in this way, the new movement to put into Scots, and in versified Scots at that, what the Scots had discussed only in English and prose, destroyed the intramural monopoly which had habitually associated philosophy with the philosophy of the classroom, and brought it out into the market place, so to speak, in the Socratic way, for anybody who might choose to listen. No doubt, in the beginning, few listened, and the poet became almost as unpopular as Socrates had been in the Athens of his time. But, as in the case of Socrates, the tide was to turn.

I will confine my remarks to the quartet of poems in *Sangschaw* which go under the title 'Au Clair de La Lune' — the first poem, 'The Man in the Moon', in the interpretation I give it, shows the poet raising the question about a traditional stereotype of the philosopical classrooms, which — at the centre of Western philosophy since Descartes — had, as anyone who has bothered to look into the facts of the matter will know, dominated Scottish philosophy more than it had dominated philosophy in other countries, viz. the problem of the relations of philosophy and common sense as formulated in reference to puzzles raised by perceptual illusion:

> The moonbeams kelter i' the lift,
> An' Earth, the bare auld stane,
> Glitters beneath the seas o' Space,
> White as a Mammoth's bane.

An', lifted owre the gowden wave,
Peers a dumfoun'ered Thocht,
Wi' keethin' sicht o' a' there is,
An' bodily sicht o' nocht.[3]

The breaking down of the barriers between textbook philosophy and poetry is achieved through the use of the antithesis, found by the poet in *Jamieson's Dictionary of the Scottish Language*, between "keethin' sicht" and "bodily sicht" — i.e. between seeing things indirectly, especially spotting the presence of underwater fish by the disturbances visible on the surface of the water on the one hand, and seeing them directly as a whole, on the other, as where one actually sees the fish. What the synthetic Scots, as used by the poet, does, is, so to speak, to make publicly palpable the meaning and interest of the philosophical distinction explained by Hume in Section I of the *Enquiry Concerning Human Understanding*, and illumined in the book on Hume by Husserl's disciple, C. V. Salmon,[4] between the unproblematic way things present themselves as objective and independent of us before we have begun to reflect on the perceptive relation we have with them, and the problematic subjective character of mere appearance which the same things present to us as soon as reflection begins on how we perceive.

How are we to escape from the egocentric predicament to which philosophy seems to condemn us as soon as we become reflectively aware of our cognitive relations to the things we perceive as mediated through the five senses of which the poet wrote the annals? This theme is central to the sequence of the four poems as a whole, which seeks a way out of the difficulty by reawakening the ancient quarrel of the poets and the philosophers, which is a familiar stock item in our inheritance of general culture, thanks to Plato's *Republic*, and for that reason not taken seriously, but converted into a routine stereotype. Poetry, Grieve claims in the last poem of the four, giving new life to the faded theme by his peculiar language, is what will enable us somehow to transcend the "chaos of thought" as exemplified by the keethin' sicht/bodily sicht dualism, thereby establishing its authority over the plain man's point of view — whether the plain man likes it or not — by the curious light poetry brings. Look at how a lament played on the pipes, says the poet, illustrating the point in the first of the four poems, can make up for the meaninglessness of death and the inevitable disappearance of things.

But the poet's attack in these two poems, though it makes some impression on the situation, is not yet entirely convincing, and philosophy can still cling to its objection, namely that the poet has not shown how we are to extricate ourselves from the subjective idealism of reflection. This objection, however, is very convincingly rebutted in the most remarkable of the quartet of poems, 'Moonstruck', in which, using the analogy of going mad, the poet produces a suspension of the reader's scepticism, by a singularly felicitous description of what it is like to break through to a different point of view. As the critic Oxenhorn says in a very stimulating analysis of the poem:

"the description [in the second verse] instantly dissipates any sentimentality that might accrue to moonlight. It prepares us for the typical third stanza shift from sensuous description into metaphysics:

> An' the roarin' o' oceans noo
> Is peerieweerie to me:
> Thunner's a tinklin' bell: an' time
> Whuds like a flee.

How much is assumed in the use of that innocent 'and'; the leap is immense! What the mind apprehends in such a state is neither supernatural nor mystical but (in the philosophical sense) metaphysical. . . . By using that folk language to convey a metaphysical experience, MacDiarmid makes it plausible and vivid. He takes us along."[5]

Illuminating, however, as Oxenhorn's analysis is, it has to be somewhat sharpened up if it is to do justice to the poet's achievement. First, it is better to speak of the language used by the poet as common speech, heightened by drawing from Jamieson in the light of memories of the Makars, rather than suggesting that it has its basis mainly in folk consciousness. Secondly, while it is illuminating to speak of what the mind apprehends as being neither supernatural nor mystical, but "(in the philosophical sense) metaphysical", one comes, I believe, still closer to the poet's meaning if one takes him to be speaking about the experience of breaking through to a new point of view, which comes about through the resolution of the contradiction which causes the philosophical problem — in this case the puzzles which have to do with the distinction between appearance and reality.

What the poet is doing, as I see it, is in fact to bring out into the open the quarrel between poetry and philosophy as seen by John

Davidson — the fellow countryman who was the hero of the poet's youth. Condemning all philosophy as unable to do anything but formulate a dualism beyond which it cannot get (a criticism which certainly applies very aptly to the arguments of the Scottish philosophers in which the scepticism of David Hume and of Sir William Hamilton was at odds with the commonsensism of Reid and his school), Davidson makes the courageous claim that it is poetry, not philosophy which is going to show how to resolve the contradictions between the "keethin' sicht" and "bodily sicht" and thereby achieve the realist (Davidson himself calls it materialist) point of view which will reconcile common sense with modern science. The point of view implicit in the metaphysical poetry of *Sangschaw* ought, if we are to do it justice, to be conceived as a kind of follow-up of Davidson's programme for a takeover of Scottish philosophy by the Scottish poets who would, in their own unique way, face up to and resolve its hereditary problem of the relations of science, perception and common sense. Read in the light of this parallelism with Davidson, the passage in 'Moonstruck' on the "apprehending" of an object which is "metaphysical" (in the philosophical sense) is much more directly concerned than Oxenhorn's language suggests with posing in poetic terms the problem of the philosophical textbooks as to how the deficiencies of dualism can be overcome so as to give rise to a tenable form of realism, or, for that matter, materialism (which is how Clerk Maxwell decribed realism).

The MacDiarmid of *Sangschaw* appreciates, I believe, somewhat better than Davidson the kind of problem with which philosophers are faced, and the intellectual drama begun in the 'Au Clair de la Lune' sequence carries on after the poems have ended, reaching its climax two or three poems later in 'Crowdieknowe', where Grieve makes the point — very important in philosophy, and more especially in Scottish philosophy — that the real impediment to the world triumph of metaphysical poetry, or metaphysics of any kind, is the steadfast refusal of common sense to take seriously the philosophical positions which claim to explain it to itself by transcending it. In a very lively illustration which brings home to us the strength and solidity of this resistance to highbrow values, the poet pictures the anger of the older generation of Langholm men at being forced to awake from their graves by the last trumpet. The heavenly host, which symbolises the metaphysical experience, seems to them a flighty gang of foreigners who do not deserve to be taken seriously. The ultimate difficulty blocking the progress of this elitist poetry which is going to clear up the chaos of thought is the anti-elitist reluctance of the majority to break away from the customary routines of life.

The poet, in these poems which illustrate so well Anderson's theory of the role of literature in breaking down the unthinking routines by forcing ultimate questions into consciousness, is therefore, in my interpretation, developing a set of philosophical ideas which, though in line with what is happening in the most advanced writing in the most advanced countries, is at the same time present in his experience, in common with that of all other Scots, due to the cultural conflict which was raging in Scotland in his formative years. The claims of poetry as a mode of intellectual cognition had been given new life, perhaps indeed introduced into Scotland for the first time, by Davidson, who had held that all philosophy was entangled in a dualism from which it could not escape, and who was making high claims for the cognitive powers of poetry as what alone could break through the dualism, so as to give free expression to the materialist vision demanded by the progress of modern science. But at the same time, the dualism of the sort attacked by Davidson was the theme of a continuing argument between three thinkers who are mentioned by Grieve in his preface to *Contemporary Scottish Studies* in 1927 — on the one hand the Earl Balfour and Professor Pringle-Pattison, both of them authors of best-selling books in defence of various versions of the traditional dualism of Scottish common sense, which they admired, and on the other hand, there was the man who criticised them from the point of view of Hegelian monism as the most effective solution — Lord Haldane.

What I am suggesting is that the philosophical point of the Moon-poems and 'Crowdieknowe' is brought home to us better if we note that they are concerned with the same issue as divided Davidson from these three philosophers who argued with one another in the academic tradition, though only one of them actually taught. After all, a fourth philosopher mentioned along with the other three in the preface to *Contemporary Scottish Studies,* J. Y. Simpson, whom the poet admired, and on whom he wrote an article, is acknowledged by name in *Sangschaw* as the inspiration of the poem 'The Innumerable Christ' which tries to work out the poet's favourite idea of how a religious idea can be given a materialistic, realistic meaning. Why then should we not suppose that the philosophers to whom the poet is not sympathetic — Balfour, Pringle-Pattison and Haldane — as well as Davidson, whose continuator the poet to some extent regarded himself as being, are not also in the back of the poet's mind in the same pages? Emerging against the background of the intellectual struggles over Ordinance 70 — which though passionately pursued, and though stimulating some of the participants to real achievements in philosophical thinking about education, were so much a part of the customary inherited background of post-Disruption Scotland as not to be very much noticed, or even to be the object of embarrassed silence — the poet's project for a Scottish renaissance did not involve merely literature and the arts, or even merely politics. It looked forward to the re-creation of a metaphysical Scotland which was no longer ashamed of itself.

To get hold of the point I am labouring, it is necessary to remember how the kind of Arnoldian methods described by Anderson led the poet to the discovery of certain cultural trends in contemporary Scotland, which it had been customary to neglect, but which even in their decadence retained a certain amount of interest. That is to say, what brought to light for the poet these unnoticed routines was the fact of his viewing the present of Scottish experience from two different perspectives — comparing it by turns to the periods of classic culture in Scotland's past and by turns to the chief movements of intellectual life in the leading countries of the twentieth century. On the one hand, the former, the contrast of Scotland's present with its past, exposed the fact that more and more areas of cultural activity among the Scots were, as a matter of custom, being accepted as being unworthy of discussion in their own right, that is to say, as being noteworthy only insofar as they might connect with the culture of the U.K. as a whole. On the other hand, the latter, the comparison of the life of the mind in Scotland of the first quarter of the twentieth century with what was happening culturally on the continent in the same period, revealed that there still remained in Scotland certain traditions of art and intellect, which, however negligible they might be when viewed in a U.K. context, nevertheless altered and increased their value when judged by standards of the European mainland in the sense of evidently deserving a certain amount of independent consideration which the present-day habitudes of the Scots ruled out. The poet gives plenty of examples of what he is talking about in *Contemporary Scottish Studies.*

I want to take a brief look at Grieve's early masterpiece — *A Drunk Man looks at the Thistle* (1926) in order to show how its main theme consists in the explicit organisation of the intellectual tensions to which I have called attention as being implicit in the early short poems. The structure of the poem, as I see it, will be made clearer by drawing certain parallels between its argument and the position developed by Anderson in his most mature works, that is, after 1940. A point to note by way of general introduction is that the thistle, in its chief sense, stands for the struggle of forces and counter-forces, through which the evolutionary process carries itself forward on a principle of the unintended consequences without any question of there being any foreseeable reconcilability of the various strands involved — a decidedly Andersonian idea which has its parallels in early Scottish philosophers like Hume and Adam Smith. What is said about the thistle in its other sense of symbol of Scotland has to be subordinated to what is said about it in this first sense, if we are to understand the poem as a whole. The ultimate problem posed by the poem is thus the universal one of how *"the thistle yet 'll unite/Man and the Infinite"*.[6] First things are therefore put first, and the national aspect does not make sense, except in the light of the cosmic aspect. "He canna Scotland see wha yet/Canna see the Infinite,/And Scotland in true scale to it".[7]

The starting point of the argument, what is taken for granted, is the historic rivalry between the national groups as well as within each national group, over the question of excellence in culture, knowledge, thought, etc., the thing which gives human life its distinctive character. In the first place there is the international struggle between groups as to the quality of their respective contributions to culture. Although they each have their ups and downs, some groups will always be superior to others, the possibility of equalisation being ruled out. In the second place, there is within each group a corresponding struggle between the elite, the intellectual few who do the discovering, and make possible the progress, and the anti-elitist many, who are not equal to participating in the general argument, and who seek, often successfully, to bring to an end "The insatiable thocht, the beautiful violent will,/The restless spirit of man"[8] by imposing egalitarianism, of which the Burns International is for our poet the great example, but which has sources outside Burns in the Reformation inheritance. "O fitly frae our cancerous soil/May this heraldic horror rise!/The Presbyterian thistle flourishes/And its ain roses crucifies. . . ."[9]

As so far sketched, the scene seems to be set for a vulgarised version of Nietzscheanism. What differentiated Grieve from this sort of fashionable life-philosophy and brings him much closer to Anderson, is that the "thocht" of the *Drunk Man* is not irrationalist in the technical sense — that is to say, it is not influenced by Shestov, who, contrary to what Oxenhorn says, was not (so far as my impression went) taken seriously by Grieve until the thirties. For the Grieve of the *Drunk Man*, the chief obstacle to be overcome by intellectuals before they are in a position to show how the thistle yet will unite man and the infinite — before, that is, they can achieve a detached view of the ubiquitous struggle in which they are caught up, and their place in it — is the classic problem of epistemology, understood in terms of the crux of perpetual illusion, that is to say, the crux already illustrated from *Sangschaw*, which provided Hume with a foundation for his scepticism, and which, because of the tradition of the free discussion of Hume in the Scottish universities long before he was freely discussed elsewhere, was familiar enough among the Scots, and not just in academic circles. Indeed, the very word epistemology, which in English seems exotic, originated, it is illuminating to note, in Scotland itself, being invented about 1854 by J. F. Ferrier of St Andrews in the course of his heroic — and unsuccessful — effort to clear up the intellectual confusion underlying the Church crisis, by distinguishing between the right way and the wrong way of reconciling philosophy with common sense.

Drawing on an independent intellectual tradition which, though weakened and somewhat ashamed of itself, was by no means dead in the Scotland of the first quarter of the twentieth century, the *Drunk Man* locates the crisis area of the intellectual's development in his encounter with the post-Cartesian conundrum, as it continued to survive right down to our own time, as to how to detach oneself from subjectivity, as to how to overcome the egocentric quality with which — to cite Hume again — the bodies originally and naturally perceived by us as existing out there beyond ourselves seem to become invested, as we turn our attention on ourselves and begin reflectively analysing our perceptive relation to the bodies earlier perceived as existing independently of ourselves. The critical moment of the intellectual's development, as envisaged in the *Drunk Man* is the very same as that described in the 'Man in the Moon', which contrasts the appearance sight with the bodily sight of things. In short, when the crunch comes, the problem the intellectual is faced with is not the Nietzschean version of the fashionable idea that this appearance/reality dualism can be got rid of and explained away by some sort of philological history of the way we have misunderstood language. Rather, the difficulty presents itself to Grieve in the same form as it presented itself to Anderson, namely, as the classic crux posed by David Hume, with some help from Bishop Berkeley, as to whether the distinction between appearance and reality might not be justified, and its apparent contradictions got rid of, by drawing attention to certain pervasively familiar facts which are neglected and hidden on account of their very familiarity, by reference to which what was hitherto dark becomes clear and intelligible.

The fact that the intellectual in the *Drunk Man* is faced with the classic problem of the textbook (the problem in a rational form) is, I believe, made quite plain at the very climax of the poem where the poet is discussing in what sense metaphysical poetry might bring at "lang last that unity" (between man and the infinite). "Oor universe is like an e'e/Turned in, man's benmaist hert to see,/And swamped in subjectivity."[10] When "thocht" asks itself whether it can use "its sicht/To bring what lies withoot to licht"[11] all the metaphysical theory "mankind/'S made yet is to the Earth confined,/Poo'erless to reach the general mind/Poo'erless to reach the neist star even/That as a pairt o'ts sel' is seen"[12] — i.e. seen in our earthbound point of view, the stars are visually indistinguishable from cats' eyes which shine in the dark, and in that sense are seen in subjective terms. How is "thocht" to transcend our terrestrial standpoint — "To grow wings that'll cairry it/Ayont its native speck o' grit."[13]

Without professing to know the answer, the poet at this point evolves a fruitful speculation, solidly based phenomenologically and capable in principle of being experimentally tested in some future circumstances, as to how we might overcome the terrestrial element in our perceptions, so as to be able to know the status and possibilities of human nature as it would be independently of its existence on earth, and as it would be if it existed in other circumstances. Suppose someone is able to reach the nearest star, and thus to put himself in a position to observe what is unobservable by us while we are here — the quality of earth which makes it appear as a star like the others, destroying its special status as a standpoint for our perceiving? "For gin the sun and mune at last/Are as a neebor's lintel passed,/"[14] "Til he has felt that he's been gi'en/The stars themsels instead o' een,/And often wi' the sun had glowered/At the white mune until it cowered."[15] In that case we would be able to see what is at present invisible, e.g. "the stishie/O' Earth in space/Breengin' by/At a haliket pace"[16] and might even be in a position to decide from observation as to whether or not there was anything in Professor J. Y. Simpson's suggestion about the innumerable Christs, i.e. whether or not such people or rational human-like beings that there were on the stars, would have a religious life like ours, organised around the central fact of a crucifixion of the Christ.[17]

Let us show that the poet is here concerned with the nature of rational knowledge of our human condition by comparing this final part of the *Drunk Man* with what John Anderson says about our knowledge of our country's culture. Now from this point of view, the important thing about these science-fiction speculations with which the poem concludes is not so much their anticipation of changes which have come over standard problems — like the one as to whether there are mountains on the other side of the moon, in this age of astronauts, where it has been possible to decide the matter by looking — as the fact that the multiplication of extraterrestrial perspectives on our earthbound perception of the moon and stars of which the poem talks, performs a function strictly analogous to that performed by the thing Anderson speaks of as necessary to the discovery of cultural standards — the multiplication of perspectives from the standpoints of foreign cultures which we are able to bring to bear on the cultural customs of our own community. Both these methods — Grieve's and Anderson's — in their different ways, enable us to detect qualities in our ordinary experience, in the one case cultural, in the other case cosmological, which, because they are always there, routinely given, could not be noticed so long as we did not go outside our own sphere — that is to say, so long as we did not manage to look at ourselves from alien standpoints — in the one case, from that of the culture of other countries, in the other case from that of the standpoint of other stars. Grieve, himself, for that matter, frequently makes Anderson's point in other parts of the poem — it is after all one of the leading theses of the *Drunk Man* that the features in Scottish culture recalling the situation of those countries which have language revivals would have remained hidden and practically undetectable if the Scots uniformly and without exception had continued to adhere to the custom, which had grown up since the time of Masson, of regarding the intellectual life of their country as worthy of being considered only insofar as it fitted into the culture-pattern of the U.K. as a whole. So too the analogous point which these final pages of the poem's speculations bring out, is that European countries were able to break with the custom universally inherited from scholasticism of regarding their earthbound perspectives as the natural and necessary mode of human perception, only because the researches of Galileo and other scientists established the fact that heavenly bodies like the moon had enough, materially speaking, in common with the solidity etc. of the earth to legitimise speculations about the possibility of their offering standing room and a viewpoint from which human-like perceivers could look back on the earth. That is to say, just as the discovery by some hitherto isolated community of the existence of other communities with cultures peculiar to themselves makes a difference to the way the former regards its culture, and makes it consider the possibility of alternative ways of doing things, as well as of its blind spots, so too the discovery by the telescopes of the Renaissance astronomers of the existence of extra-terrestrial bodies, which observation showed to be material in much the same sense as the earth was material, altered our customary ideas about the limitations of our experience and setting aside the belief of human nature as tied to a terrestrial standpoint, inspired speculations like those of Giordano Bruno.

The illusions, the subjective and uncritical attitudes, which arise in connection with the routinisation of our acceptance of some ends as useful are discussed in the poem in connection with the national/international distinction as it exists for the intellectual class in a country in a situation similar to that of Scotland. "I micht ha'e been contentit wi' the Rose"[18] the poet says — but for the fact that he "saw hoo ither countries' genius drew/Elements like mine that in a rose ne'er grew . . .".[19] That is to say, if one compares Scotland not only with England, but also with continental countries, so as to note affinities and lack of affinities, one discovers that the kind of traditional view of unity typified by the thistle depends on a tradition of life as composed of mutually conflicting forces, which jostle one another, giving rise to a kind of "antisyzygy", that is to say, unyokableness, unpredictable changes, due to internal pressures — such as are also found present in Russia, as described by, say, Dostoevsky,[20] but which are absent from the tradition of those countries which value toleration and play social harmony. (Compare Anderson's distinction between the view which accepts struggle as endless and incapable of being eliminated, and the view which regards struggle as capable of being eliminated.) This unity of intolerance, this acceptance of endless struggle and debate, in respect of which the poet's comparison shows Scotland and Russia to be alike, is absent from, or not prominently present in England, where "th' owre sonsy rose/That roond aboot its devotees/A fair fat cast o' aureole throws/That blinds them, in its mirlygoes,/To the necessity o' foes",[21] i.e. to the inevitability of endless struggle. It is this contrasting which, looking beyond Britain, compares Scotland and England to Russia and to other continental countries, including the small countries characterised by literary renaissances, that brings to light the sharp difference between the thistle and the rose, as the poet has formulated it. Suppose the comparison of Scotland with these non-Anglo-Saxon countries not to have taken place. Suppose the Scots to be so wedded to the habit of regarding themselves as part of Britain and not looking outside it, and the distinctive nature of Scotland which the poet has brought to light — the character of evolution through endless struggle and debate — would cease to be noticeable, even though it was always there:

> O drumlie clood o' crudity and cant,
> Obliteratin' as the East rouk
> That rows up frae the howes and droons the heichs,
> And turns the country to a faceless spook.[22]

Now, just as the *Drunk Man* can learn the possibilities and limitations of his country's culture only by comparing it with the culture of other countries, and by looking at his own from their point of view, and just as he doesn't know the possibilities and limitations of human life as it is led on earth, without seeing it in a cosmological setting and looking at it — if that were ever possible — from the standpoint of the stars, so too, in regard to the personal aspects of his life, he cannot know the limits and possibilities of his own personality until he is in a position to compare what he knows about himself by direct observation of his behaviour with other aspects of his behaviour, which are directly observable, not by himself, but by those living in day-to-day contact with him, and which he learns about from them, and could know nothing about apart from them. The theme of this inter-personal basis of self-knowledge is elaborated with great verve and insight through the parts of the poem which treat of the relation of man and wife. The topic is introduced one-fifth of the way through in a passage which has become well known:

> A luvin' wumman is a licht
> That shows a man his waefu' plicht,
> Bleezin' steady on ilka bane,
> Wrigglin' sinnen an' twinin' vein,
> Or fleerin' quick an' gane again,
> And the mair scunnersome the sicht
> The mair for love and licht he's fain

Till clear and chitterin' and nesh
Move a' the miseries o' his flesh. . . .[23]

The experience of the partner's responsiveness is thus a very important and essential part of one's self-knowledge — a point which is made several times throughout the poem, as in these lines:

E'en as the munelicht's borrowed frae the sun
I ha'e my knowledge o' mysel' frae thee,
And much that nane but thee can e'er mak' clear,
Save my licht's frae the source, is dark to me.[24]

To make sense of what the poet is saying here, it seems to me reasonable to point out that his self-description in these passages on personal relations, depends upon the fact — familiar enough in modern phenomenonology (e.g. Sartre's discussions of the Body and the Look, in *Being and Nothingness*, and certain parallel passages in Merleau-Ponty's *Phenomenonology of Perception*), as well as in some traditional philosophy (especially that of Scotland, notably Adam Smith and J. F. Ferrier), but in any case obvious enough to his readers without their having to study philosophy in detail — that our powers of self-observation are systematically limited. In the case of sight and of smell, the applicability of this rule isn't easy to dispute. When we are looking at a body like a table, which comes and goes in our experience, it is possible to see it in the round, from all sides, but when we are looking at that body of ours, which does the perceiving, and is always there, we see it differently, and important parts of it — those intimately connected with the visual perception — remain invisible to us (except in mirrors, an exception however which does not break the rule). So too, in the case of these things which come and go, and are objects in that sense, their characteristic odours are readily noticeable by us, whereas in the case of our bodily odours, when their relative constants like bad breath escape our notice, their existence can be brought home to us only by others. In the case of the hearing of sound, the principle has been disputed by Jacques Derrida, in an argument[25] which, however, is not difficult to answer. We hear no doubt the sound of our own voices (that is, of our auditory responses to the things and persons around us) but we do not hear the sound we make with our voices in the way we can hear or attend to the sound made by other things, as the shock of hearing ourselves for the first time on a tape recorder makes clear — the fact being that certain features of our voices which are constant, e.g. the local accent, etc., are inaudible to us in the sense of being unnoticeable, so long as they are invariable. We cannot vary our auditory standpoint in regard to our own speaking as we can in regard to the speaking of others. So too, it is not so difficult to rebut the theory that the principle does not apply in the case of touch and tactual feeling. It is, I grant, true that I can feel my right hand with my left, and even give myself a sort of experience of their clasping one another in some kind of handshake. But in contrast to what I can learn about from other people in the case of shaking hands with them, and studying their responses to me, it is not revealed to me in the experience of shaking hands with myself whether my clasp is or is not, for example, cold and off-putting, because the left hand of mine which I feel with my right is always felt as the hand of a friend, which beats in tune with me, and is always in sympathy with what it feels.

This principle of the limitation of one's self-observation is, in my view, what gives sense to these passages in which the *Drunk Man* says that the communications of his wife are what enables him to correct his partial view of himself in relation to his circumstances — the thistle on the hillside, the moon etc.

> O Jean, in whom my spirit sees,
> Clearer than through whisky or disease,
> Its dernin' nature, wad the searchin' licht
> Oor union raises poor'd owre me the nicht.[26]

Unusual experiences like being drunk or ill — compare Anderson on what can be learned by being an odd man out in one's own nation — the poet is saying, can, by breaking the habitual rhythm of one's life, make one conscious of qualities of one's nature which so long as they are unfailingly present, in health and sobriety, are not noticed. For example, one learns in illness how much one's habitual way of looking at things depends upon the confident flow of health. But, the poet goes on, the effects on one's knowledge of one's nature, which result from the experience of being looked at by one's wife, are incomparably more far reaching than that which arises from the experience of drink or illness. Illustrating what he says by reference to the facts, already noticed, of the limitation of our visual knowledge of our bodies, the poet points out that whereas he only half experiences himself when he looks at himself in solitude, he is able to complete the picture of himself — to get a knowledge of the half which hadn't been visible — when he looks at himself in the light of what his wife communicates to him, that is to say, when he — to speak the language of Adam Smith — uses his wife's responses to him as a mirror which draws attention to aspects of himself which escape his direct observation. "Be thou," the passage continues, "the licht in which I stand/Entire, in thistle-shape, as planned,/And no' hauf-hidden and hauf-seen as here/In munelicht, whisky, and in fleshly fear."[27] That is, when I depend for knowledge of myself on my direct experience of myself and on nothing else, I get only a "keethin' sicht", that is to say, a partial and misleading view of myself in relation to the things I perceive, whereas I get a "bodily sicht" of myself and my situation, and see myself whole, only insofar as I let my attention be drawn by others to those parts of myself which are hidden from my vision.

Oxenhorn[28] speaks of Ouspensky as the source of the poet's ideas here, but on my reading of the poet's argument, the point he is making (whatever its immediate source) has more affinity with the doctrines of thinkers who are much less exotic, and much more close to logic, in the technical sense, than the Russian mystic would want to be. John Dewey, for instance, in the Smithian passage from the beginning of *Democracy and Education*[29] — to which I have already called attention in other connections — enunciates the same sort of principle that lies behind Grieve's argument and gives life to it. In communicating information to a pupil, according to Dewey, the teacher discovers something new about himself and his relation at the viewpoint of his pupils, and therefore has to look at himself and his own life through the pupils' eyes. Moreover, the same sort of doctrine is advanced in a source far closer to Grieve than either Dewey or Ouspensky — the well-known lines of Robert Burns, in which, watching a louse crawling over the bonnet of a young lady in the pew in front, he remarks that our blind spots are due to its being impossible for us to see ourselves as others see us, a phrase which he directly borrows from the famous passage in Adam Smith's *Theory of Moral Sentiments* (a book admired by Burns) in which what is true in Hume's scepticism about perception is deftly disentangled from what is false and misleading.[30] According to Smith, the unquestioning belief of common sense that the bodies perceived by me exist independently of myself and my perception of them, is shaken, or brought into doubt, in the reflective analysis of perception, only insofar as the philosopher takes account in his analysis of what direct experience of himself tells him about himself and his relation to the bodies perceived, and insofar as he omits to consider in his analysis the parts of his commonsense belief in the externality of things to himself which come to him indirectly from others, and which enable him to see in imagination that the relation of himself to the bodies he perceives — the distance between them, the independence of the one on the other — is precisely analogous to the relationship of the other perceivers to the things they perceive, as he knows from his direct observation of them. That is to say, to translate once again into the language of *Sangschaw*, in my direct experience of myself, I get only the "keethin' sicht" of my relationship as a perceiver to the bodies perceived, and it is the indirect knowledge of this relation, conveyed through my direct experience of others' responses to me, which give me — indirectly — the "bodily sicht" of the relationship as it is believed in by common sense. On this view the real affinity of Grieve's thought was with the tradition of the Philosophy of Common Sense as it was developed by philosophers he knew nothing about — Adam Smith and Ferrier — rather than the texts of Ouspensky, though these may have set him off.

A closer reading of Oxenhorn, however, makes it clear that his interpretation of this central theme of the *Drunk Man* does not differ materially from my own. In adapting Ouspensky's ideas, the poet effects a logical restructuring which transforms it into something like Common Sense Philosophy:

"[The poet's thought] is all quite abstract — perhaps excessively so — in the tradition of 'Scotch metaphysics'. Yet the crucial point about these speculations is that they are worked *through*, that they ultimately issue not in rigid abstraction but in a refreshed commitment to one's own place and kind. If individuals 'canna look on nakit licht', if darkness 'comes closer to us than the licht, and is our natural element', then our efforts to overcome it must become collective."[31]

Thus Oxenhorn's, view of the poet's philosophy — give or take certain modifications — brings out the poem's point in an illuminating way. The poet arrives at the conclusion — by some kind of logical process — that sceptical views about the possibility of knowledge of oneself in relation to the thing perceived arise from a failure to grasp the social element in it; what I learn about myself I can only learn about myself by paying attention to the others and their look. What is questionable in Oxenhorn's account is the negative way he speaks of the rigid abstractions of the "Scotch metaphysics". The poet Grieve, one must remember, was notable — and, I might say, very Scottish (in a philosophical sense) — in respecting the role of abstraction as a necessary element in thought. In *To Circumjack Cencrastus* he speaks of the "abstract disciplines we sairly need"[32] and, as I remember, he admired Kemp Smith's article on 'The Fruitfulness of the Abstract'[33] without, no doubt, understanding in the technical sense the details of the philosophical argument, but at the same time managing to catch its general drift.

Thus though the thought of the *Drunk Man* may have its source in the exotic and off-beat philosophies which the poet liked to read, it nevertheless seems to be the case that as the philosophical argument of the poem develops, it transcends the limitations of its starting point, and its intellectual affinities are in the end less with Ouspensky than with certain systematic mainline thinkers, old and new, in the Scottish tradition, who were neglected by the poet because, aligning himself here with the vast majority of his countrymen, he didn't find Scottish philosophy immediately stimulating. John Anderson, in his theory of history, puts over a similar view to that of the *Drunk Man*, expressed however from a quite different point of view. Anderson's position, one might say, is a generalisation of the thistle and the rose theme, in which, without any mention of England and Scotland, contrast is drawn between a pair of group attitudes or movements of society, one of them working to suppress strife in countries and between countries, and the other accepting strife as ultimately uneliminable. As against this, the poet's position is a sort of a particularisation of Anderson's very abstract antithesis between history as the discontinuing of struggle and history as continuing struggle, the former being in the work of the poet exemplified by the tradition of English society which the rose emblem symbolises, the latter being exemplified by the spirit of Scottish society as symbolised by the thistle.

The point of identity between the poet and the philosopher, is summed up in a dictum of Nietzsche, which the latter cites with approbation. "Man does not aspire to happiness, only the Englishman does that."[34] Their difference is summed up in the fact that, for the philosopher, the Nietzschean anithesis between man and Englishman is universalised into that between anti-utilitarianism and utilitarianism, whereas the poet individualises it into a contrast between what he regards the universal-human attitude expressed in the Scottish scepticism or pessimism, and the heretical point of view of Anglican Pelagianism with its optimism about things.

To get the parallel and the difference clear, we have to see

Anderson and Grieve as defending much the same sort of Scotticism — as Masson calls it — meaning by that in this case the criticism of the utilitarianism and the happiness-seeking philosophy from the Calvinist point of view — which is put over by the philosopher in the internalised form, but by the poet in the externalised form, to borrow Masson's phrases:

"A Scotchman, when he thinks, cannot so easily and comfortably as the Englishman repose on an upper level of propositions co-ordinated for him by tradition, sweet feeling and pleasant circumstance. . . . It amazes Scotchmen at the present day to see on what proximate propositions even Englishmen who are celebrated as thinkers can rest in their speculations. Quietism, mysticism; that soft, meditative disposition which takes things for granted in the co-ordination established by mere life and usage, pouring into the confusion thus externally given, a rich oil of an abounding inner joy, interpenetrating all and harmonising all — these are for the most part alien to the Scotchman. No, his walk as a thinker is not by meadows and wheatfields and the green lanes and the ivy-clad Parish churches where all is gentle and antique and fertile, but by the bleak seashore which parts the certain from the limitless, where there is doubt in the sea-mew's shriek, and where it is well if, in the advancing tide he can find a footing on a rock."[35]

This was said in 1852, but before the decade was out (indeed within two years) Masson was calling for a switch of line:

"Scotticism is not an invariable thing, fixed and intransmutable. It does not consist in vaunting and proclaiming itself, and in working in Scottish facts, Scottish traditions and Scottish reminiscences — all of which have perhaps been done enough; it may be driven inwards; it may exist internally as a mode of thought, and there may be efficient Scotticism, where not one word is said of the Thistle, and where the language and activity is catholic and cosmopolitan. And seeing this is so, need we suppose we have seen the last of the Scotchmen, the last of the men of Edinburgh? No."

But the Union having made Scotland a partaker in an intellectual accumulation and an inheritance of institutions far richer than her own:

"while much of the subsequent effort of Scotland had been in continuation of her own development, much had been necessarily and justly been ruled by the law of our fortunate partnership. And so for the future, it may be internal Scotticism working on British or still more general objects, that may be in demand in literature and other walks."[36]

What the philosopher of Sydney and the poet of the *Drunk Man* have in common, as well as where they differ, is made clear enough in the contrast between Masson's two statements. Both Anderson and Grieve uphold the anti-utilitarian or, as one might say, realist attitude for which life is a walk by the bleak seashore which parts the certain and the limitless, and both likewise criticise a superficial and rosy-spectacled attitude which reposes on an upper level of propositions co-ordinated by traditions, sweet feeling, etc. and which seem to them to take for granted the co-ordinations established by inner life and usage.

The difference between the poet and the philosopher is thus over the question of whether Scotticism (understood as a realistic or anti-utilitarian way of life) ought or ought not to uphold its bleak logic in abstraction from the Scottish facts and traditions in which it grew up. Anderson, one might say, was responsible for a vigorous restatement in an internalised form which, by removing the references to Scottish history and traditions, made it easier to put over to his Australian audience. But the poet was not going to be working in Australia but in Scotland, and he therefore rejected the idea of a Scotticism in which nothing was said of the thistle, and which set out to be British and cosmopolitan, because his wide experience of foreign literatures, both in great countries and in small, had made him aware that the internalised Scotticism which he had, like other people, simply taken for granted, was something which could, at that juncture, be replaced by externalised Scotticism with great advantage to the culture of the country.

We will understand better the coincidence of the *Drunk Man*'s position and Anderson's in their common opposition to the happiness principle and to defences of it which were being put forward in the name of anti-elitist democracy, if we bear in mind that the thought of the two men in each case arose indirectly out of their reaction to the culture-crisis of the Scottish twenties, in which a 200-year-long tradition of the intellectual upholding of classicist standards broke down as the result of the Ordinance 70 struggles. From the mid-eighteenth century to the early twentieth century the universities and the educated classes of Scotland had been more or less continuously involved in a series of intellectual engagements in which they had been seeking to uphold the anti-utilitarian values of a commonsense philosophy against the increasingly confident assaults of the greatest happiness principle as put forward by the protagonists of radical reform. Brought out into the open about 1770 in the attacks of Priestley on the Scottish philosophers, the argument for and against utilitarianism surfaced anew in the exchanges between the Benthamites and the Edinburgh reviewers as represented by Jeffrey and Macaulay in one direction, and by Thomas Carlyle in another. Always simmering in the background, the intellectual tensions boiled over once again, and this time in a decisive manner, in J. S. Mill's onslaught on the Hamiltonian school in 1865 which, without extinguishing the Scottish philosophy in Scotland, destroyed its credit in the rest of Britain, at least from the majority point of view. Still very much alive in Scotland, the conflict of principles reappeared in the eighties and nineties in the more gentlemanly form of the disputes between Caird of Glasgow, who spoke in the name of a Hegelianised version of Mill's utilitarianism, and the Edinburgh-based philosophers, S. S. Laurie and Pringle-Pattison, who stood — the latter explicitly — for a Hegelianised version of Reid's Philosophy of Common Sense. Finally, in the first decade of the twentieth century, the struggle began to take on a more violent form with the growing prominence of the outspoken Darroch, the Edinburgh Professor of Education who, in the opening stages of the Ordinance 70 affair, was attacking the classical common sense of the Edinburgh academic establishment in the name of a neo-utilitarianism inspired by American pragmatism and not least by Dewey.

Throughout this long period, the outcome of each new crisis was that the anti-utilitarian resistance of the Calvinist north more and more lost ground to the confident utilitarianism which had inspired the reform of the British state, and which the state itself, with the encouragement of Hegelian philosophers like Green and Caird, was progressively identifying itself with — not least in the work done by Caird's pupil Struthers as head of the S.E.D. Finally, the tension boiled over in the later stages of World War I, when the Scottish universities found themselves with no alternative but to do battle with the state, as represented by the S.E.D. planners, who, in loose alliance with the popular forces of the country, were preparing to destroy the traditional academic standards in Scotland. At first sight it seemed as if the stage was set for a new outbreak of the philosophical war between utilitarianism and anti-utilitarianism which had been intermittently going on every generation since 1770, and Burnet's *Higher Education and the War* was evidently published with the idea of striking a first blow in a campaign which would defend a philosophically based classicism against the utility principle associated with Darroch and the American pragmatists.

However, instead of starting up once again a discussion of the traditional issues of philosophy and first principles versus pragmatism, the Scottish universities decided to make themselves safe against the anti-elitist assault of the people and of their planners, by the very modern tactic of an academic reorganisation which, by cutting off the universities from the S.E.D. and at the same time making philosophy safe from its competitors by putting it into a sort of ivory tower, would silence their critics by breaking contact with them instead of arguing with them in the market-place. There must, it was felt, never again be one of these public fights between philosophers over the question of utilitarianism and anti-utilitarian common sense, which, it was felt, had damaged the dignity of the Scottish universities in the eyes of the English-speaking world almost as much as the disastrous debates and splits over disestablishment-arianism had done in the nineteenth century.

It is when we read the *Drunk Man*, as well as Anderson's posthumous books, against the background of the intellectual struggles of the Scottish twenties that the meaning of the philosophical innovations of both men reveals itself to us in the fullness of its profundity and force. Both poet and philosopher, in their different ways, were seeking to restart the long continuing intellectual argument among the Scots, which the universities had decided to avoid. The poetry of the one, the philosophy of the other, constituted a practical proof that the ancient argument was still very much alive. The state-planners might behave as if the large-scale developments of British civilisation had brought about the irreversible triumph of the utilitarian principle. But in their timely reactions against these over-confident and very superficial claims, Grieve and Anderson were resurrecting the dying tradition by restating the case against the anti-elitist utilitarianism in a philosophy which, not merely in its vigour and depth, surpassed anything there had been for nearly 100 years in Scotland, but which, in the case of the poet at least, broke with immediate routines by taking its stand, unashamedly, on a re-externalised Scotticism.

Leaving Anderson till later, let us study in more detail how, in contrast to the arrogance of the Scottish universities of the twenties, who, instead of meeting the intellectual challenge of the teachers, broke off relations with the schools and the S.E.D., the *Drunk Man* affirms the inescapable necessity of argument from first principles. The point of special note here is that the poet prepares the way for his — as Oxenhorn rightly says — legitimate and effective argument against scepticism, the argument from social roots of knowledge, by emphatically calling attention to the persuasiveness of the evidence for the existence of pervasive contradictions in empirical knowledge, and by repeatedly reminding us of the well-foundedness of the sceptical case. The verve and lucidity as well as the frequency of the poet's expositions of the strong points of philosophical doubt is a feature of the *Drunk Man* which Oxenhorn, however, does not seem to appreciate. This is because, I believe, of his being much more at home with the "oil on troubled waters" philosophy of the rose than with the thistle philosophy of the bleak seashore where it is next to impossible to avoid slipping on the rocks. He seems to forget that what distinguishes the Scottish tradition of philosophy from the tradition in the other countries of the West, is the fact that the two thinkers who did most to keep the Scottish argument in motion were both sceptics — David Hume and Sir William Hamilton. The poet, however, whatever his actual "examination-knowledge" might be on the subject, does not, so far as his poetry is concerned, forget the fact, and the argument of the *Drunk Man* is a continuing battle against a scepticism which is no sooner refuted well and truly in one form than it reappears in another and more difficult form.

The intellectual situation of the human being is, in this poem, a perpetual struggle against doubts which are not thrust on him from outside, but inevitably arise from within his own thinking:

> Aye, this is Calvary — to bear
> Your Cross wi'in you frae the seed,
> And feel it grow by slow degrees
> Until it rends your flesh apairt,
> And turn, and see your fellow-men
> In similar case but sufferin' less
> Thro' bein' mair wudden frae the stert! . . .[37]

In explaining this scepticism, the poet gives a fairly accurate and striking portrayal of what he sees as the main difficulty which stands in the way of our understanding the detachment from self which allows us to see ourselves as others see us. "I perish o' a nearness I canna win awa frae"[38] — this central paradox of the human situation

JOHN ANDERSON AND C. M. GRIEVE

applies to each of the three levels of experience: the familial, the
national, and the cosmological, which are systematically discussed in
the poem. First, the horizons in which one perceives the world are
limited by the behaviour pattern imposed by one's experience of
being brought up in a certain family, and the characteristics resulting
from that are not noticeable until one has experience outside the
family, as in marriage. Second, the way one perceives the world is
determined by one's national inheritance of which one cannot
become conscious until one is able to put oneself at the point of view
of other nations. Thirdly, the way one perceives the world is limited
by one's terrestrial situation. That is, the earth on which we stand
exists for us only as an obscurely perceived foreground of whatever
else we perceive beyond the earth, and it is difficult to discount or
allow for this foreground if we are not able to perceive it from the
standpoint of other heavenly bodies.

Of course, as we have noticed before, the sceptical difficulty which
arises at each of the three levels can be overcome, but that does not
prevent it from always coming back, as the result of certain characteristics of our perception which are well described by the poet:

> Oor een gi'e answers based on pairt-seen facts
> That beg a' questions, to ebb minds' content,
> But hoo a'e feature or the neist attracts,
> Wi' millions mair unseen, wha kens what's meant
> By human brains and to what ends may tell
> — For naething's seen or kent that's near a thing itsel'![39]

We can distinguish between the lasting qualities and the accidental
qualities of our nature in the case of qualities that come to us from our
family background or from our national background or from our
background as earth-dwellers, because of our being able to look at
ourselves from the standpoint of other families, other nations and
perhaps one day other planets, but we cannot make an analogous
distinction between the permanent and the temporary in our
qualities, when we raise the question as to which are going to develop
and which are going to die out in the evolutionary changes which are
liable to overtake our species:

> Juist as man's skeleton has left
> Its ancient ape-like shape ahint,
> Sae states o' mind in turn gi'e way
> To different states, and quickly seem

Impossible to later men,
And Man's mind in its final shape,
Or lang'll seem a monkey's spook
And, strewth, to me the verra thocht
O' Tocht already's fell like that![40]

Our claim to know what is there, i.e. to distinguish the false from the true, may have been able to hold its own against scepticism at the previous stages of the argument. Granted the onward march of evolution, it seems to follow incontestably, not only that our present points of view about things, however carefully worked out, are bound to be superseded as false, but also that we have no means whatever of discovering where the weakness of our present-day orthodox opinions lie, owing to the absolute ignorance we are in as to what the outlook of the race of superbeings that may follow us is going to be like.

In the event, however, the *Drunk Man* is able to turn the tables on scepticism, at least in principle in the cosmological meditations in *terza-rima*, which form the finale of the poem. The line the poet takes continues the principle affirmed in the poem on the 'Innumerable Christ'; questions which appear unanswerable from the point of view of terrestrial experience because the requisite evidence is lacking, become answerable, and so meaningful, in the light of the kind of evidence which might conceivably be provided by a cosmological extension of our experience. The point here is that the stars are at varying stages of development, some more advanced than the present situation on earth. If therefore — and it is a big *if* — we ever could identify with the point of view of the superbeings near one of these developed stars, we might begin to get some clues as to what was defective and false in our terrestrial point of view. Repudiating thereby the characteristically sceptical position (Hamilton's) that we have to accept the nature of ultimate reality as being absolutely beyond our ken, the poet is working his way towards the more logical (and more hopeful) counter position put forward by Ferrier in his *Institutes of Metaphysics* (1854), and reaffirmed by Burnet in his Romanes Lecture on 'Ignorance' of 1923, that the knowable and the ignorable are one or that we can be ignorant only of what might possibly be known.[41]

Affirming the value of intellectual standards in a Scotland which was deeply divided about them and losing faith in them, the argument developed in the *Drunk Man*, taken as a whole, is remarkably consistent. Oxenhorn seems to me to have lost touch with the *Drunk Man* as a philosophical drama of ideas when he declares it to be quite out of keeping with the cultural aspirations of the central character in the poem that he should be married to a small-town scold like Tam o' Shanter's Kate, and not to a "faculty wife". At the same time as emphasising the sharp separation between the elite-figure of the poet and the others, the poem itself never forgets that the former has his roots among the latter, and preserves the closest connection with them. Having as one of its main themes the contemporary breakdown of the symbiosis between democracy and intellect which had been traditional among the Scots, the *Drunk Man* deserves to be read as a kind of re-run of John Davidson's poem on growing up in Greenock — 'A Ballad in Blank-verse on the Making of a Scottish Poet'.[42] Both poems are on the theme of an autodidact whose culture is alienating him from his family and fellow-townsmen with their orthodox anti-elitist point of view. But the distinguishing feature of the later poem as opposed to the earlier is that the drunk man is still able to identify himself with the anti-elitist point of view and to see himself through the eyes of the others. In the first one third of the poem when the main theme is being established, the philosophical flights which express the point of view of metaphysical elitism alternate with a down-to-earth self-commentary in which the elitist shows himself to be uneasily aware of how his enterprise looks from the point of view of the kind of people he is surrounded with — the people of 'Crowdieknowe'. The result is that in "the battle of the two philosophies" — to borrow the name of a book about the Hamilton-Mill controversy — the drunk man is able to do a certain amount of justice to the standpoint he is opposing, that of the many, as well as to the standpoint he defends, that of the few. No doubt the effect, as Oxenhorn suggests, is that of self-parody, but to my mind the tension between sublimity and bathos which thereby finds expression gives scope to the poet's *vis comica* and, as such, is a strength of this poem which struggles with a philosophical theme.

Seen in this perspective the *Drunk Man* is not to be regarded as a mere literary exercise in synthetic Scots, but rather as a contribution to the Ordinance 70 debate, just as much as was the poet's *Contemporary Scottish Studies*, published in 1927, the year after the poem. From one point of view the *Drunk Man* may be the opening of a new epoch in Scottish poetry, but from another point of view it is not too much to see in it a renaissance of Scottish philosophy, understood in its traditional sense as the upholder of standards and the critic of aberrations in regard to the continuing debate between the opposed *weltanschauungen* of the grimly deterministic orthodoxy of Calvinism on the one hand and the optimistic voluntarism of the Pelagian minority on the other hand.

Grieve's attitude to the position taken up by the leading Scottish philosophers in the debates of the twenties is to a great extent paralleled by that of Anderson. Though the latter's first concern was doubtless with the development of philosophy in Australia, the very considerable currents in his thinking which derived from Burnet may be illuminatingly viewed as carrying on Burnet's criticism of the philosophy establishment of the Scottish universities, for their betrayal of its distinctive inheritance. What had gone wrong with philosophy in Scotland? Looking at the question in the light of Arnold's method of comparing the country with the intellectual culture of the other leading nations, Anderson decided the weak spot in the Scottish tradition of philosophy as compared not only with that of the continental countries but even with England and America, was their refusal to take seriously the study of logic. This shortcoming, Anderson notes, is already present in Hume. The sceptical outcome of Hume's philosophy, his readiness to accept an inextricable tangle of contradictions as the inevitable outcome of systematic thinking about fundamentals, is, in Anderson's eyes, identical with the failure of the *Treatise of Human Nature* to develop a constructive doctrine of formal logic.[43] Perpetuated by the leading philosophers who came after Hume, whether they were critical of him or admired him, this blind spot about the crucial importance of logical studies had been the Achilles heel of Scottish philosophy, being more than anything else responsible for its failure of nerve in the face of the attacks by the Deweyite Marxism which was flooding into Scotland in the wake of the teachers' movement. In contradistinction to Burnet's brave stand for principles, the other philosophers in Scotland seem, from Anderson's point of view, to have settled for sorry compromises, and his irritation against them seems to have known no bounds — as witness the fact that he was so carried away by passion in his review of *Scepticism and Construction* by C. A. Campbell, the respectable Glasgow Professor, as to fail to draw properly some fundamental distinctions, as Professor Gilbert Ryle was later to point out.[44]

To understand the problem confronting Anderson here, it has to be borne in mind that in regard to the nineteenth and early twentieth-century innovations in logic, the Scottish tradition as inherited by

Anderson from his teachers had taken up the same kind of reserved attitude as it had adopted towards the analogous (and interconnected) phenomena of the modern movement in mathematics. While prepared to acknowledge the valuable contribution made by the movement which was producing a non-Aristotlean logic and a non-Euclidean geometry, the Scottish professors of mathematics and professors of philosophy, under whom Anderson studied, and in whose departments he was to work, regarded the mainstream of development in logic as well as in geometry as continuing to move in the direction originally given it by the Greeks. By comparison, the alternative line of development, which, instituted by the innovators, sought to carry logic and mathematics along paths uncontemplated by the Greeks, was regarded with suspicion among the Scots, as being a divergence which was leading logic and mathematics away from the central highway, in the sense of obliterating basic distinctions in the interests of what looked like simplistic reductions. Robert Adamson, for example, the philosopher most respected in Scotland at the beginning of the present century, had suggested, in his short book on the history of logic, that the developments in the line of mathematical or symbolic logic depended upon an atomistic view of knowledge and perception, while, in an analgous way, the Scottish mathematicians, headed by men like Anderson's teacher, Gibson of Glasgow, without denying the power and the fruitfulness of the new developments in continental mathematics like those of Cantor, nevertheless tended to regard them as philosophically ill-founded, insofar as they departed from the Euclidean objectivism, and opted instead for a view of space according to which the characteristics it showed depended upon the way we chose to describe it.

Meantime, just when Anderson was first attending university classes, i.e. in the two years before 1914, a considerable body of opinion had crystallised among the Scots which was in favour of the new mathematics and the new logic. The appointment of Whittaker to the Edinburgh Chair of Mathematics had, as I have pointed out earlier, created a situation in which the fluid and unorganised opposition to Scottish scientific conservatism had crystallised into a movement for introducing the new physics, and along with it the innovations in mathematics and logic, which were so suspect. The conventional wisdom of the time might naturally have thought — indeed John Maclean did express himself along these lines in a letter sent to a friend from prison during the war[45] — that the new generation of students of mathematics, physics and philosophy in Scotland — that is, young men like Anderson who were ambitious and were no respecters of traditions for their own sake — would have been caught up in the currents of advance which under Whittaker's guidance were seeking to bring to the Scottish universities what was accepted as the physics of the future by the universities of the world. In the event, however, Anderson's response to the challenge of this new scene of thought was characteristically "thrawn". Sympathising with the reservations of his mathematical and philosophical teachers in regard to the new developments and even in some respects being more royalist than the royals, he set his sights on a renaissance of traditional geometry which, restoring it to the pristine strength and beauty of its Hellenic origins, would check the undoing of intellectual standards which he saw as likely to be the most important results of the reforms in logic and in mathematics. Identifying (one might think) with Adamson's criticisms of the new logic as resting on a metaphysical atomism, Anderson went on to bring against it the accusation that, by authorising a description of the world which would obliterate or obscure the connection of things with one another in the way they interacted, the revolt against Aristotle was making it more and more impossible to refute the pragmatism which was seeking to sell itself as the passport to universal happiness all round. A philosophy which wanted to be genuinely progressive ought to be moving back and not forward. Taking its cue from Burnet, it would have to return to the Greek consideration of things; to the Hellenic objectivity.

By way of clarifying Anderson's position, I want to draw attention here to the parallelisms between the way the poet responded in the *Drunk Man* to the cultural problems of the Scotland of the early twentieth century and the way Anderson responded some twenty years later, when the educational problems he had encountered in the Scotland of his youth reappeared in an intensified form in the educational reorganisation in the Australia of the post-war years. The aim of both is to justify the unity of knowledge against the defeatism of an academic generation who are acquiescing in the fragmentation of knowledge. Just as the *Drunk Man*'s aim is to show, in the face of the counter-claims of the sceptic, how the thistle unites man and the infinite in virtue of an intellectual progress in which knowledge of what it is to be a family man, knowledge of what it is to belong to a certain nation and knowledge of what it is to have the cosmic status of earth dwellers, systematically illumine one another, so too

Anderson replies to the claims of modern logicians on behalf of the utility of the intellectual tools which they claim to be superior to the traditional forms handed down from Aristotle that, whereas the old logic made the various subjects intelligible to one another by enabling us to think of them as connected, the new logic destroyed the mutual intelligibility of subjects to one another by imposing on them a pattern of disconnectedness. Not only may we say of Anderson what Oxenhorn said of Grieve, in regard to the *Drunk Man*, that he thought *through* the problem, systematically working it out and not resting content with genial *aperçus*, but it is even the case that Anderson did his own "Back to Dunbar" in the three late articles on logic — 'Hypotheticals' (1952) and the posthumous pair 'Relational Arguments' and 'Logic and Empiricism'[46] — in which, reintroducing Burnet's theme of the defence of generalism in order to answer Gilbert Ryle's criticisms, he exhibits a mastery of the techniques of formal logic unequalled in Scotland since the days of Lokert the logician, and John Mair in the sixteenth century.

8

DRUNK MAN OR LUCKY POET?

MacDiarmid and Anderson were, as has been noted, both much preoccupied with the great question of how far the insufficiency of human nature in the individual can be compensated for on a collective plane.[1] Both of them had one phase in which they regarded collectivisation in the form of socialism as a means of liberating man from his insufficiency, and another phase (finding expression in the case of the poet in his nationalism) in which they regarded collective action as incapable of ending man's insufficiency in the way of evening out the contradictions and reconciling one form of human life with another.

At the same time their unlikeness shows up very clearly against this background of what they had in common. In the first place, whereas Anderson moved away from an original socialism to a more pessimistic awareness of the limitations of the human situation, MacDiarmid's move was the other way about — a difference accounted for in part by the contrast between their respective fathers. In the case of Anderson, a caustic, anti-clerical dominie, in the case of the poet a genial, but God-fearing postman. In the second place, and even more important, is the fact that Anderson's socialism was always obsessed by the problem of scarcity; a revolutionary progress is, in his case, associated with the idea — taken over from Sorel — that the co-operation of intellectuals with the artisans will be able to carry forward the victorious struggle against nature beyond the limits possible to private industry.[2] But MacDiarmid's socialism rests on his belief that modern science has put into our hands the means of ending forever the reign of scarcity, and replacing it with a reign of plenty — a difference which seems to be illustrated by their relationship to their favourite paper, The New Age. Anderson, as his article on the paper shows, strongly deplored the conversion of the editor, Orage, to C. H. Douglas's Social Credit doctrines, whereas MacDiarmid in this matter was one of Orage's strongest supporters.

As this comparison with Anderson brings out, the salient fact of

MacDiarmid's shift of position is that it is much the more radical of the two, a leap from one extreme to another, from the "Churchiness" which lies behind the *Drunk Man* to the Leninist "Command Economy" illuminism of *Lucky Poet*, as can be quickly illustrated by contrasting what is said in the *Drunk Man* on "the social question" with what is said in the incidental verses to *Lucky Poet*. The 'Ballad of the General Strike' in the former seemed much less close to the reflections of a revolutionary on the failure of a rising than to the meditations of a medieval cleric on the collapse of a peasants' revolt, with the aims of which he has been in sympathy, but which he is aware of as doomed from the start, owing to the failure of the participants to take the measure of the difficulty and seriousness of their task. In the later poems, on the other hand, the view he once had about the limitations of human nature and the impossibility of changing it beyond a certain point, have completely disappeared as a result of his conversion to the point of view of modern science. The ultimate triumph of mankind is already implicit in a revolution in physics which has found expression in Russell's non-Aristotelian logic, but for the new era to materialise properly, the Russellian logic has to be simultaneously brought down to earth by the strong hand of Lenin, while at the same time the beauty of the whole process has to be brought out by giving it wings of song.

But, as a consequence of all this, another fact follows, of even greater moment. Over and above forecasting, in his own development from classical to modern, the stages through which the institutional culture of twentieth-century Scotland was to pass, the poet's dramatic change of front by reason of his constant insistence on taking back the issues discussed to first principles, succeeded in posing anew, in terms of education and general culture, the ancient argument of the Scots with themselves about God or Mammon, which, in the past six centuries had been so often debated among them in reference to the question of the country's political sovereignty or to its distinctive religion. Acting like a Socratic gadfly he confronts his countrymen with the question of their culture and their universities in its full philosophical difficulty, whether in the twenties he is arguing in passionate defence of the old metaphysical Scotland of literature and oatmeal or whether, in the second half of his career, he is making an equally passionate defence of the new scientific or technocratic Scotland as part of a materialist Utopia where man to man the world over would brothers be. Considered in their practical effect, these gadfly tactics were to prove as ineffective in arousing the Scots as they had been in arousing the Athenians some 2,500 years before, but theoretically speaking the outcome was somewhat different, and, like Socrates, MacDiarmid, by bringing things back to philosophy and asking the proper questions there, was to initiate an intellectual renaissance which, as far as the English-speaking world goes, compares very favourably with the better known efforts of larger countries.

Let us make good this claim by a rapid run-through of the poet's intellectual development between the two plateaus of the *Drunk Man* and *Contemporary Scottish Studies* of 1926-27, on the one hand, and *Lucky Poet* of 1943 on the other. A notable exception to T. S. Eliot's claim as to the natural inferiority — as compared with the real thing — of the homespun philosophy of an autodidact poet, the *Drunk Man* actually makes a contribution of some weight to Anglo-American philosophy in the sense of reviving the forgotten doctrine of Adam Smith, Schelling and Hegel that self-consciousness is inseparable from mutual consciousness, i.e. from being aware of oneself as an object to the others. Buoyed up with a sense of intellectual achievement, MacDiarmid set about writing another metaphysical poem, more extensive and more ambitious, which, taking its stand on the first principle of a Hegelianised teleology, sought to justify the timeliness of the Scottish Renaissance, by showing it to be a necessary stage in the self-liberation of mankind. (The Russian revolution had shown how to master the machine, a Gaelic revolution would show how to humanise the machine age.) But as the poem's "argument" develops, it becomes abundantly clear that the teleological *a priori* on which it rests amounts in practice to a Panglossian principle which is incapable of establishing the timeliness of anything contingent because all it assures us of is that *whatever is, is right*.[3] The energy in the poetry of *To Circumjack Cencrastus* falters and sags in proportion as it becomes clear that God's inscrutable purposes, for aught we know, may involve the consignment of Scotland to the dustbin of history rather than its re-emergence on the world-map. The Russian revolution is doubtless sanctioned by the divine plan because it has happened, because it is a fact, but who knows if a Scottish Renaissance will make any historical impact? The Scots may have already done the work God expects of them.

The problems with *Cencrastus* seems to have resulted in the poet's complete disillusionment with the classic project — known to him through the 1929 translation of Husserl's *Ideas* — of justifying knowledge-claims by appealing to the unshakable basis of a self-evident *a priori*. When the true nature of the *a priori* has been worked out in practice — as happens in *Cencrastus* — what results is a metaphysical idea with which the poet finds himself in complete disagreement, both intellectually and morally — namely that (as Bradley puts it) this is the best of all possible worlds, and everything in it is a necessary evil. Abruptly turning his back on Husserl whose *a priori* had been respectfully celebrated in a neat little poem at a vital turning-point in the argument of *Cencrastus*,[4] the poet identifies with the most intransigent opponent of Husserl and his *a priori*, the Russian irrationalist Lev Shestov (incidentally, also one of Husserl's intimate friends), for whom in the last analysis, the truth of things lies not with the Husserlian self-evidence of two and two equal four, but with the refusal of Dostoevsky's *Underground Man* to believe that two and two equal four.[5] Henceforward, MacDiarmid will enthusiastically embrace the Shestovian view of the rational *a priori* of classical philosophy as a fetter on the human spirit, which, condemning us to the nightmare view that "what is done cannot be undone", blinds mankind to the biblical insight that to God all things are possible, or as the poet put it himself in his 'First Hymn to Lenin', that whoever takes Christ's message seriously has it in him to do not just the things Christ did but things still greater. Penetrating beneath the surface of Shestov to his essential philosophy, the poetic autodidact had seen that it amounted to two propositions — first that David Hume was right to reject the *a priori* in favour of experience, and second that where Hume had gone wrong was in failing to see that his critique of the causal nexus had reinstated the possibility of miracle.

This passionate attachment to Shestov might have led the poet into the intellectual wilderness or worse,[6] but by reason of the poet's natural feeling for philosophy, the result of the contact was not an aberration but a genuine if minor contribution to the subject which could very well be remembered. The special relationship of Shestov to Husserl to which the poet draws attention, not only illumines the, as yet in important respects unknown, greatness of the former, but was the personal link which brought Husserl to Paris at the end of the twenties and was thus responsible for his historic lectures there (as is made evident by Shestov's — I cannot call it anything else — *magnificent* obituary tribute to his friend, written in 1938, and available in English in the 1961 volume of *Philosophy and Phenomenological Research*). Equally creditable to MacDiarmid's intellectual acumen, however, is the deft way in which Shestov's biblical miracles are transformed by the poet into the miracles of modern science, the connection being made in the light of the work of David Hume who, the poet knows, is spoken of by the leaders of the revolution in physics in exactly the same terms as Shestov uses, namely as a thinker who fails to follow out the radical implications of his destruction of the causal *a priori*.[7] In the light of Korzybski's book (see below) and the numerous testimonies in its favour from "progressive" scientists of the first rank, MacDiarmid now gives a new reading of Shestov. Valid insofar as it is an attack on reason in the sense of the old logic of Aristotle, Shestov's irrationalism is perfectly compatible with a new non-Aristotelian logic as developed by Bertrand Russell and the Poles as a kind of methodology for the scientific revolution of the twentieth century. Aligning himself with the scientific orthodoxy of the twentieth century, the poet now reformulates the central question of philosophy in a shape which, at the time (the thirties) was acceptable only to the radicals in the Scottish universities but which since that time has increasingly become a mark of intellectual orthodoxy not only in faculties of science but in the other faculties. How is it that poverty and ignorance still persist on an enormous scale in a world where science has given us sufficient know-how to be able to end them? The "backward-looking" MacDiarmid of the *Drunk Man* and *Contemporary Scottish Studies* has now become the "forward-looking" MacDiarmid of *Lucky Poet*.

According to what Grieve tells us, this new development in his *weltanschauung* crystallised for him in the course of reading Count Alfred Korzybski's *Science and Sanity: An Introduction to Non-Aristotelian Systems and General Semantics* (1933). Appealing strongly to the poet because its ambitious programme of seeking a solution to the problems and contradictions of modern social theory by applying thereto the logic evolved with the more direct purpose of evading the problems and contradictions thrown up by the crisis of modern physics, corroborating and clarifying the lines taken in *Lucky Poet*, Korzybski's 800-page blockbuster of a pedagogical book restates and updates, in view of the political and intellectual crises of the thirties, the progressivist ideas which John Dewey had put forward twenty years earlier. Like Dewey, it calls for a clean break with the scholastic logic inherited from the Greeks and for its replacement by a modern logic endowed with sufficient flexibility to do justice to the advance of science as well as to the new and more

more hopeful crop of social ideas. The way forward for Korzybski as for Dewey depends, in the first place, on getting rid of what the latter had called the dualistic legacy of Greek philosophy. One of the immediate results of the non-Aristotelian disciplines is — Korzybski says — the elimination of the elementalism of body *and* mind, intellect *and* the emotions. Like Dewey, Korzybski has no patience with the Greek idea of intellect as a kind of spectator which has detached itself from involvement in experience. Intellectual work has to be connected directly with what is experienced in experiment, but in addition, as in Dewey, the experience isn't to be considered as merely private or inner, but as behaviouristic "since perception is to be conceived as a response to a stimulus".[8]

The starting point of Korzybski thus resembles Dewey in regard to science and society, but what is novel about *Science and Sanity* is, in the first place, that it seeks to face up to the problems created for philosophy and pedagogy by the revolution in twentieth-century physics. Let us set forth the Korzybski programme by quoting from one of the many testimonials of his merit from well-known scholars which he prints at the end of his book:

"We still teach classical science on Mondays, Wednesdays and Fridays, and modern science on Tuesdays, Thursdays and Saturdays, as Sir William Bragg lately said. Within the bounds of the Aristotelian system, there appears to be no hope of finding the requisite unifying principle. Mathematics has rapidly been outgrowing the old forms of so-called logic, but mathematical physics has been slow to appreciate the value of the efforts. Korzybski's *Science and Sanity* will be of great value to science because it contains the basis for a new and wider and unified form of scientific determinism."[9]

A great self-publicist, Korzybski is careful to draw his testimonials from the most respectable sources. Let me cite two further references from scientists whose names are not yet forgotten in order to give a clue to the distinctive nature of Korzybski's contribution. According to E. T. Bell, author of *Makers of Mathematics*:

"Korzybski among personal contributions of his own concerning the law of identity has succeeded incidentally in making current the fundamental revolution in mathematics which goes under the name of non-Aristotelian logic, and of bringing to educated people an account of the most significant development in abstract thought of the last millenium."[10]

An intellectual propagandist for the advances made by others rather than an original thinker, the nature of Korzybski's achievement consists, according to a sponsor with an authority even greater than Bell's (Bridgman of Harvard) in showing how the modern reforms in logic may be said to be the basis of a pedagogical revolution which affects not merely the language of mathematics but all language, and therefore all departments of life:

"Of late years, the realisation has been growing that a large fraction of the difficulties of society, civilisation and science, is verbal in character. Among the few serious attempts to waken full self-consciousness of what the situation is, and having awakened it, to provide a technique by which the vicious consequences of verbal habits may be avoided, I believe that the work of Count Korzybski must be valued as of the greatest importance."[11]

What particularly commends Korzybski's pedagogy to Grieve is that, while reaffirming the social optimism of Dewey, and of Grieve's friend A. S. Neill, it concerns itself primarily with something to which perhaps Neill gave insufficient attention and which Dewey took up only rather late, the necessity of finding educational techniques for communicating, so to speak, to the masses due respect for, and a certain amount of understanding of, the higher standards of intellectual rigour demanded by the revolution in the sciences. Remarkably confident at having discovered the secret of how to diffuse throughout the community the standards appropriate to a scientific age, Korzybski can be as intemperate as Grieve himself in his attacks on the various political establishments for their sins against the light and for their indifference to the needs of philosophical culture. What shields him from the charges of intellectual crankiness which were brought against the poet's more homespun efforts in the same direction, was the respect in which *Science and Sanity* was held by leading intellectuals of the West. Bertrand Russell, for instance, is recorded at the end of the book as having cabled to Korzybski that without having read the whole, he strongly approves of the parts he had looked at and in general is struck with some admiration for Korzybski's wide range of learning in various fields. Read against this background, Korzybski's work thus went far towards confirming for Grieve his dream of a renaissance of polymathic poets, who, working under the banner of Leninism, would diffuse the advance of the sciences and help to sort out the conflicts between them in accordance with what he conceived as the "becoming tendencies of the age".

Considered in a more particular light, Korzybski's thesis, as I understand him, rang a bell with the poet through its programme for making the sciences intelligible educationally, the methodology *of* which was to spread, throughout the scholastic system, the abstractive approach so much approved of by Grieve, and the materials *for* which were to be got from a judicious popularisation of a philosophy already known to and respected by Grieve, viz. the Whitehead of *Principia Mathematica*. The new teaching, said Korzybski, must encourage the pupils to familiarise themselves in regard to an ordinary word like apple, with four distinguishable but inseparably connected meanings which had always been inherent in the thing and its situation, but which the Aristotelian tradition had not been able to differentiate properly. The first has to do with the apple as a scientific object, consisting of processes of a physical and chemical nature, inexhaustible in their complexity and still largely unknown, in the process of which it reacts with other things; reactions which are perceived by us not directly through the senses, but indirectly by studying experimentally the way the apple interacts with these other things. Missed by Aristotle, this aspect of the apple can be observed by finding things which observably react to qualities in the apple which are hidden from our direct observation — as for example we observe the electrical qualities of another's brain by devising machines which observably react to them. In the case of this first set of the apple's qualities, we are dealing with what, according to Whitehead, was studied through perception in the mode of causal efficacy, whereas in the case of the second set of the apple's qualities we are dealing with those which are "manufactured by the lower senses", that is to say, with the small selection of the apple's qualities to which our sight, hearing, etc., can be got to react directly in separation from one another. This side of the apple was, of course, known to Aristotle for whom the sense qualities of the apple, its colour, the sounds associated with it, etc., were its chief qualities.

Called by Korzybski "the psychological picture" probably manufactured by the higher centres, the third aspect is the only one on which, in the modern world, there is any great controversy as to the way in which it relates to the first two, out of which, however, in some sense, it arises. Aristotle, because of missing the contribution to the nature of the apple of the submicroscopic qualities referred to under the first head, treats the apple in the third sense as a sort of self-contained thing or substance, existing or capable of existing exclusively or in independence of the other things, lying below its perceived sense qualities, and holding them together. By contrast, philosophers like Whitehead, who are aware of the thing as existing at the submicroscopic level as well as the macroscopic level, accuse Aristotle of the fallacy of misplaced concreteness and consider the apple as consisting in continuous interaction with other things and changing in response to the changes which occur in their behaviour to it.

An unsettled problem arises at this third stage because Whitehead and his celebrated collaborator Russell, though agreeing as to the inadequacy of Aristotle's position, differ as to what is to replace it. More pluralist than is Whitehead, Russell is unable to sympathise with the view, which, I think, is also Korzybski's (at least in a modified form), that the apple is ultimately one distinguishable process in a web of inseparably and organically connected processes. This disagreement of Russell and Whitehead may, however, be disregarded here, because on the final and fourth stage of the apple's meanings — the one which Korzybski regards too as the really important one for the philosophical problems raised by modern physics — the two Cambridge men whose joint efforts make them, from the Korzybski point of view, a sort of second Aristotle, are agreed not only that the old Aristotle is wrong, but also as to what it is that puts him wrong.

In this fourth stage, then, we are concerned with the apple in the sense of something that can be spoken about and "verbally defined" and the objection Whitehead and Russell have to Aristotle — to use the traditional jargon — is that Aristotle's notion that the third stage of the perceived apple as something self-contained and exclusive which has qualities, led to what is a demonstrable error in logic — the privileging of the subject-predicate form of statement as against the relational form. To speak somewhat more precisely, what Whitehead and Russell mean when they say that Aristotle privileges the subject-predicate form or reduces the other forms to it, is that, according to Aristotle, the statements that all apples ripen, or that all apples rot, are tested for their truth and falsity in the same way as a statement to the effect that this apple reddens, or rots, etc. Just as observation enables us to decide whether or not this apple reddens or whether or not it rots, so too observation is supposed by Aristotle to enable us to decide whether or not all apples rot, whether or not all apples redden, in the same way as it seems to decide whether or not this apple reddens or is red, or whether or not this apple rots. But as Whitehead and Russell see it, this alleged parallelism is not justified, because, in the light of one of the things Hume said in his critique of causality, it is not possible to establish by observation whether or not all apples rot in the way in which it is possible to establish by observation that this apple is red or not or rots or not, etc. (The point is, in our time, common property on account of Popper's work in publicising the principle that you cannot verify, positively, universal propositions.)

These Russell-Whitehead condemnations of Aristotle are a commonplace of modern teaching of logic and are accepted as a matter of course, without being much thought about. But what brings them alive for the present study is that John Anderson, as a result of taking a fresh look at what others were taking for granted, set aside the Russell-Whitehead logic in favour of a return to a modified Aristotelianism the importance of which, for the argument of the present book, will emerge in due course. For the present, it will be enough to note that universal propositions can be tested in experience in the same way as singular propositions:

"Of course [universal propositions] might, when taken to be the case [i.e. tested], turn out to be false; but so might any finding of ours. I may wrongly take it to be the case that all fires burn, but so, too, I may wrongly take it to be the case that this is a fire, that it burns, etc."[12]

Just as experience can establish the truth of a singular proposition it can, for Anderson, do the same for a universal proposition. In short, whereas Russell and Whitehead, following Bradley, want to reduce universal propositions to the status of being hypothetical, Anderson goes back to Aristotle's view of them as categorical. In the same way Anderson, in developing his criticism of the non-Aristotelian logic of Russell, has no patience with the latter's "contradiction of classes". But these matters will be discussed later. The point to bear in mind is that these Russell-Whitehead doctrines, so generally taken for granted, are not so taken by Anderson.

In contrast Korzybski is a great enthusiast for the Russell-Whitehead logic — he devotes a chapter to Russell and the theory of types — but he is well enough aware that the anti-Aristotelian philosophy itself gives rise, by a further extension of its distinctions, to logical difficulties of a peculiarly complicated and intractable kind. Grieve, however, for his part, accepts the system hopefully as a definitive turning-point for the better in the intellectual history of man. The "irresistible superiority" of this Cambridge view to anything which has gone before shows itself, according to Grieve's way of thinking, in a characteristically intellectual flexibility which, arising from its epoch-making boldness in making explicit these distinctions between inseparables which have never before been brought to light, allows the mind to work on two different planes and to move in two different directions at once, so to speak, and all at the same time. By contrast the Aristotelian system, as the result of its limitation of viewpoint which arises from its failure to make the requisite abstraction, confines the minds of men to a single track. The attractive feature of the new philosophy from Grieve's point of view was thus its discovery, made through its persistence in abstractiveness, that the exploration by scientific instruments of aspects of bodies inaccessible to our senses reveal them to exist in a world governed by different and opposed rules to those apparently regulating the behaviour of things of that same sort in the dimension of the world which is directly accessible to us by ordinary observation. Thus, while spatial things are Euclidean insofar as we can handle them as well as see them, the indirect knowledge we get through the measurement of astronomical bodies which are beyond our reach and impossible to properly see, suggests that — insofar as they may be considered denizens of interstellar space — they are subject to the rules of non-Euclidean geometry. Or again, there is the somewhat analogous fact associated with the quantum theory that bodies behave according to the law of causality insofar as they are surveyed and dealt with on the macroscopic level, but insofar as we are able to study their behaviour at the microscopic level revealed in exploration in laboratories, such regularities as we do discover are statistical only, and are governed by a strict law of causality. Paradoxes of this sort, which delayed the dissemination of the ideas of the revolution in physics, are what first attracted Grieve to it. He delights in the outlandish names of Lobachevsky or Schrödinger which are associated with the boldest discoveries.

However, what Grieve welcomes most from Korzybski is not these particular applications of his position, but his very general thesis that Aristotle's two-valued logic which depends on the fact that bodies are as we directly experience them to be, and nothing else, and for which therefore, a body either has or has not a certain quality at a given time, has been ousted from its privileged place by the many-valued logic of Lukasiewitz and Tarski. This, bringing in a new submicroscopic plane as well as the macroscopic, alone accepted by Aristotle, makes it possible to speak meaningfully of the same body as existing simultaneously in the ordinary kind of macroscopic plane with its ordinary qualities and in the other unobservable plane with a very different set of qualities; therefore it is no contradiction to speak of the same body as having the opposite qualities at the same time or alternatively as having optional qualities at the same time, according as it suits one's line of research and without any danger of logical difficulties. This view of logic fascinates the poet, because it makes it possible for him to reconcile his positivistic hopes acquired before 1914 in his early socialist days — for the progressive spread of the values of modern science for the amelioration of humanity — with Shestov's attack on the tyranny of general ideas as expressed for example in the sympathetic study he does of Dostoevsky's *Underground Man* who refuses to acknowledge the necessity that two and two equal four. The possibility of the social contradictions which worry the poet is therefore shown to be avoidable in principle by the achievement of the Polish logicians in their many-valued version of the Whitehead-Russell logic:

"I have [Grieve says in *Lucky Poet*] fully in mind that unique characteristic of the structure of human knowledge (as revealed through the Polish logic) by which, as Korzybski says: 'If we pass to higher orders of abstractions, situations seemingly insoluble, matters of fact, quite often become matters of preference so that one question can sometimes be answered yes or no, true or false, depending on the order of abstractions the answerer is considering. The above facts alter considerably the former supposedly sharply defined fields of yes or no, true and false and, in general, of all multi-ordinal terms. Many problems of fact on one level of abstraction become problems of preference on another'."[13]

Korzybski illustrates this, Grieve proceeds, by giving a remarkable instance, among other examples in the mathematical work of Lobachevski, namely the discovery of the possibility of kinds of space different from and alternative to the Euclidean space. If man is to progress beyond the classical view of the human situation which sees it as the scene of an endless struggle of warring opposites, he can only do so, Grieve thinks, by taking abstractive thought more seriously than the Greeks did, and by systematically employing it in directions undreamed by them to explore the new paths opened out by the new logic. The follow-up of Shestov's irrationalism has therefore brought Grieve, in the end, to the Polish version of Russell's logic. (Lukasiewitz himself mentioned to me when I met him in Ireland that his reading of Russell's articles had been the turning point of his intellectual life.)

In a remarkable finale to his discussion[14] Grieve clarifies and consolidates his position in regard to abstraction by taking up some disparaging remarks made by Edwin Muir about the Scottish passion for distinctions without a difference. "I have quoted elsewhere in the book," Grieve says, "what Mr Edwin Muir had said about the intellectual complement of Scottish republicanism as manifested in my work of the drawing of subtle distinctions." In fact, the citation from Muir, so far as I can find, is not anywhere in *Lucky Poet* as we have it now, doubtless because it had to be shortened for publication, but we may guess from the context that Muir might be calling attention to the analogy between Grieve's pronouncements of the later thirties and the anti-nomianism of the last remnant of the Covenanters who exhibited the same combination as Grieve does of an impossible dream of a Scottish Republic set apart in starry separateness with an obsessive passion for going to all lengths in the differentiation of meaning, like the distinction in Hogg's *Confessions of a Justified Sinner* between the fifteen different species of faith. This excessive abstractionism, Muir is perhaps wanting to say, is likely to have the same provincialising effect on Grieve's work as it had on that of the anti-nomians, cutting him off from the mainstream of culture as effectively as it cut them off.

What Grieve strongly objects to here is not so much Muir's vague charge against anti-nomianism in general as his disparagement of the abstractive processes which, in Grieve's view, constitute the central principle of the particular sort of anti-nomianism which he has been recommending to the younger Scottish poets — the radicalisation of Scottish scepticism in the tradition of Humean intellectuality, brought up to date in the light of Schrödinger and Shestov. It is because Mr Muir "is not scientifically informed" that he misses the key significance of abstraction for modern literature. "Was it not Sylvester," Grieve bursts out in a sentence borrowed without acknowledgement from Korzybski, "who said that in mathematics we look for similarities in differences, and differences in similarities?" The meaning of this reference to an English nineteenth-century mathematician of genius who showed some interest in the connection between mathematics and poetry is, I think, that the principle enunciated by Sylvester does not apply to mathematics only, it "applies to the whole abstracting process" (apparently Grieve's own words) as manifested in poetry equally with the sciences. Surely Muir himself sometimes seemed to be aware that abstraction, i.e. "this drawing of subtle distinctions between matters as similar as possible", is characteristic of Grieve's own metaphysical poetry? Far from having nothing to do with poetry, analysis, or in other words abstraction, is what poetry and science have in common. The younger Scottish poets of the present age, Grieve goes on, if they are to rise to the height of their times, must make themselves better acquainted with scientific abstraction than Muir is, precisely from the point of view of their task as poets:

"It is for this reason that if I were asked to frame a test paper for literary aspirants, I would ask: (1) a poem on the fact that what is known as the 'Lorenz transformation' *looks like* the 'Einstein transformation'. When manipulated numerically both give equal numerical results, yet the meanings, and the semantic aspects, are different. Although Lorenz produced the 'Lorenz transformation' he did not, and *could not*, have produced the revolutionary Einstein theory. (2) A short paper discussing the fact that the semantic aspects of practically all important mathematical work by different authors often involve *individual semantic presuppositions* about fundamentals."[15]

This latter question recalls the phrase in *Cencrastus* "nationality in algebra even"[16] where — according to Kenneth Buthlay — Grieve is indebted to Valéry, but where the Einstein-Lorenz reference comes from, I have no idea. Possibly from Korzybski somewhere, but it does not sound like the sort of thing he says.

The second part of Grieve's argument against Muir presses the old claim that the restatement of the findings of the sciences in terms of the new philosophy will do wonders in overcoming the barriers of disseminating their results:

"If Mr Muir had been scientifically informed he would have realised the key significance of abstraction as a *humanising* factor not only in the aspect of it already discussed in which a consciousness of abstraction bridges the gap between the two cultures of science and poetry, but also in a second aspect in which the spread of consciousness of abstraction in the sense explained, that is to say through the co-operation of the Whiteheadian philosophy and the Polish logic, will bear fruit for 'the future of the *human* development of mankind' — i.e. the humanisation of man — by giving the sciences a direction as well as a diffusion which 'will promote' the achievement of a general sanity in place of the almost universal insanity . . . "[17]

which obtains at the present day. The condition of this great advance is that the new philosophy, as put over by Korzybski, prepares the way for the long overdue synthesis of the findings of the new sciences as well as for their wider diffusion — two tasks which have not been accomplished by the traditional Aristotelian logic, the poverty of whose apparatus of distinctions rendered it unequal to the challenge. Korzybski's claims that his own philosophical pedagogy will put all this right evidently raises Grieve's enthusiasm, and chimes in with his deepest notions.

Perhaps it is Korzybski's intellectual self-confidence which delights Grieve. In any case, he quotes with approval Korzybski's most far-reaching claims. "As this enquiry shows, science involves some structural metaphysics and semantic components which once discovered, *are childishly simple and can be given in elementary education.*" Italicizing the phrases in the quotation which bring out the essential novelty of this pedagogical revolution, Grieve goes on to describe its results in Korzybski's own words in order that Muir and his friends will be made sensible of what they have missed by their apathy towards science:

"Such education allows us to give very simply to children the 'cultural results', or to impart the semantic reactions which are the aim of university training, in a relatively short period and instruct any technicalities. These benefits, under an Aristotelian education, are too rarely acquired even by university graduates, and impossible to impart to the masses who are left, helpless with archaic, delusional structural assumptions."[18]

In company with the leading philosopher, anthropologist and physicist of the age — Russell, Malinowski and Bridgman — Grieve enthusiastically endorses Korzybski's programme for a philosophical reform in pedagogy which will enable the kind of work which is now done inefficiently at the university level, if indeed it is done at all, to be accomplished efficiently at the level of the schools. "The above statement may appear visionary," but "what the present theory verifies 'empirically' is that it can be done in an extremely simple way, provided we study the neglected non-elementalistic aspects of mathematics and science; namely their structural and semantic aspects," which the leaders of the modern movement like Russell and the Poles have brought to light.

But in addition to its services in drastically simplifying the process of imparting high quality knowledge in the classroom, the

Korzybskian synthesis also appealed strongly to Grieve because of its claim to facilitate the interchange of knowledge across frontiers and in that way to create the conditions for the kind of intellectual co-operation between nations which would allow each nation, each racial group (especially the Celts) to make its contribution to the common pool without losing its cultural distinctiveness:

"Count Korzybski points out later in his book—this corresponding to the internationalism or world-thought I have adumbrated elsewhere in these chapters as one of the prime-factors of my poetry — that a non-Aristotelian provision 'will have an international and inter-racial application, requiring a very thorough revision of all the doctrines, a better acquaintance of specialists in one field with the accomplishments in other fields and an up-to-date epistemology. Modern conditions of *life* are, to a large extent, affected by non-Aristotelian science, but exploited by the thoroughly Aristotelian doctrines of the commercialists, militarists, politicians, priests and lawyers — which results in a bewildering chaos, resulting in needless, great, and imposed suffering for the great masses of mankind as exemplified by such cataclysms as wars, unemployment and different economic crises...."[19]

One must, of course, recognise the partisan nature of Grieve's acceptance of Korzybski. This pedagogical synthesis, which appeals to him because it fits in with and rounds off his progressivist philosophy, repels people of equal standing who are of another way of thinking. John Anderson, for instance, though he is at one with Grieve on the necessity of keeping up the fight against over-specialisation, nevertheless differs entirely from Grieve on the question of the philosophical foundations of the inter-disciplinary synthesis. Accepting the Aristotelian principle that a proposition is either true or not true, that something is either the case or not the case, Anderson has little patience with the claims of the new logic favoured by Grieve, that the spatial qualities of body may be regarded as either Euclidean or non-Euclidean according to choice or that the behaviour of bodies and their parts is both governed by the laws of causality in the strict sense and at the same time in some way breaks the laws of causality according to the way one looks at them. The distinctions introduced by Russell and Whitehead's logic were, he thought, in many cases, ill-founded and on that account liable to darken and complicate the question of the interrelation of things and levels with one another, instead of producing a new clarity about them, which was required if the progress of depart-mentalisation in the sciences was to be checked.

From Anderson's point of view, the extensive claims made by Korzybski for the great benefit of mankind likely to result from the universal acceptance of the anti-Aristotelian logic — the elevation of the culture of the masses in regard to the knowledge of science as well as the facilitation of communication between different races — were doctrines unworthy of a serious philosophy. Indeed the testimonials to the merit of Korzybski's book from Russell, Bridgman, Bell and Malinowski, could be seen as confirmations of Anderson's foreboding that science was increasingly unmindful of the need to adhere to objective standards and was subordinating itself to the service of the dream of social happiness. Similarly unworthy would be Korzybski's effort to support his glowing predictions by asserting that mankind was at last in a position to break away from the inheritance of ancient Greek ideas which had outlived their usefulness. Thus, for example, the geometry of Euclid was considered worthless and could be discarded like the logic of Aristotle. But the new non-Euclidean geometry which was supposed to have ousted the old — in the version of it put forward by Russell in his book on geometry — was, Anderson claimed, nothing but an extended version of the spherical trigonometry which derives from Euclid and forms the concluding part of traditional textbooks on the subject, such as that of John Playfair.[20] Consider, for example, Proposition XII: "The three angles of a spherical triangle are greater than two, and less than six, right angles". Already in spherical geometry we are dealing with triangles which have non-Euclidean properties and, as Thomas Reid showed in his remarkable discussion of the subject in Section IX, Chapter VI, of his *Inquiry into the Human Mind*, an extension of the geometrical analysis which leads us to the view that "of every right-lined triangle, the three angles taken together are greater than two right angles" enables us to establish, in regard to our spherical geometry, the main paradoxes of non-Euclidean geometry such as "right-lined triangles that are similar, are also equal", or "if two lines be parallel — i.e. everywhere equidistant from each other, they cannot both be straight".[21] As Anderson saw the situation, the claims made by Korzybski for non-Euclidean geometry are as questionable as his claims for non-Aristotelian logic.

But, leaving aside Anderson, let me get clearer the difficulties and tensions in Grieve's "thocht" by comparison of the philosophical line sketched out in *Lucky Poet* with that developed in the *Drunk Man*, which will bring the difference between standpoint of each book into clearer relief by contrasting it with the considerable areas of common ground. Under the latter head, it may be noticed at once that in reference to the problem which has been fundamental in philosophy since Descartes, that of one's knowledge of the external world, and which on that account reappears in both Grieve's works, *Lucky Poet* repudiates subjective idealism, scepticism, etc. in favour of a realist position similar to that taken up in the *Drunk Man* and (what is very important) defends it by the same sort of argument — an appeal to the social fact of my experience of others and their communications. So far, the two are the same on this topic, but where they differ is that whereas the *Drunk Man* thinks his way through the traditional problem, drawing attention, in the course of his arguments with himself, to the phenomenological facts — the kind of thing you get in Merleau-Ponty or Sartre — and, exhibiting in the process, autodidactic though he is, a real feeling for the difficulty, in *Lucky Poet* on the other hand, taking his materials from what seems to be some review article on the problem, rearranging them no doubt, and at the same time interposing appropriate comments by Chesterton and no doubt by himself, Grieve writes a competent enough page on the subject.[22] This, however, doesn't in the least illumine or add anything fresh to the accepted way of looking at it, but simply proves Grieve's ability to master the standard way of speaking and thinking about the problem with the easy confidence of a practiced journalist of the sciences. What he gives us on this problem of perception in *Lucky Poet* is reportage rather than original thought.

By contrast, the *Drunk Man*'s treatment, as I have suggested, is amazingly good when judged from the point of view of a stimulating contribution to the same topic. In a varied development, he gives to the theme of our perceptual situation the same vital aspect which Hume and Adam Smith speak of, in terms less personal and more general but equally metaphorical, when they point out that in our perception of the world, we experience the people around us, that is the people in their bodily form, as *mirrors*. That is to say, when Grieve[23] speaks of our experience of the other as supplying us with a light which reveals to us parts of ourselves, hidden from our direct inspection because overshadowed by dark from our point of view, he too is exploring our perceptual situation in the light of the fact that by using other people and their responses to us as mirrors, we are indirectly made aware of an epistemologically important quality of ourselves which is not available to us in direct observation — the dependence of our ability to make sense of the continued existence, out of our sight, both of the parts of the body with which we see, the eyes, as well as of numerous bodies in our vicinity which are other than our own and other than that at present eyed by us and consequently seen. What confirms the philosophical value of Grieve's work here in a genuine sense is that he is aware of the facts he is metaphorically describing as being not peculiarities of our vision but as extending to all our senses *mutatis mutandis*. That is to say, like the various philosophers we have mentioned as exploring this territory, Grieve is aware of the fact in question as a general fact, the interest of which is the light it may throw on the empirical foundations of our belief in the existence of bodies which are unobserved by us. The distinctive quality of these passages in the *Drunk Man* is thus that the poet is not just *talking* about philosophy, but is actually in what he writes *doing* some philosophy.

By comparison with the *Drunk Man* passage, that in *Lucky Poet* is intellectually far more orthodox and far less interesting. "The clearly defined 'perceptual object' which we see, transcends the vague mass of sense-data presented to our visual organs; it is more than these sense-data or any combination of them because it is permanent and public to many observers, whereas the sense-data are shifting and private."[24] But, clearly, this sentence throws no light on the difficulty that the bodies of the other observers are given to us also in shifting private sense-data. Nothing said here nor in the rest of Grieve's page throws any light on the problem as to how we become aware of "the perceptual object" as transcending "this vague mass of sense-data presented to our visual organs". The superiority of the *Drunk Man* remarks depends on the fact that it does try to throw some light on the difficulty, by suggesting, in metaphysical terms, the theory according to which we do not become aware of the sense-data as objective — that is to say of what is given to us in seeing as being independent of our sight — until somehow we are made aware of a fact which we cannot learn from vision, that the parts of the thing seen by us exist somewhere beyond and at a distance from the (to us) invisible parts of ourselves which serve us as our organs of sight. Thus whereas the *Lucky Poet* passage tells us nothing, or in other words describes a problem without offering any solution, the corresponding theme in the *Drunk Man* seeks to fill the gap by speaking of our experiences of the others as affording the light which reveals to us the existence of certain parts of ourselves, as being vital to the visual process, but at the same time notable by their absence from the visual field made possible by themselves.

When we compare the *Drunk Man* and *Lucky Poet* in respect of the further reaches of the problem of our knowledge of our relation to the world, that is to the part of the problem which concerns history and man's place in it, we find that the two are better matched. Keeping up the same high standard of metaphysics, the *Drunk Man* continues to explore the foundations with the metaphor of light, which was his clue to unravelling the mysteries of perceptual process. Here he finds that, thought out in its further implications, the idea of light reveals the existence of unshakably necessary truths which set limits to the human situation in the sense of showing the impossibility of progress. "Deep surroondin' darkness, I discern,/Is aye the price o' licht",[25] or in other words every pleasure has its price, that is, pleasure can be felt only in contrast to pain.

The idea here is an old one, which may have come from Calvinism and which the Scottish economists made so much of, that when you change things, the change is going to have unexpected, unpredictable consequences which will raise new problems every bit as awkward as those the change was meant to eliminate, and which will in part neutralise the advantage, being in this way counterproductive. By contrast, *Lucky Poet* sets aside the pessimism about the possibility of progress by accepting the Shestovian position that general ideas in the sense of the *a priori* principles of classical philosophy are a Medusa's head which have no power over those who disregard them. That is to say, the classical argument which denies the possibility of change for the better really depends on an unjustifiable deference to general ideas. Fire burns here and in Persia, but how do we know fire burns on distant stars? "Who can guarantee that two and two,/Are not five on Jupiter".[26] It follows that the so-called unshakable general truths like the claim that darkness is always the price of light, or that pleasure is always felt by the contrast to pain are not categorical propositions which observation confirms for us once and for all but simply hypotheses which observation cannot confirm, and may refute. How do we know that there cannot be such a thing as unalloyed pleasure in certain circumstances not yet experienced? How do we know that we cannot discover a world where nobody is in the shadows and everybody is in the spotlight? In the end, *Lucky Poet* finds that modern logic confirms Shestov's objection against the time-honoured paradoxes by reference to which the *Drunk Man* presents the human situation as in some sense unalterable.[27] Identifying with the point of view of modern science, Grieve salutes David Hume as the man responsible for this great advance. It was his critique of the idea of necessary connection that opened the eyes first of philosophers and then of the world to the fact that all general propositions are not only unprovable, but may have exceptions.

From the point of view of the quality of the thought, the poetic expression, in the *Drunk Man*, and also in *Cencrastus*, of the necessary truths which deny the possibility of progress, achieves a high standard in philosophy, not altogether unworthy of the passages in the *Gorgias* and the *Philebus* of Plato, in which "the might of general ideas" was first exhibited to the world. But let me quote from the latter poem in order to show the consistency and the power of the poet's development of the idea:

> Shaddows that feed on the licht for aye
> Hauntin' the waters that canna win free,
> The wild burn loups but you haud it fast
> As the hands o' the past haud me.
>
> A burn may dream o' a warld aince mair
> O' water and licht an nocht beside,
> But has aye as faur to gang as it's gane,
> And a burn in the dark roots' clutch'll bide.
>
> Tint in a windhaw or siller swirl
> Bigger and blacker the roots strike back,
> As whiles through a high-falutin' o' love
> I hear my body mockin' my talk. . . .[28]

By comparison, Grieve, in his poetic defence of the progressivist idea in *Lucky Poet*, does not bother to think out the fundamentals of the position for himself, but instead puts it over by means of appeals to scientific authority. What he wants to do evidently is not so much to prove a thesis as to put over a thesis which he thinks is already so strongly backed by evidence as not to need any more:

> Yet what are all our intellectuals saying?
> All victimised by repetition-compulsion
> They are denying these huge horizons opening out
> And crying 'Fundamentally man cannot change'
> And bleating 'After all there's but one kind of man.
> Men's ways of thought can never become
> So inconceivably different from ours!'
> Can't they? They have already. Mine have
> And every fit member's of the I.U.R.W.
> And are speedily disposing of the bourgeois notions.[29]

Addressed 'To the Younger Scottish Writers', the poem makes its point simply by appealing to the authority of science:

> There is nothing whatever in contemporary biology
> Either the science of heredity or of genetics,
> Nothing we know of the mechanisms of inheritance,
> Nothing in the nature of the genes or chromosomes
> To stand in the way of the radicals' enthusiasm
> For social transformation — the revolutionists'
> Advocacy of profoundly-altered social systems.
> On the other hand there is a vast accumulation
> Of evidence from the sociological sciences,
> Economy, anthropology, sociology,
> Politics, the philosophy of history, to substantiate
> The necessity, the sanity, and the wisdom
> Of deep changes in all institutions, customs,
> Habits, values — in short, civilisations.
> Human nature is the last thing we need to worry about.
> Let us attend to the circumstances that condition it.[30]

Up to the mid-thirties, Grieve however seems to have been still very much aware of the force of the arguments of *Cencrastus* and the *Drunk Man* against the possibility of a fresh start because of our being held back by the hand of the past. His main resource in justifying progressiveness in the face of these arguments was to appeal to the fact of evolution in the animal world. One can feel strongly the tension within his mind as it experiences the pull of these competing alternatives, the one serious and metaphysical, the other jaunty and debunking, as they appear, eyeball to eyeball, in the same poem 'Envoi: On Coming Home' from *Scottish Scene*. The poem begins by Grieve's giving his impression of Scotland as a land where nothing ever changes or can change:

> Scottish Jews comin' doon frae the mountains
> Wi' the laws on their stany herts;
> Minor prophets livin' i' the Factory Close
> Or ahint the gasworks — fresh sterts?

But his spirits perk up again when he remembers the accounts of evolution in the manuals of popular science:

> The Sauria in their ain way
> Had muckle to commend them.

Fell fearsome craturs, it's a shame
That Nature had to end them.

Grieve in the year this was published (1934) was moving evidently towards progressivism but quite as evidently still had his reservations which, if I am not mistaken, find their classic expression in 'On a Raised Beach', published in *Stony Limits and Other Poems* (also 1934), a poem ranked by Oxenhorn and other critics with the *Drunk Man*, and considered the second high-point of Grieve's achievement. The poet calls attention to "These stones, with their resolve that Creation shall not be/Injured by iconoclasts and quacks".[31] The poet reflects: "So these stones have dismissed/All but all of evolution, unmoved by it,/(Is there anything to come they will not likewise dismiss?)/As the essential life of mankind in the mass/Is the same as their earliest ancestors yet".[32] He isn't forgetting his vocation as a poet-propagandist of progress which was to lead him to identify with Korzybski and all the scientists who supported his pedagogical reform, but for the moment he is thinking about the aspect of it which the others tend so often to forget — its difficulty. "The empty hand of my brother man,/The humanity no culture has reached, the mob./Intelligentsia, our impossible and imperative job!"[33] Thinking things over in the perspective provided by the present argument, I can't help feeling that Korzybski, Bertrand Russell and Grieve himself (of the *Lucky Poet*), furnished good examples of the kind of thing he had in mind when he spoke of iconoclasts and quacks.

9

THE PROBLEMS OF A PRIVILEGED SUBJECT

Whether or not poets are the acknowledged legislators of the world, there is certainly a sense in which they are among the first to draw the attention of a society to the changes in its direction and the new set of problems which are raised by the impact on it of the world situation. This role of the poet is borne out by the changes which came about at the end of the third decade of the present century at the time of the resolution of the Ordinance 70 affair. Originally the poets had formed a group loosely united around MacDiarmid — Edwin Muir in the twenties, and in the thirties Sorley Maclean and Robert Garioch — but with the impact on Scottish life of the events of the thirties, in particular the impact of the revolution in science, the unity of the group suffered a break. The character of this emerges fairly clearly in the work of those of them with a special interest in science. On the one hand, MacDiarmid, as we have seen, took up with Korzybski and shared in the bright vision of science he put forward. On the other hand, Garioch, younger, and reacting after the war, responded to Oppenheimer's more sombre view. In his very interesting poem 'The Muir' he suggests that if the physical foundation of things is as paradoxical as Oppenheimer says, we should not boggle at *Genesis*. Rather earlier, and acting independently, Edwin Muir had also moved away for much the same reasons, put off by MacDiarmid's confident scientism.

But in the division thus indicated in the work of the poets, new features became evident, namely that, unlike what had happened in previous centuries, but in a manner very like what was happening elsewhere in the world, the optimistic ideas generated by the revolution in physics and the promise of a new technology overshadowed the classical view of the limitations of science. This began to recede into the background along with the disappearance of the Renaissance tradition of Greek studies. The confidence and consistency seemed to be on the side not of the classicists but of the modernists and the line pioneered by MacDiarmid, in *Lucky Poet* of the forties, was given new life in the sixties by Alexander Trocchi, also a great admirer of Korzybski.

This movement from classicism to scientism among the poets of the Scottish Renaissance is interestingly borne out by the line of development taken by the Scottish universities during the same period. The posts of classicist professors who had fought the S.E.D.'s scientistic modernism were later held by professors who, whatever their private views, were the institutional standard-bearers of modernism.

During the sixty years between 1908 and the post-Robbins era, the honours Arts degrees, with two outside subjects, as well as the degrees in the faculties of Science, continued to develop in their own way, more or less independently of the Arts settlement of 1927, the effects of which were confined to the peculiarly Scottish institution of the three years' Ordinary Degree. But the fact that this privileging of philosophy was confined to a single sector does not mean that it was unimportant as an educational experiment, either quantitatively or qualitatively. Given that over 60 per cent of the Arts students still took an Ordinary Degree till well after 1960, and given that the Arts faculties attracted nearly a third of the student body in Edinburgh and in Glasgow in the thirties, when the former as a whole had about 3,500 and the latter upwards of 4,500, it follows that a substantial number of students were annually exposed to philosophy at that time in these two institutions alone — a number which would have tended to increase — though not perhaps proportionately — up to the fifties, when Edinburgh, having overtaken Glasgow, had now more than 6,500 students to the latter's 6,000. The numbers thus being considerable, and the kind as well as the calibre of the students fairly definite, it seems fair enough to raise a question as to the long-term effects of the liberalising reforms which gave the "useless" subject of philosophy a central position in the curriculum, in preference to its old rivals, history and educational psychology, in which, under Darroch and Sir Richard Lodge, students had been encouraged to question the status quo.

At this point, however, we come up against the difficulty that whereas the Scots were relatively speaking outspoken in the self-exploration of themselves and their society in the twenties, a shyness seems to inhibit this inwardly directed curiosity in the thirties. Not only is there nothing in the later stage corresponding to the fresh and probing analysis of the atomisation of Scottish society which came from the pens of Burnet and of Grieve during the Ordinance 70 crisis (the latter writing also in the *Pictish Review*[1]), but the thing which, in a retrospective view, seems to be the most remarkable event of the period — the initiative in re-establishing Scottish independence in the matter of cultural standards (against the advice of the S.E.D. and against the whole trend of things in the Britain of the thirties) by the restoration of philosophy to the central place in the Ordinary Degree — was left to work itself out in the shadows without so far as I know being publicly monitored or publicly discussed. Almost overnight, the noisy argumentation of the prolonged culture-crisis had died out in one of those unpredictable turn-arounds so common in Scottish history, the nature of which is appropriately symbolised in a verse of MacDiarmid's published in the *Scottish Education Journal* in 1931, and thereafter left unregarded in its files until the *Collected Poems* came out in 1978:

> Catch it noo — for even as I speak
> The fish may be gaspin' on dry land there
> And the hindmaist wave o' the Esk gang roon'
> The curve at Land's End to be seen nae mair
> And the silence still waur for a sang to brak'
> Follow the row the waters mak'.[2]

But though the quantitative, well-documented methods may not help us here, we are not without resources to find out what really happened. For example, leaving aside the term by term account of the Scottish Arts curriculum in order to measure its accomplishments against a decade by decade account of the public impact of books produced by Arts faculty members, the long-term results of 1927 may be summed up in a challenging schema which I leave others to criticise. After some thirty years of effectively enough sustaining the role prescribed for it of standard-setter and metaphysical leaven to the Ordinary parts of the Arts curriculum, the philosophy departments no doubt began to cut themselves off from their generalist functions by letting themselves be caught up in the fashionable wave of interest in merely technical and specialist problems of the subject. But while this change of direction no doubt reconciled the philosophers to losing the privileged position which their subject had established in the struggles of the twenties, over and against the rival claims of psychology and of history, the remarkable thing about the development of philosophy is that it was displaced by psychology and history from its central position in the Arts curriculum only in proportion as psychology and history, transcending the limited particularised topics normally associated with them, showed themselves in some sort competent to take upon themselves the responsibility for the metaphysical and transcendental questions which had formerly been the field of philosophy, but from which philosophy, with apparent self-satisfaction, was in the process of cutting itself loose. Bringing to light a feature of twentieth-century Scottish education, which the Scots themselves never publicise and perhaps never even think about, a long-term survey of the results of the 1927 settlement shows its reintroduction of intellectual values into the Scottish Arts curriculum to have had lasting results, at least in this sense, that the great questions of "man's place in the universe" and "man's chief end" are still very much alive in the Scottish universities even at the present time. Indeed, the central drama of their history as twentieth-century institutions would seem to be the struggle between philosophy on the one hand and human sciences like psychology and history on the other, as to which should be responsible for intellectual values.

In order to prepare for this denouement, it will be sufficient to look briefly at the role of philosophy in the Scottish universities between the end of the twenties and the end of World War II, confining our account to the two universities whose rivalries and mutual stimulus constitute the central thread of Scotland's academic history, namely Edinburgh and Glasgow. On the one side, intellectual enthusiasm was the great quality of the Glasgow department, as it descends from Edward Caird through Henry Jones to C. A. Campbell. The leading idea seemed to be that philosophy in Scotland never achieved a first-rate quality until the displacement in the nineteenth century of the ideas of Reid and the Common Sense School by those of Hegel and English idealists like Bradley and Green. By contrast, the leading quality of Edinburgh was a kind of unenthusiastic detachment, according to which intellectually speaking there was really nothing new under the sun. Hegel and the Germans had been, of course, very good, according to Edinburgh opinion circa 1900, but then so also had been Reid, who, if not quite so deep as Hegel, stands for something remarkably similar, the defence of our natural wholeness of view, and the attack on an atomisation in which our understanding of things is frittered away. The advent of Kemp Smith to Edinburgh in 1919 and Campbell to Glasgow in the early thirties made less difference to the traditional spirit of the two departments than one might think. A pupil of Jones, Campbell, in general, held to the position that the ideas of T. H. Green marked a turning point in British philosophy, but at the same time he insisted that the moral ideas of Green would never get the appreciation that they deserved until they had been detached from Green's own determinism, and restated in terms of a freedom of open alternatives doctrine which was Campbell's chief contribution. The effect of his teaching was to induce in the students an enthusiastic belief in free will, and a corresponding loathing of scientific determinism. So too, in Edinburgh, although Kemp Smith did not think so very much of Hegel and even less of Reid, his fresh and penetrating views of the history of philosophy found expression in a new version of the doctrine that in the matter of intellectual ideas there is nothing new under the sun. The three greatest thinkers of the modern world, as he saw it, Descartes, Hume and Kant, were all occupied in evolving variations of the theme that knowledge consists in a battle against illusions which keep constantly returning to us in new forms and which, if probed to the bottom, present us with insoluble problems. In contrast to Campbell's buoyant belief in freedom, Kemp Smith's social pessimism (or realism, as he himself would have called it) implied, as we have seen, a kind of secularised version of original sin, according to which Campbell was nothing else than a modern version of the Pelagian heresy. In spite of all these sharp differences, Kemp Smith and Campbell were nevertheless at one in what they disapproved of. No doubt, public enemy number one in both cities was the Deweyite pragmatism which had until recently had such a hold among teachers and training colleges. But Dewey, by the thirties, was not being taken so seriously, and the real danger in both philosophical classrooms came from the scientific philosophy of Bertrand Russell, which had by this time established such a hold, directly or indirectly, on the great seminaries of the South. It was not that Russell himself was much mentioned, but the parts of him which were recommended reading — like the *Problems of Philosophy* — were clearly the target of the passionately felt and often subtly argued doctrines which were pronounced from the rostrum to the large Ordinary classes.

It was on the part of the philosophy classes' curriculum which is devoted to logic — a relatively small part — that the case against Russell was finally clinched, both in Glasgow and in Edinburgh, by the adoption of W. A. Sinclair's very clear and very brief *Traditional Formal Logic* (1937) by Edinburgh (where Sinclair taught) in the year of its publication, and by Glasgow two or three years later. In contrast to the type of textbook previously used in Scotland, which argued about the problems of logic by comparing Aristotle with Mill and with Bradley, Sinclair put forward a very sceptical view of the value of logic which he expounded in later publications (e.g. *The Conditions of Knowing* in 1955). Where writers on logic, and above all Russell, went wrong, was in claiming autonomy for their discipline, which in fact was really a part of philosophy. The doctrines of logic did not have any privileged position in regard to the more metaphysical parts of philosophy. It followed that it was beside the point, and indeed a worthless endeavour, to refute metaphysical positions like those of Campbell or Kemp Smith by pointing out that they were unverifiable or contradictory from the standpoint of Russell's logic. Campbell and Kemp Smith might be both wrong, and Sinclair thought they were, but their positions were not to be refuted by reference to those of Russell, who, though very clear, was perhaps very superficial.

The *Traditional Formal Logic* no doubt did not say anything like that, but put its position over in a more indirect way, which was likely to stick. Explaining the central doctrine of the tradition very clearly, Sinclair then refrained from criticising it on the ground that it was now only of historical importance, because of its having been studied in such a widespread way through Western history. Sinclair, no doubt, didn't forbid people to study logic, but the impression he certainly gave was that the questions it dealt with were side-effects and secondaries to the main line of philosophical discussion. The arguments of Kemp Smith and of Campbell, whatever their worth, were just as well founded as those of Russell and Hegel, differing from these latter only in virtue of their very different philosophical presuppositions.

But there was more to Sinclair than his writings in logic, and the direction in which his work was moving up to his tragic death in the Cairngorms in his fiftieth year (in 1955) reveals better than anything else I know the hidden potentialities, the secret meaning of the revolutionary step taken by the Scottish universities in 1927 of restoring philosophy to a privileged position in the curriculum. Reversing the anti-intellectual currents which, throughout the rest of Britain, were cutting philosophy off from the other subjects and were getting it to withdraw into itself in a self-complacent exclusiveness, philosophy in Edinburgh, as the results of Sinclair's initiative, began to reforge its broken links with the sciences, human as well as natural. Having first established the credit of philosophy in the eyes of the scientists by personal participation in the circle of Professor F. A. E. Crewe who, in the course of defining the place in the map of knowledge of his novel subject of animal genetics, had found himself obliged to raise explicitly fundamental and philosophical questions as to its relations to the existing sciences, social as well as natural, Sinclair was, before the end of the thirties, accorded the rare privilege of delivering an annual course of lectures in the Faculty of Science on the nature of knowledge, in which the foundations of the new physics as well as of those of the new biology were discussed. Following on that lead, as his posthumously published book *Socialism and the Individual — Notes on Joining the Labour Party* (1955) shows, Sinclair went on to canvass in a typically clear-headed style which simplifies, without vulgarising, the problems raised by the new sciences of society which were beginning to find a place in the Edinburgh syllabus (e.g. the relation of Marxism to the Sociology Department). Without therefore explicitly involving himself with the Burnet programme (of which, however, he would certainly have been aware) Sinclair shows how the 1927 reinstatement of philosophy at the centre of the curriculum made it possible once again for the Scottish universities to take on the role envisaged for them by Burnet of being the training grounds of a distinctive elite.

A puzzle outside the Arts faculties of Scotland, and sometimes even within them, owing to its being an experiment which was conducted, so to speak, in silence and in the dark, this reinstatement of philosophy to its place in the centre of the curriculum turns out to have had cultural consequences more interesting than it is generally given credit for. Discouraging simple-minded evaluations, it put before the Ordinary classes the view that our scientific civilisation would degenerate into the atomised world of Sir Humphrey Appleby if its claims were not limited and checked by reference to metaphysical ideas like free will, original sin or, in the case of MacMurray, interpersonal knowledge. Metaphysical thinking, therefore, far from being something which, as Russell urged, was an impediment to science and ought to be got rid of, was a fundamental prop of civilisation. No doubt, in the work of the Ordinary classes, positions like these were developed in somewhat of a rhetorical manner, but the gaps in the argumentation were to a great extent filled out, both in the work of the Honours classes, which tended to be much more outward looking, and in the books written by the professors and lecturers which, on the whole, stand up very well to the test of being re-read in our own time.

Because of the public reticence of the Scots on the subject of their cultural conventions, not a lot was known in the seminaries of the South about what was going on beyond the Tweed in the philosophy departments which, in consequence, began to be regarded — inaccurately indeed — as "intellectual backwaters". This natural impatience with what was going on in Scotland, however, did not develop into anything very serious until after World War II, when Oxford, having assimilated the Cambridge ideas, came forward as a great teaching university whose mission was to spread the new scientific philosophy throughout the West. Others things being equal, the pedagogic zeal of the Oxford philosophers would not perhaps have made much impression on the philosophy classes in Scotland. But as it happened, the rise of the Oxford School was followed by a State-organised expansion of the British universities, which, as applied to Scotland, produced the situation in which the increase in the staff numbers proceeded at double the rate of the student numbers. The consequent creation of all these extra posts, which had to be filled in a hurry, gave the critics of the Scottish Arts faculties, both inside and outside, their chance; and by the mid-sixties the new philosophy of science, evolved at Cambridge and systematised at Oxford, had extruded from the philosophy classrooms the older and more metaphysical approach.

Moderate and sensible men who had made their mark by their scholarship, the new incumbents were in nearly all respects well equipped to carry on the standards and the traditions of the philosophy departments. There was, however, a real innovation in the new direction given to the courses, which though their theme continued to be an elementary survey of the relations of philosophy to the sciences, sought to put over the view that philosophy, when it functioned properly, was the handmaiden of the sciences, and not, as men like Kemp Smith, Campbell and MacMurray had maintained, their metaphysical critic. Descartes, though in some ways a great champion and pioneer of modern science, had nevertheless hindered its advance, and obscured its character as observational, objective or public, and non-arbitrary, by tying it to a philosophy which saw sciences as *a priori* rather than observational, and which destroyed the objective, non-arbitrary character of science by insisting on the necessity of approaching it through the inward-looking decisions of the free will. So too David Hume, the next man on the list of great modern philosophers, though he helped along the advance of science by pointing out the errors of the a priorist, free-willist approach of

Descartes, nevertheless put new obstacles in the way of science by emphasising, even more strongly than Descartes, the value of an inward-looking private approach to it. Philosophy, therefore, had never done proper justice to science until the great revolution of the twentieth century which has liberated science from the metaphysical impediments to its progress like free will or subjectivism, and which has limited the role of philosophy to its just bounds, by showing that the only real contribution it can make to the sciences is the relatively humble one of coming to their help when called for, to clear up their logical confusions, by using its technical expertise in Russell's system.

The introduction of this new philosophy to the large Ordinary classes did not, however, have the happy results that many expected of it, but rather tended to confirm an observation once made to me by Campbell, that the technical scientific philosophy of the Russell type could not be put over in the Ordinary classes of the Scottish universities without destroying their *raison d'être* by making nonsense of their cultural role. After all, the whole point of restoring to philosophy its privileged position in the curriculum in 1927 was so that it should draw attention to the permanent value of metaphysics to civilisation, as providing a means of criticising organised science as a check on its pretensions to dominate everything. On the other hand, the general idea of philosophy which would be picked up by the students under the new style of Ordinary class teaching was that the kind of metaphysical ideas put over by Kemp Smith and Campbell had simply been a hindrance to the advance of science, and that this old style philosophy with a metaphysical drift could safely be left to specialists in a modern world in which the sciences, as the result of the defeat of their philosophical foes by the technical logicians, were now poised to leap forward in an irreversible progress. The effect of this sort of thing on students who had conscientiously enough struggled through an Ordinary course in philosophy was to make them wonder, looking back on it at the end, whether their journey had been really necessary. What was the point of being obliged to take on a philosophical survey course, telling one all about the intellectual crimes and follies of mankind, as a preparation for a career in a world in which, the same course seemed to imply, science was now able to advance freely without being hindered by the unnecessary ministrations of officious metaphysicians. The interest began to go out of the Ordinary classes of philosophy as it increasingly became clear that this new style of philosophical analysis, which, whether it liked it or not, drew its chief inspiration from Russell's logic, was far better fitted for putting over as a speciality in Honours courses in the subject than for providing materials for one of the general courses of the old type.

Successfully reorganising the Honours and postgraduate schools so as to make Edinburgh the Scottish centre of what the Oxonians still liked to regard as their "revolution in philosophy", the new management was much less at home with the generalist side of the philosophical tradition which, indeed, it was inclined to dismiss out of hand as provincial or illiberal. Philosophers in a Scottish style, it was felt, had been far too given to meddling in the affairs of sciences which had nothing to do with them. Sinclair's achievement in establishing the philosophical bridgehead in the Faculty of Science, if it was taken note of at all, was regarded as a move in the wrong direction. There was, if possible, even less sympathy with the idea of keeping up the contacts Sinclair had formed with the liveliest parts of that faculty, especially the School of Genetics, which, under its new chief, Waddington, had become a centre of ferment of general culture. The sort of thing for which Edinburgh genetics was now becoming known, such as the exploration of the relationship between the sciences on the one hand, and arts like painting on the other,[3] was regarded as beyond the intellectual pale, from the point of view of philosophers who aspired to establish their subject on a professional footing. The object of Edinburgh philosophy was no longer to encourage personal curiosity about large questions like "the universe and man's place in it", but to train up competent expositers of anti-metaphysical systems of philosophy which had already proved their worth by being acceptable in the centres which constituted the mainstream of culture.

Not so much an eclipse as a slow fade-out which, as far as affecting the calendar courses is concerned, is much more evident in Edinburgh and Aberdeen than in the other universities, this change in philosophy's status was on the whole acquiesced in as being appropriate to the change which had come over the Scottish universities' relation to the State since the end of the Second War. After all, the 1927 settlement, which had restored philosophy to its old role, had represented a sort of gesture of defiance on the part of the Scottish universities against the utilitarian values which the part of the British State they then dealt with — the S.E.D. under Struthers and McDonald — had sought to impose on them. But in the new situation created after the war by the welfare state, Burnet's ideas about culture seemed to make far less sense than those of the bureaucrats, and the Scottish universities, detaching themselves from the narrowness, as it was thought to be, of the S.E.D. and connecting with the State by way of the Department of Education and Science in London, seemed to have become reconciled to the utilitarian principles which they had formerly repudiated. In any case, privileged subjects were again coming under fire in the years after 1945, and the old claims made for the "priority of epistemology" — for the values of the head as opposed to those of the hands — were denounced in the name of "Christian equality" by the Robertson committee which spoke for the Scottish teachers. Soon the fundamental prop of liberal values in the Scottish Leaving Certificate scheme — the entrenched position of English literature as something everybody had to take — was removed without institutional protest, except from Glasgow University, which took its three sister institutions to the Court of the Privy Council, but lost its case. If English literature couldn't be saved, why make a fuss about a subject like philosophy, which, it was felt, would be more likely to hasten the end of its suspect privileges by speaking out in their defence than by remaining silent?

It might have been thought that a subject like the metaphysical part of philosophy, which, everybody seemed to be agreed, was useless, was on the way out in the Scottish Arts faculties and would gradually disappear altogether. In the event, however, the reverse seemed to be the case, and driven out from what used to be its legitimate home, it has found new quarters elsewhere. Once again, it is a case of "Philosophy is dead, long live Philosophy".

From the sixties onwards a remarkable transformation had come over the well-established Scottish tradition of taking an interest in metaphysical problems. In Edinburgh, as the Philosophy Department, under the influence of the scientific observationalism which had now become its ruling position, gave up its responsibility for discussing the larger questions about man and his place in the universe in order to accept the more limited role of an under-labourer engaged in smoothing the way for the sciences, new departments and schools suddenly began to blossom in the fields of the human sciences, which, without giving up the limited area of regional researches to which they had formerly restricted themselves, took upon themselves the great task of resolving, by experiment, observation and measurement, the grand problems of metaphysics — especially that of the relation of mind and matter — i.e. of the nature of conscious intelligent behaviour — which from ancient times had been the central preoccupation of philosophy, but which philosophy was now giving up. The first proof of this shift in responsibility for metaphysics from philosophy to psychology was the creation of a School of Artificial Intelligence, unique in Britain, which soon began to restore the fame of Edinburgh metaphysics in the international scene by its well-publicised projects for manufacturing robots, which might not only throw light on the way human beings think, but which would, it was hoped, ultimately achieve the property supposed to be unique to man, of thinking for themselves. Soon after, an interdisciplinary programme began to develop, which was to attract to Edinburgh leading figures in psychology, physiology and linguistics. Finally, after various vicissitudes, this was consolidated by the creation by the university of a School of Epistemics, the explicit programme of which is to provide a definitive solution of the metaphysical problems formerly associated with philosophy, by using a combination of experiment with Russell's logic as its means of investigation.

One might well wonder why this disappearance of the old metaphysical interests of Edinburgh from the Philosophy Department which had harboured them so long, coincided with the reappearance of the same sort of metaphysical interests and problems in Edinburgh departments of psychological and biological science which were committing themselves before the world to a programme in "experimental philosophy", meaning a subject bridging the gap between the large-scale trascendental speculations about reality as a whole, formerly discussed only in the *a priori* speculations of the old philosophy departments, and the observationally based mechanical model-making familiar in psychology departments but hitherto reserved for investigations more concerned with the part than with the whole. At first appearing merely arbitrary, the relationshop between the disappearance of metaphysics from one department and their reappearance in another in the same institution, begins however to appear as something more than a mere coincidence as soon as we take account of the fact that the acknowledged hero and inspirer of the artificial intelligence movement in Edinburgh, Kenneth Craik, began to evolve his views about the possibility of exploring thinking by inventing robots in Edinburgh in the course of doing a joint degree in philosophy and psychology under Kemp Smith and James Drever (Senior) in the later thirties. James Drever's connection with Craik is, of course, well known, as the result of the informative

Cambridge obituary being printed as a kind of preface to Craik's posthumously published papers. But the influence of Kemp Smith may be, I suspect, just as important as that of Drever, in that the starting point of Craik's programme for the experimental investigation of artificial intelligence is to be found in the view of the nature and role of abstractive thought, which, constituting by far the most important of Kemp Smith's original contributions to philosophy, is explained in the third of his three articles on 'Universals' in *Mind* (1927), and is further explored in the 1928 Paper of the Aristotelian Society on 'The Fruitfulness of the Abstract'.[4] The relevance of Kemp Smith's very clear and well-worked-out speculation into the kind of experience the eye would have to undergo in order to be able to make the commonsense distinction between inseparables like colour and shape — it would have to involve, he says, the experiences of same shape/different colour, same colour/different shape and the comparison of these experiences — would seem to prepare the way for the approach to abstraction which Craik develops in his first and only book *The Nature of Explanation* (1943) — presented to me in that year by Kemp Smith. "How should we set about designing a mechanism to respond to these different kinds of identity, and identity in diversity?"[5] "The hardest part of the process is the act of representation itself — the representation of something variable in size and location, by a definite natural process."[6] These questions of Craik focus on the topic of recognition of identity in difference in much the same way as Kemp Smith does, although the latter, as I read him, makes the problem considerably clearer, because he seeks to bring to light the experiences which enable us to recognise identity in the midst of difference, sameness of shape in spite of different colours, by contrasting it with the kind of experience which would not be sufficient to enable us to distinguish the shape aspect of the thing from its colour. Craik, on the other hand, sets about speculating as to how to invent a mechanism which will pick out identity in the midst of difference without bothering to enumerate to himself the kind of circumstances in which it would not do what he wants it to do. Nevertheless, this does not prevent Craik from having written on the subject of abstraction a book which is worthy of being compared with Kemp Smith's stimulating remarks.

Of course it would be easy to criticise what I say about Craik on the principle that one swallow does not make a summer. But the quality which distinguished Craik — the fact that he takes up one of the great problems of philosophy and seeks to give it a psychological solution by experimental means — is paralleled by a great deal of work produced by the Department of Psychology in Edinburgh University. The work associated with the names of Professor Bower, Professor Donaldson and Professor Trevarthen, though not metaphysical at all in the way in which Craik's work is, nevertheless must have drawn a certain inspiration from the ideas canvassed in the philosophy departments while they were still centres of metaphysical speculation. Professor Trevarthen, for example, is certainly indebted to MacMurray while Professor Bower seems to take his starting point from a Kantian view of the *a priori* in mind which came to him from James Drever (Junior),[7] himself more a philosopher than a psychologist by training, and owing more perhaps to Kemp Smith than he did to his father. In seeking to line up these three later contributions to psychology with that of Craik in order to make claims about the philosophical inspiration of the work of Edinburgh psychologists, I am not of course concerned just with any contribution that makes the grade of "the year's work in . . .", but with books and articles of a high quality which is acknowledged far beyond the bounds of Edinburgh and Scotland. Moreover, the tradition, as I understand it, is still very much alive, manifesting its existence most recently the selection of the Edinburgh department as the proper place in which to locate the new Chair in Parapsychology, which was set up in accordance with the terms of Arthur Koestler's will. Significantly, Dr John Beloff, a psychologist with a strong interest in philosophy, played a key role in this. Recent developments in the Psychology Department thus seem to confirm what Craik said in the first sentence of his book namely that, "Philosophy seems at present to be in a stage of transition between the *a priorism* of the past and perhaps an experimental philosophy in the future."[8]

The tension between philosophy and the human sciences in Edinburgh has not been ended by the former surrendering its responsibility towards metaphysics to the latter. An ancient and proud movement of intellect such as Scottish philosophy does not give up provinces and pull down flags. Accordingly, round about 1960, when it was becoming clear that the privileged position regained for philosophy in 1927 was in danger of being lost as the result of the spread to Scotland of an analytic philosophy in the Russellian vein, which was dubious of the value of general culture, defences of the threatened tradition were put forward in Sydney and in Belfast, which, quite independently of one another, invoked the name and doctrines of John Burnet. The Australian arguments formulated by John Anderson in the last two or three papers written by him before he died in 1962, made the point that the sense of wholeness which was Burnet's great quality and which inspired his critique of specialisation was being emptied of meaning by a modern and superficial attitude to logic which destroyed the unity of science by developing a doctrine of every branch of science having its own logic. The way to defend what was valuable in the Scottish philosophical tradition was, according to Anderson, to renew the problem of Scottish logic by going back beyond his erstwhile pupil Sinclair (whose work he doesn't seem to have liked much) to Latta and Macbeath's *Elements of Logic* (which he used in Australia as a textbook), and then, as the result of criticising the latter, to inaugurate a revised Aristotelianism, which by restoring the lost sense of the unity of logic, would at one blow reinstate Burnet's views of the whole, and frustrate Russell's efforts at atomising analysis.

Much less philosophical than Anderson's, the effort made by myself in *The Democratic Intellect* to defend the philosophical tradition, claimed that the twentieth-century crisis in the Scottish curriculum, by blotting out the memory of Burnet's critique of specialisation, was a further manifestation of the provincialising pressures to which Burnet himself had drawn attention, but which, as I argued, had begun much earlier than he suspected, namely in the eighteen-twenties with the debate occasioned by the earliest of the three University Commissions of the nineteenth century. Starting from a discussion of Burnet (unfortunately, for reasons I have explained above, excluded from the book as published) I had sought to awaken a new sense of the value of the endangered tradition of philosophy teaching by suggesting that, in turning their backs on the country's intellectual past, the Scots were not merely giving up pedagogical methods which might be objected to as over-abstract and general, but were also dissociating themselves and their universities (for what seemed a mere temporary convenience) from a long, continuous line of philosophical thinkers of very high quality, through Hutcheson and Hume in the early eighteenth century to Ferrier in the latter part of the nineteenth, who were acknowledged throughout most of the world as having made a contribution of great and permanent importance to human culture.

Increasingly read outside Scotland, Anderson's contribution has so far had little or no effect on Scotland itself, although perhaps its day may yet come. My own contribution, however, is much more relevant to my present thesis, since, in the event, my effort to make the Scottish departments of philosophy aware of the great value and interest of the historical philosophy of Scotland evoked on the whole little response from the teachers and, what mattered most, no response whatsoever from the students but, to my surprise and, ultimately, satisfaction, provided a considerable stimulus to the great and growing movement of historical studies in the Scottish universities which had developed far beyond their relatively humble beginnings with Lodge, and which were now becoming among the most popular subjects in the Arts faculties. Just as metaphysics, in being given up by the departments of philosophy, was taken over with striking results by the studies in the field of psychology, so too the classic debate of the Scottish philosophers on the relations of ethics and economics and of science and common sense, having ceased to be the responsibility of the philosophy departments, were taken up by the history departments to be reanimated and rethought out with notable results. Previously, the history departments were known for producing work of quality which had made no impact on the general reader and the Scottish people. Suddenly this defect was remedied as historians took upon themselves the task of making the historical debate on Scottish philosophy come alive in relation to the social circumstances of the Scotland of the time. In particular, one might mention Professor T. C. Smout, whose *History of the Scottish People* has been admitted into many houses which do not often welcome books, simply because he has given the Scottish intellectual debate a new look and a new liveliness, by showing that just as in our own time the fundamental philosophical tension was between the Platonic world of high culture championed by Burnet and the levelling subworld of the *Scottish Educational Journal* which for a time looked to Darroch as its spokesman, so too in the classic age of Scottish philosophy the storm centre of debate was not the argument between Hume, Adam Smith, Reid and their friends, but rather the intellectual tension between their group and another group much less able and original philosophically, but equally strong-minded, which took its standards from the utilitarian-minded radicals and democrats from south of the border.

Pulling the whole argument together by reverting to the question from which it originally started — as to whether philosophy was of much importance in the evolution of the twentieth-century curriculum — I want to conclude by making two points. As regards the first three-quarters of the century, the question of philosophy certainly had great importance, I think, not only because the main issue of the curriculum was whether philosophy should hold its own against the human sciences, but also because the latter were ultimately able to win out against philosophy only because they successfully took upon themselves the responsibility for the metaphysics and for the morals which philosophy had given up. As regards what lies ahead, one cannot be sure, and it may be that philosophy will be content to occupy a subordinate position in the curriculum, dissociating itself from its traditional role of guardian and critic in regard to an ancient and intellectual tradition, the responsibility for which it has let others take over. On the other hand, it is just as difficult for departments as for individuals to break away from their past which, in the present case, has lately begun to return upon it, in the form of a group of belatedly published books, which bring to life the standpoint of Scottish philosophy during the period of the twenties to the fifties when it had regained its privileged position and knew what to do with it. There are the *Von Hügel-Kemp Smith Letters* from the Edinburgh of the early twenties, there are the two collections of John Anderson's papers and lectures, *Education and Inquiry* and *Art and Reality*, there is the posthumously published book on the relations of *Analysis and Dialectic* which brings to us the ideas of J. J. Russell, the brightest intellect in Campbell's department at Glasgow, and there is *Ferrier of St Andrews* by Mr Arthur Thomson, a distinguished pupil of Stout, which brings home to us the continuity of the Scottish intellect of the nineteenth century and that of the twentieth century as well as the continuing vitality of its ideas.

No doubt, the philosophy departments, as they now are, would be ready enough to leave the work of assimilating and assessing this legacy from the recent past of the Scottish Arts faculties to the historians or psychologists. But here we must remember that academically speaking "there are hills beyond Pentlands and lands beyond Forth" and more particularly there is the great University of Glasgow which, ever since the Robbins Committee sanctioned the breaking up of the united front between the Scottish universities and allowed each to go its own way, has pursued a very different course from Edinburgh. As the result of being left to its own devices, traditional patterns have begun, without anybody's willing them, to re-emerge in Glasgow University. As Andrew Macpherson[9] points out, the average age of entrance has, in the West, begun to drop back to that of about seventeen years old at a time when the other Scottish universities are seeking to raise the entrance age to that of universities elsewhere by keeping it at eighteen-plus. Once again, in the public discussions which have arisen in the eighties as to whether the Scottish universities should reform their broken unity by organising themselves in a committee which would approach the Government by way of the S.E.D. or would continue to do what they have done since the Robbins Report — each one seeking quite independently of the others to do the best for itself by making direct contacts with the Grants Commission and the D.E.S. in London — Glasgow, as it has often done before, has sought to revert to the historical position in which the Scottish universities approached the Government together through an independent body, whereas each of Edinburgh's two universities take their stand on the more modern position that a country the size of Scotland is ill-placed to afford great universities, and if it wants to continue having such luxuries must go on subordinating itself to a wider whole.

Remarkably enough, this tendency of Glasgow to reanimate a traditional point of view has coincided with the emergence of a new concernedness with the nature and value of Scotland's intellectual tradition, which directly and explicitly raises in a fresh and challenging way, questions long neglected by all the Scottish universities, including, of course, Glasgow itself. Keeping in view the great changes which have come over the intellectual climate of the Scottish universities in the last twenty-five years, Alexander Broadie fairly and squarely faces us with the problem as to whether the major development of these years — the coming into Scotland of the mathematical logic — is as incompatible with the native philosophical tradition of Scotland as men as different as Kemp Smith, Campbell and Sinclair apparently had believed it to be. Giving an answer which is as challenging as it is unexpected, Broadie propounds the thesis that the new logic is incompatible with the Scottish tradition in philosophy only insofar as this latter is identified with the Scotch metaphysics which have prevailed in the universities from the days of David Hume and the Enlightenment right down to Campbell, Kemp Smith and MacMurray in our own century, but becomes readily reconcilable with the Scottish intellectual tradition if one takes a more extended view of it and does not date its origins to the curriculum reforms of the last decade of the seventeenth and the first decades of the eighteenth centuries, but instead traces its origins back to the first founding of the universities, and in particular to the famous achievements of the Scottish logicians of the sixteenth century — the school of John Mair and *Lockert the Logician*, about whom Dr Broadie has written. Just as C. M. Grieve, sixty years ago, sought to make the Scots more conscious of their poetic tradition by enunciating the slogan "Back to Dunbar" as providing a standard which accords far better with modern excellence in poetry than anything Burns did, so too Dr Broadie, from his vantage point in Glasgow, seeks to stimulate a revaluation of the Scottish intellectual tradition by arguing that the logical work of the philosophers who were the contemporaries and sometimes the friends of William Dunbar and Gavin Douglas, has far closer affinities with the modern advances in logic, not only in spirit and potentiality, but in actual achievement, than have all the social, psychological and meta-physical speculations which were produced under the auspices of the Scottish universities before the invasion of the Scottish departments by the new ideas from the South. In short, the view from Glasgow advises the Scottish universities to accommodate their intellectual traditions to the twentieth century, not by leaving them in cold storage, but by revising them so as to "burn what has been adored, and to adore what has been burned" — to quote a slogan of Grieve in the twenties.

Constitutionally speaking, the idea of Scottish universities as centres of an autonomous tradition within the U.K. seems to have lived on in twentieth-century Glasgow at a time when it was dying our or being discouraged in Edinburgh. However, this difference between the East and the West in the matter of the constitutional positions of the two universities within British education as a whole does not seem to have affected very much the fact that in the more particular matter of their attitude to the Scottish intellectual tradition, the developments in Glasgow closely paralleled those in Edinburgh. That is to say, the metaphysical inheritance in both universities in proportion as it faded out within the philosophy departments as the result of the influx of the new philosophy which had been developed at Oxford and Cambridge, was taken over by the human sciences, and in due course, in Glasgow, as in Edinburgh, provided a stimulus to notable work in the fields of psychology and of history.

Carried through in a spirit very different from that manifested in the parallel process in Edinburgh, the eclipse of philosophy by psychology — the take-over of the former by the latter — as it expressed itself in the Glasgow tradition, depended on the fact that from Caird through Jones to Campbell, the driving force of philosophy in the West had been, as we said before, the enthusiastic commitment to a German-Hegelian idea of philosophy — mediated to a certain extent by the work of Green and of Bradley at Oxford — which repudiated both the Scottish philosophy of common sense and the English atomistic empiricism as *insular*. The really distinctive feature of the Glasgow situation is that as developed by Campbell's pupils like J. J. Russell, this interest in continental philosophy in the Hegelian form naturally enough — as happened also in France — began to be combined with an interest in Edmund Husserl and phenomenology which was regarded, not so much as opposed to but as complementary to the dialectic of Hegel. Close to Campbell, and regarded by some as his appropriate successor, Russell made clear enough his interest in phenomenology in the course of the book he was writing from the fifties onwards by giving it in its original form a title borrowed from Husserl's *Ideas* — 'Reason and Reality'. When, however, in the early sixties, the Glasgow Philosophy Department was invaded by the Oxbridge version of analytic empiricism which Russell's phenomenology was meant to refute or correct, he took a transatlantic appointment, carrying with him his manuscript, which was finally published posthumously in the early eighties under the title *Analysis and Dialectic* which, perhaps, in deference to the changed climate of opinion, draws attention to his interests in the dialectics of Hegel and Marx while retaining the commitment to phenomenology. However, the departure of Russell did not mean the extinction of the phenomenological interests within the Glasgow Arts area of studies. Suppressed within the Philosophy Department, Russell's project of using phenomenonology to reanimate the intellectual life of Britain reappeared among Glasgow psychiatrists, and was realised in practice with striking success by Ronald Laing, the author of the well-known books on *The Divided Self, Self and Others*, as well as the analysis (with David Cooper) of Sartre's *Critique of Dialectical Reason*, published under the title of *Reason and Violence*. Without being the equal of Craik's work, either in originality or fruitfulness, Laing's contribution is nevertheless parallel to it, in the sense of showing how ideas originating in the old philosophy departments could provide the inspiration of books written by psychiatrists, which were to have a real measure of public success.

So too in Glasgow, as in Edinburgh, the work of reassessing the philosophical traditions of Scotland, for which philosophy departments might be expected to be responsible, but which no longer interested them, was taken over by the historians, and especially those concerned with the effects of economic development on intellectual life. The philosophers' apathy towards the distinctive tradition is evident enough in the contribution of Campbell to the volume published at the Glasgow Quincentenary — *Fortuna Domus* — who, though confessing to being much more impressed than he had expected by the quality of the philosophical work done in Glasgow by men like Hutcheson and Reid, nevertheless continued the policy of the Glasgow Philosophy Department as set by Caird and Sir Henry Jones of seeing the incoming of the German ideas into Scotland as the crucial turning point in the progress of philosophy, in the light of which all previous work by Scots — Hume apart — turns out to be limited and provincial. Neglected by the philosophers, the theme of the continuing interest of the Scottish intellectual tradition — especially as illustrated by the work done by Adam Smith in his years as Professor of Moral Philosophy at Glasgow — continued to survive and flourish in the West of Scotland as a major preoccupation of the Department of Political Economy. A line of reflective-minded economists — Professors W. R. Scott, A. L. Macfie, and latterly Andrew Skinner — set about exploring the relation of Smith's economics to his ethics and theory of science, then went on to discuss the relation of his work to the philosophical economics contributed by other Scots like Hume and Sir James Steuart, and finally took advantage of the 200th anniversary of the publication of the *Wealth of Nations* to launch the Glasgow edition of Adam Smith's works which, supervised by Skinner, constitutes a landmark in Enlightenment scholarship. Moreover, the development along these lines did not stop here, but was carried much further by Professor Sidney Checkland in his book on the *History of Scottish Banking* (1973) which brings to life the whole story of the Scottish intellect from the end of the seventeenth century by exhibiting the relation of the innovations in banking practice made by the Scots to the economic-philosophical discussions which were started by men like Law of Lauriston, David Hume, Adam Smith and Sir James Steuart in the eighteenth century and which were resumed without much decline of quality among the leading bankers of the Scottish nineteenth century like Alexander Blair of the Bank of Scotland. Bearing somewhat the same relationship to the Glasgow studies of the Scottish Enlightenment as carried out by Professor Skinner and others as T. C. Smout's *History of the Scottish People* bears to the Edinburgh discussions of the Scottish intellectual heritage, Checkland's enthralling and authoritative book provided a remarkable example of how intellectual history can be publicly important in the sense that the decision of the Commissioners as to the future of the Royal Bank of Scotland seem to have been to some extent influenced by their reading of it.

However, this parallelism between the West and the East in reference to the way they treated the common intellectual inheritance of the country has to be qualified in several respects if we are to make sense of the present day situation. In Edinburgh, Scottish philosophy faded away from the Philosophy Department gradually, and in circumstances unlikely to cause a crisis. Pringle-Pattison's popular presentation of Reid gave place, after 1920, to his successor Kemp Smith's scholarly studies of the importance of Hutcheson and the Scottish religious background, if one is to do justice to David Hume's philosophy, while Kemp Smith's work in its turn provided stimulus in the sixties for the Scottish Enlightenment studies which were now arising in the history departments of Edinburgh. By contrast, the disappearance of the Scottish philosophy from the Glasgow Department took place in a much more sudden and dramatic manner, and was, moreover, attended by circumstances which kept constantly in view the possibility that the philosophers might be wrong in regarding Hume's Scottish critics like Reid as having deflected philosophy into a backwater. In the first place, the study of Scottish philosophy was terminated by Jones only after a thirty years' struggle, in which Professor John Veitch had stood up for and advertised its virtues not only by denouncing the Hegelian doctrines of his colleague Caird from the rostrum — "Pure Being is pure nonsense" — but also by planting giant thistles along the driveway up to the door of his country house in Peeblesshire, to show that however ashamed Caird might be of Scottish philosophy, he himself thought well of it. But in the second place, the triumphant propaganda for Hegelianism put forward by Jones from the nineties onwards, though it might silence the voice of Scottish philosophy within the Philosophy Department, was powerless to prevent it from being heard outside the Philosophy Department, in widely read books produced by the new Glasgow school of economists, like James Bonar's *Philosophy and Political Economy* (a product of the nineties) where Hume and Adam Smith are fully treated, or in W. R. Scott's books on *Francis Hutcheson* and *Adam Smith as Student and Professor*. Salving the self-esteem of the West of Scotland by a kind of doctrine of a double truth which allowed Scottish philosophy to be valueless in metaphysics but valuable on the question of the relation of ethics and economics, this Glasgow compromise was to last a very long time without being challenged. In the end, however, in the new situation created from the sixties onwards by the necessity of finding a place in the philosophy curriculum for the modern logic and the new analytic scientific-minded philosophy of the Gilbert Ryle generation, the compromises presupposed in the distinctive Glasgow tradition of intellect began to be brought to light and rethought with results to which I now wish to call attention.

Illustrated by *Lokert: Late Scholastic Logician* and by the more extensive *John Mair and his Circle*, as I have suggested, the new departure is provided by Alexander Broadie's work, of which "Back to John Mair" could be the slogan, the significance of which, not only for Glasgow but for all the Scottish universities, can best be brought out by distinguishing within it two separate but related recommendations. The first of these gives new life to the Hon. Rory Erskine of Marr's reply to A. J. (later the Earl) Balfour's assertion, in a private argument, that in the new conditions created by international co-operation, there was no longer any room for the idea of Scotland as the centre of a distinctive type of tradition of philosophy. In questions of this kind, where we are to think not in terms of decades and generations, but of whole epochs, what we have to remember is, Erskine of Marr retorts, that during the past five hundred years the Scottish tradition in philosophy has died out and been reborn two or three times, one of the most notable of these renaissances being that headed by the long-lived John Mair (before 1470-1550). It is therefore shortsighted and unphilosophical for the future Prime Minister Balfour (himself no mean philosopher) to write off the possibility of a revival of Scottish philosophy. A week may be a long time in politics but it is a short time in philosophy.

Equally impressive and equally unfamiliar, the second point implied by Dr Broadie follows from the first. The reawakening called for in the slogan "Back to John Mair" has, Broadie's argument tells us, already in some sort come into being in Edinburgh without anybody's noticing what was happening, in the course of the revolution in which epistemics — a kind of interdisciplinary grouping of psychology, artificial intelligence and computer studies under the presidency of symbolic logic — shows signs of taking the central intellectual position in the curriculum made vacant by the demise of the old Scotch metaphysics. Essentially involving the replacement of the old Aristotelian logic as associated with the old metaphysics by a non-Aristotelian logic, the new line opened out by epistemics corresponds closely to what is intended in Broadie's call for the return to the logic of Lokert the logician and of John Mair.

Valuable for its percipience, however, this diagnosis of the present situation in Scottish philosophy can, in my estimation, be accepted as a whole only by qualifying in certain respects the latter of the two points. The possibility of a distinctive contribution to philosophy by the Scottish universities which Broadie envisages, consists, it may be argued, not so much in the victory for the new logic which can claim affinities with, and might even draw inspiration from, that of John Mair, but in a fresh outbreak of the twentieth-century argument in which the claims of this new logic as well as the analytic movement it has inspired in so many places, is going to be challenged in the name of the old logic in works which draw their inspiration from John Anderson as well as from J. J. Russell's *Analysis and Dialectic*.

PART III

"BACK TO JOHN MAIR"?

COMMON SENSE AND LOGIC

From the late spring to the late autumn of 1985, the *Edinburgh University Bulletin*, in its extra as well as in its regular editions, made exciting reading. It was not so much the fact that, as in other universities, there was a growing movement away from pure specialisation to interdisciplinary arrangements — brought into being through governmental prodding — but that, in the metropolitan university of Scotland, this reorganisation of studies seemed to promise the re-emergence of a generalism of a new type in which the central subject was not, as of old, philosophy in the classical tradition, but a version of modern logic, co-operating on a *primus inter pares* principle with psychology, linguistic theory, artificial intelligence, computer science, etc. To ratify this new status of non-Aristotelian logic it has been made into a regular department of the Faculty of Science, its name being changed from Epistemics to Cognitive Science for the purpose, and the importance of its work recognised by its being granted special funds at a time of great stringency for the rest of the university. At the same time, and apparently in furtherance of the same principle, a check has been put on over-specialisation in the Faculty of Social Sciences by setting up a general class, open to all, on the subject of the relationship of technology to society, also to be conducted on an inter-disciplinary principle but without the involvement of traditional philosophy. It seems we are fast moving into the new era, looked forward to by the poet MacDiarmid, when the curriculum will once again be organised around the principle of generalism, but a generalism which was modernist in its values and had left classicism behind it.

But, for all its claims to revolutionise philosophy in Scotland by going back to the anti-Aristotelian logic pioneered in the sixteenth century by John Mair in much the same way as the "Back to Dunbar" movement has revolutionised Scottish poetry, this reorganisation of the sciences around the School of Epistemics on lines sketched in Korzybski's *Science and Sanity* does not involve as radical a break as one might have thought with the intellectual tradition which it seems set to expurgate from Scotland — the presbyterian humanism which was introduced by Buchanan, which was carried further by the Scottish Enlightenment, and which in our own century staged a notable comeback in the work of John Burnet. Just as the central problem for philosophy in Scotland in the Enlightenment and in the nineteenth century was that of reconciling philosophy with common sense (to use Ferrier's phrase), and just as the primary issue faced by Renaissance and Reformation philosophy arose out of the tension between what Descartes called the teaching of nature (common sense) and the light of nature (logic), so too the new Department of Cognitive Science, according to the public description given of it, sees its task as that of exploring how far the language of common life (natural language) can be clarified and even revitalised in the light of the new ideas about meaning for which we are indebted to modern logic. This intellectual revolution is thus a somewhat more limited affair than it is advertised to be, the innovation it represents consisting of not much in a fresh and systematic effort to grapple with the great problem of the conflict between traditional ideas of nature and those of the new physics, as in the fact that, whereas from the fifteenth to the nineteenth centuries the relations between logic and common sense were discussed by philosophers who took both these terms in the sense given them by Aristotle, the great leap forward promised by our modern epistemists consists in discussing the relations between common sense and logic in the new senses given the two terms by Bertrand Russell, G. E. Moore, and Gilbert Ryle. The progress to be achieved by the reforms thus, it would seem, amounts only to this, that if the Scottish universities are to regain their intellectual reputation in the world the favourite problem of the relation of logic and common sense must be detached from the values of Athens and rethought, in modern terms, against the background of Oxford and Cambridge.

And yet, to do justice to the modernists, it has to be pointed out that this sharp break with the past in which their new ideas achieved official status within the Scottish universities, without, so far as I know, ever being seriously discussed, and so to speak in deference merely to fashion, was in considerable part due to the refusal of the men on the spot representing tradition to have any truck with the innovations. Entering into the Scottish philosophy departments in the early sixties at a time when the staff numbers suddenly increased, the ideas of the Oxbridge "revolution in philosophy" were allowed to achieve a central place in the curriculum with very little resistance, not because they were acceptable to all the teachers, but because they were regarded by many of the traditionalists as too full of nonsense to be worth arguing against. This somewhat unreasoning hostility to the innovations is evident not only in the weak writings of MacMurray and C. A. Campbell on the subject, but also in the remarkable quartet of articles — 'Hypotheticals' (1952), 'Classicism' (1958) and 'Relational Arguments' as well as 'Empiricism and Logic' of 1963 — produced by John Anderson in response to some provocative criticisms of him by Gilbert Ryle, during the latter's missionary tour of the Antipodes in 1951.[1] Not content with the forceful attack on the foundations of the Russellian logic in 'Hypotheticals', Anderson undoes the effectiveness of his critique by seeking to distance himself at every point from the new philosophy. The facts of ordinary language and of common sense which it takes as a starting point and in terms of which it poses its problems are rejected by Anderson as contemptuously as he rejects the atomistic tendency of its analyses. This failure to find any point of agreement makes it difficult for him to be clear as to what he is disagreeing with, and he puts still more obstacles in the way of our understanding him by treating Russell's arguments as errors which can be disposed of in a single sentence. In spite, therefore, of their soundness and subtlety, his ideas dazzle the readers in a kind of firework display and fail to make a permanent impression.

These denunciations by Anderson of the appeals to ordinary language etc. seem particularly unjust to Moore and Russell, whose doctrine on the subject of common sense is the result of a sustained and prolonged effort, on the part of the universities of the South, to make sense of what had been for them, to begin with, the very strange and alien phenomena of the Scottish Enlightenment in general and the philosophy of Thomas Reid in particular. This interest originally shows itself in the blend of amusement with genuine curiosity which is illustrated by anecdotes like George III's "Fie, fie, Mr Dundas, no more of your Scotch Metaphysics", in response to the ministerial recommendation that he resolve the deadlock on the Irish Emancipation Bill by signing it *qua* King, while at the same time putting on record his dissent from it *qua* person, or Sydney Smith's fragment of conversation overheard in an Edinburgh ballroom, "what you say, my lord, is true of love in the abstract". From the mid-nineteenth century onwards, at the very time when the Scots were beginning to lose confidence in their intellectual tradition,

Reid and his Common Sense were taken up in earnest by the Southern seminaries, now emerging from their century of hibernation, and a succession of thinkers of excellent quality, from Mansel and Case to Pritchard at Oxford and from John Grote through Sidgwick at Cambridge, prepared the way for the emergence of Moore, of Russell and later of Ryle, who, to the embarrassment of the Scottish departments of philosophy, gave a certain privileged status to the point of view of the plain man and of the language he expressed himself in which had long been dismissed as irrational in Glasgow and somewhat later too in Edinburgh. All the same, Edinburgh and Glasgow, in spite of the ebbing of the creative urge, still remained pretty good judges of the intellectual quality of writings, and knew what they were doing in repudiating the appeals to common sense by Moore and company. "Consciousness," said Kemp Smith, meaning thereby what he would have later called 'the vulgar consciousness', "is inherently metaphysical" in the sense of inseparably involving beliefs in causality, the external world, other minds, and one's own mind, all of which as objects are in one sense transcendent to experience.[2] To make the central question of philosophy, as Moore seems to do in the humorous self-mockery of the passage "hens' eggs are generally laid by hens", into an inquiry into how certain parts of our ordinary knowledge which go beyond sense can be founded on other parts of our ordinary knowledge which do not go beyond sense, is, the Scottish philosophers saw well enough in their own way, to make a fool of philosophy by making it ask questions which, because they are unanswerable, are by that very fact unaskable and spurious.[3] Looking at Russell and Moore with a serious critical eye which had little patience with their wit, a philosopher in the northern tradition might well be excused for regarding them as reducing philosophy to a frivolity by making its central question the logical analysis of common sense.

But all this took place over twenty-five years ago and, in the interval, the new interest among the universities of the world in the achievements of the Scottish Enlightenment is revolutionising our picture of Reid by showing that his views on the relation of common sense to its logical analysis is far more subtle and original than either Russell or Moore on the one hand, or Kemp Smith or Anderson on the other, could have imagined. I quote from Reid's *Curâ Primâ on Common Sense* a passage which calls attention to a fact, which is never, so far as I know, mentioned in his previously published works, namely the affinity between his view of common sense and that of Aristotle:

186

"Aristotle observed that the faculty by which we distinguish the object of different senses, e.g. white from sweet, must be a faculty distinct from both sight and taste. Some of his followers gave the name of common sense to this faculty, some of them made it to be the intellectual faculty. They thought vision imperfect without this faculty. See Aguilonius *Opticorum* Lib. 1, Prop. 91: *Externus visus sine ope sensus communis perfectam visionam non producit.*"[4]

Reid says no more, but what he is driving at seems evident enough from his other works. The function of common sense as the source of the knowledge we get by comparing sight with taste, as Aristotle (and Plato) pointed out, is analogous to the function of common sense as the source of our visual knowledge in the sense that, according to the theory of vision which Reid starts from — that of Bishop Berkeley — and which in some sort is the inspiration of the Reidian philosophy, the seeing of things cannot be properly carried out, that is, cannot be carried out so as to give us reliable information about the shapes and sizes of things, except by means of the comparison of sight with touch. The important point about the relation of Aristotle's and Plato's common sense to Reid's common sense is that just as the comparison of sight with taste or with hearing, as Plato and Aristotle pointed out, gives us a knowledge of certain qualities of sensible objects as, for example, the difference between colour and sound or the existence of colour and sound — which are transcendent to the senses because of their being the object neither of sight nor of hearing, when each is taken by itself — so too the comparison of sight with touch throws further light on what is meant by claiming that there are qualities in the bodies sensed which transcend our experience of them, because it is by comparing sight and touch with one another that we discover, by touch, the continued existence out of sight of bodies we formerly saw and, by sight, the continued existence of bodies which we once felt to be solid but which we see now to be out of reach of our tactual organs. Common sense knowledge is thus knowledge of bodies which we could not get from the senses when they are in isolation from one another but which can be got from the senses when they are employed in co-operation so as to enable us to compare them together. The importance of this common sense knowledge is that it gives us a knowledge of aspects of things which in a genuine way transcends the senses and which thus is rightly called intellectual knowledge. Providing us with an analysis of common sense in terms of the separate senses, which is different from that envisaged by Moore and Russell, Reid thus, at the same time, provides us with a means of, up to a point at any rate, answering the doubts of Kemp Smith and of Anderson as to the possibility of explaining how we know what is beyond the senses by means of knowledge of nothing but what is present to the senses.

Carried only a little way by Reid himself through his usual caution, this Platonic-Aristotelian principle of how common sense knowledge takes us beyond sense is taken further by certain philosophers who are opposed to Reid on account of his limitations. Thomas Brown, for example, makes a beginning of showing how the same principle might be used to justify our belief in the causal connection of things; Ferrier, in very subtle articles, explains how the same principle might be used to justify in a certain limited way, the belief in the bodies perceived as being independent of us who perceive them; and Adam Smith, in the boldest move of all, indicates how an extension of the same principle can throw light on the very difficult question of our knowledge of one anothers' minds.[5]

Considered in themselves these facts about Reid and the others are irrelevant to my present purposes except in so far as I find myself able, with their help, to reorganise in terms of them the excellent ideas which Anderson, in a kind of race against death, wrote out in such a hurried, passionate way as to make it very difficult for them to be systematically understood. Availing myself of Reid's principle, I try to show how Anderson opposes to the generalism of the School of Epistemics, which seeks to illuminate natural language and common sense by analysing them in terms of a logic of a modern type, a revitalised version of classicist generalism which seeks to analyse and illuminate common sense in the light of a logic in the Aristotelian tradition though not necessarily identical with that of Aristotle. The systematisation of the ideas in Anderson's last articles in the light of the philosophy of common sense, understood in its classic sense, will, it is hoped, prepare the way for the argument between the old philosophy and the new, which has hitherto failed to materialise in the Scottish universities, to their great loss. My concern is that there should be an argument in which Anderson's case for classicism and against modernism receives a considered assessment in its own intellectual terms and is not hurried over because of the apparent challenge it offers to the fashionable principle of the subordination of the sciences to economic utilities.

Besides its Aristotelian meaning of a faculty distinct from each of the five senses which allows us to establish intersensorial relations, the notion of common sense also appears in the argument which follows with the meaning of shared or public sense, i.e. as social (intersubjective) as well as intersensorial. Each of these meanings of "common sense" can be seen as complementary to, and indeed as implying, the other. Only through other individuals' recognition of us, and through what they communicate to us, do we become aware of our identity as beings who feel and hear and see, etc., that is, as selfsame even while diverse and as continuing as the same (even through periods of unconsciousness) over time. Others give us our sense of bodily continuity and, conversely, it is only in virtue of the relations obtaining between our senses that we can recognise others as other, i.e. as discrete bodily existences in their own right, and so afford to them the recognition which in their turn they are able to afford to us. Reid, although he used "common sense" with both of the meanings here mentioned, never explicitly brought the two meanings together. His failure to do so appears to have stemmed from his concern not to compromise individual free will even by situating it within a network of communal relationships.

Watchwords like "Back to Dunbar", "Back to John Mair" no doubt point in the right direction. But it is too often forgotten, that, properly understood, "Back to Dunbar" points forward, through David Lindsay and George Buchanan, admirer of Dunbar and pupil of Mair, to the Scottish Reformation, the key note and distinguishing feature of which was formulated in Dunbar's lines, "Jok, who was wont to keep the stirks,/Can now draw him ane cleik of kirks,/With ane false carte intil his sleeve".[6] A mixed blessing in many ways, the Reformation in Scotland seems nevertheless to have been remarkable in creating conditions in which, for over three hundred years, the problems of the spirit (especially in reference to intellectual appointments) were discussed independently of the problems of matter, and were, in addition, elevated to a kind of equality with the latter by allowing the populace to participate, to a certain limited extent, in the philosophical debate. Looked at in this light, the slogans "Back to Dunbar", "Back to John Mair", instead of being recommendations to get behind the gloom and doom of 1560 and to work for the achievement of the material Utopia (which, according to Korzybski and many, many others, has been made possible by the reinvention of the non-Aristotelian logic), point forward to the necessity for a revival of a philosophy like that of John Anderson or J. J. Russell which draws attention to the limitations of logical atomism as put forward in the name of the other and far better known Russell.

A side-issue to my present theme, the tensions within the university tradition between the claims of intellectual disinterestedness on the one hand and those of public utility on the other, can be left to readers to study for themselves in Anderson's articles in *Education and Inquiry* as well as in *Studies in Empirical Philosophy* (e.g. 'The Servile State').[7] Concentrating here on the purely epistemological side, I will seek to bring out the value of Reid's Aristotelianised version of common sense as a means of getting round the continuing deadlock between the modernist logic developed in the great universities of the South by men like Russell and Ryle, and the resistance to it on the part of the classical tradition which so long remained alive in the universities of the North, both English and Scottish, and which was subsequently carried on by what one could call the Scottish diaspora — Anderson in Australia, J. J. Russell in the United States and, more recently, MacMurray's pupil Alastair Hannay, lecturing at the University of Trondheim and known internationally as the editor of *Inquiry*.

At first sight difficult to discuss in a well-balanced way, because of the entanglement of traditional and regional loyalties with questions of first principles, the decision between the two sides is facilitated by the circumstance that, in regard to the philosophical point at issue, the poet who identified so closely with his country had turned against the classicist standards still upheld by its universities, and enthusiastically identified with the modernist position as put forward by Russell and those who followed him. Detached, in this way, from national considerations, my argument with Ryle and with Russell is thus at the same time an argument with MacDiarmid, in which it is conceded to him that a logic worked out in modern terms ought to have a more central place in the Scottish curriculum than it has had for a very long time, but in which, it is at the same time implied, the proper way to give logic its due pre-eminence in reference to the other studies is not to impose a non-Aristotelian logic, but to promote some kind of public discussion between its consistency with the rest of philosophy as compared with that of the renovated kind of Aristotelianism introduced by Anderson.

ANDERSON VERSUS RYLE

Launched two years after the war, into a world which was ripe for a change of intellectual fashion, *The Concept of Mind* (1947) made an instant impression. The new generation of philosophical teachers and students were enthralled by the message that philosophy should cease to pontificate to the sciences from a metaphysical pedestal and turn itself into a service industry which could supply them with technical assistance when they called for it. The author's appearance at a philosophical congress was, for the next year or two, regularly greeted by outbursts of applause. Philosophy was evidently once again on the move and vice-chancellors took particular note of the new trend when soon afterwards the universities began to expand. Adherents of a different tradition, the older generation of philosophy teachers were, no doubt, less impressed but, being ill-prepared for the technicalities of the Russellian logic from which the new movement in philosophy drew its inspiration, preserved a prudent silence and refrained from public criticism. The exception, though a somewhat reluctant one, was John Anderson of Sydney who, drawn into conflict with the new philosophy, as the result of a provocative article, 'Logic and Professor Anderson' (1951)[1], from the pen of Professor Gilbert Ryle himself, was slow in meeting the challenge, replying to Ryle some twelve years later in an article posthumously published in 1963. Making up for this lack of immediacy by the vigour of its arguments, Anderson's response concentrated on the Russellian doctrine which, taken over by Ryle and made the centrepiece of his philosophy, has in our time become conventional wisdom as a result of being popularised by Popper. Why, asked Anderson, should there be so widespread a tendency, not only among philosophers but among scientists, to accept as self-evidently true the doctrine that general propositions cannot be established positively but only refuted by experience. Commonly supported by an appeal to the authority of Hume, this claim as to the impossibility of knowing a generalisation to be true on the basis of experience depends, as Anderson pointed out, on accepting as irrefutable the Humean doctrine that experience does not enable us to grasp a necessary connection between two successive events. But this idea of experiencing a causal connection between successive events in on-going experience has become incredible, Anderson says, only because of the impoverished and excessively simplified view of experience which, taken over by Russell from Mill, has in recent times been successfully sold to the public by Popper and Ryle.

Arguing the counter position, Anderson states what is to be, one might say, the first principle of his philosophy. The reason why philosophers of the Russell group deny the experience of causality stems from an over-simplified view according to which things are experienced, not only as cut off from other things, but as being in themselves nothing but bundles of separate qualities. On the contrary, what is given to us in experience are situations consisting in complex and interrelated states of affairs. Properly understood, "empiricism" is the doctrine not of the discontinuity but:

"of the continuity of things — a continuity which would be broken if we could admit different kinds of reality. Professor Gilbert Ryle who [in the article referred to above] criticises my position . . . and particularly endeavours to show the inadequacy of my situational view of things, seems to me to fall conspicuously into errors of discontinuity, of dualism, or division in reality".[2]

This complex view of the nature of the objects of knowledge makes room within the latter for an experience of causality to which Russell, because of his simplified and narrow view of experience, is blind. For Russell what is given, in the first place, is merely the experience of this thing as having some quality, e.g. blue, or this thing as standing in relation to that thing. For Anderson, on the other hand, the experience of this thing as having a quality is inseparable from, and not, as in Russell's doctrine, alternative to, the experience of this same thing as being in a certain relation to that thing. Without denying that the thing's relationship to other things is, as given in experience, distinguishable from the thing's possessing certain qualities, Anderson holds a view not very different from that put forward by Thomas Brown in his *Inquiry into Cause and Effect* "that *the qualities of substances . . . are only another name for their power of affecting other substances*" (italics mine).[3] The point is that, for Anderson, experience conveys to us what the quality of the road surface is, i.e. tarmac and not stone or concrete, only in so far as experience shows it to be melted, i.e. causally affected on a very hot day. The experiences, as it were, gives us knowledge of what the road surface is made of only in so far as they confirm one another. Russell's over-simple description of our root-experience of things, by treating the perception of their qualities as entirely independent of the perception of their interrelationships, leaves no room for any causality-experience:

"The attempt to have separate *relational* and *qualitative* logics [which follows from Russell's making the experience of a thing as having a quality independent to that of its having relations] can only lead to confusion and insoluble problems; what this attempt misses is the fact that any object (any known thing and any existing thing) is a complex situation involving both relations and qualities, so that there will always be connections to be found between any object and any other object."[4]

In the event Anderson's argument seems to have made little impression. Carried away by their belief in the scientific revolution of the twentieth century as providing the means for a materialist Utopia for all mankind, the philosophers against whom he was arguing refused to take seriously what he had said about their over-simplified view of our cognitive situation. In a summing-up of Anderson's position which is meant to be genial and generous but which, in retrospect, sounds somewhat patronising, Ryle tells him that if he had properly understood the contributions made to logic by Russell and his school he would not have denounced them as revolutionary simpletons. Anderson's own position, though he may not himself realise the fact, is really not so different from Russell's. The Russellian logic recognises and faces up to the inextricable complexities which Anderson finds in things just as conscientiously as does the Andersonian situationalism. The difference between the two is that Russell, building on foundations laid by Frege and Peano a logical system which was later to be perfected in the light of work by Wittgenstein, Tarski and Gödel, had provided a scientifically rigorous formulation of the said complexities by discovering his famous contradiction of the "class of all classes", and then gone on to unravel the tangle by inventing "the theory of types".

Far from conciliating Anderson, Ryle's bluff, tough overtures to him provoked a passionate outburst. Putting into print what most of the philosophers of a similar persuasion had always felt about Russell but had cautiously kept to themselves, he denounced the contradiction of classes as an egregious blunder into which Russell had been led through his failure in not making a serious study of the old logic:

"'The contradiction' depends simply on confused views of the notion of 'class'; the class X is just the various things which are X (distributively), what Russell calls 'the class as many', and the question whether this is or is not a member of the class X is the 'question' whether or not the Xs are X, i.e. no question at all. To suggest that there is a problem Russell has to introduce the conception of 'the class as one' and to ask whether *it* is a member of 'the class as many' — but this 'class as one' is just the various things which are *taken collectively*, or *the collection of Xs*, and this is not the same thing (it is not a 'class' at all), which means that there is no such thing as the 'class as one' and the question of what is or is not 'a member of itself' simply does not arise."[5]

Significant enough as a breakthrough of the embarrassed silence which the other philosophers of a Scottish background had universally maintained on the subject of Russell, Anderson's brusque write-off of the contradiction about classes is inadequate as a reply to Ryle. But it contains the germ of an argument which Anderson, if he had lived, could have worked up into a sequel to the two articles written against Russell and in favour of Aristotle — the 'Relational Arguments', also posthumously published, and the 'Hypotheticals' written as a riposte to Ryle in 1952, without however containing any explicit allusion either to Ryle or to Russell. It is, however, difficult to conjecture the precise form Anderson's criticism of Russell on "the theory of types" and "the contradiction of classes" would have taken or whether indeed he would have been able to get over the mental block which had hitherto hindered him from organising for publication his many ideas on the subject. For years he had been projecting a book on the subject of logic which would condemn the modern movement as an aberration, but had found it impossible to sort out his ideas on the subject, even going the length of appealing to Kemp Smith to help him out — in return for a similar service for Kemp Smith in 1922-23 in connection with the latter's *Prolegomena to An Idealist Theory of Knowledge*. Leaving it till later to comment on the value of Anderson's charge that Russell confuses "classes" with "collections", let us take an independent look at what lies behind Russell's contradiction in order to see what we can make of it.

I will begin by stating the main thesis of the "philosophical revolution", as summarised by Ryle in his article on Anderson.

When Russell came across the contradiction of the class of all classes which are not members of themselves, and then found the parallel contradiction of the Liar etc., he was forced to look for a solution in some sort of theory of Logical Types.[6] And the solution, according to Ryle, lies in distinguishing sentences which do not "express" propositions at all from those which do, the "nonsensical" from the "significant". The importance of the theory of types is that is made possible the breakthrough to the twentieth century's discovery of philosophy as being a different *type* of inquiry from science. The former is concerned with distinguishing meaningful utterance from meaningless utterance, the latter with testing the meaningful utterance empirically so as to distinguish the false from the true.

In the light of Anderson's reply, as restated by myself with the help of ideas drawn from thinkers like Samuel Alexander and Kemp Smith, it becomes necessary to cut down to size the claims Ryle makes about Russell. This reworking of Anderson will, I hope, confirm his contention that "the contradiction of the class of all classes which are not members of themselves", far from representing a real discovery on Russell's part, depends on confused views of the nature of class. There is thus, for Anderson, no parallel between the so-called contradiction of classes which results from a mere blunder on Russell's part and the parallel contradiction of the Liar, as brought to light by the Greeks and as kept alive by medieval logicians like John Mair, which as a paradox seems to be much better founded. Our business in this section is wholly with the Liar paradox and, in particular, with the question as to how far its resolution does indeed necessitate the modern notions of the relation of philosophy to science which assigns them to separate spheres and treats them as quite different sorts of inquiry. Anderson, for his part, is far from impressed by the Russellian solution in terms of the theory of types. The clearing up of the paradoxes, he claims in his laconic way, when it is properly done by philosophers who know their business, carries with it "no suggestion of divisions (or higher and lower regions) in reality".

The great objection of Anderson to Russell's innovations in logic and in particular to the doctrine about the paradoxes in logic which forms Ryle's starting point depends on making, in regard to this field, the charge that the revolution in philosophy which the theory of types is said to have sparked off presupposes an atomising view of the world which denies the traditional claims about it as being inextricably complex. When, in the light of their theory of types they assert that science talks about the world while philosophy talks about talk about the world it is only because they divide the world into two unrelated parts — one which is the province of science, the other the province of philosophy.[7]

At first sight this Russell-Ryle position seems to be saying that the sphere of philosophy is not of this world, that to engage in philosophy is to engage in an endless process of self-levitation in which the philosophers soar upwards in search of some ultimate platform affording an overview of the world as studied by natural science, in a quest always doomed to disappointment. But after being warned by Wittgenstein that by treating philosophy as an endless regress one condemns it to be silent, Russell, followed by Ryle, gave philosophy something to say, allowing it to keep its distance from the sciences and yet comment on them by describing the one as talking about the world and the other as talking about talk about the world. The regress is avoided by the pragmatic tactic of pointing out that, practically speaking, one does not need to go beyond talk about talk. The main feature of knowledge, therefore, is the work of the natural sciences in formulating hypotheses about this or that region of the world and testing them experimentally, while philosophy has a kind of back-up role in using its logic to clear up any contradictions in the hypotheses of the sciences which lead them to waste their time discussing meaningless questions.

Anderson has no patience with this redefinition of the relationship of philosophy to the sciences because, as he keeps repeating, it depends on the idea of the world as fragmented. "There is no basis except 'different orders of being' in which it (philosophy) *could*" do that sort of thing, i.e. occupy itself in talking about the way in which the sciences talk about the world. Hence the characteristic claims made by the new philosophy — the belief in divorced realities, the suggestion of fields of inquiry (or fields of reality) which cannot interpenetrate.

This discussion about regions of reality which stands in the way of any coherent theory of mind and body is summed up, for Anderson, in Ryle's characteristic doctrine of the "category-mistake". The great error of traditional philosophy, in Ryle's view, was to have failed to note that the mind-body problem can be discussed clearly and fruitfully only by separating very sharply the investigation of human behaviour so far as it is concerned with movements which can be studied physiologically or actions which can be studied psycho-logically or sociologically, on the one hand, and the investigation of our verbal behaviour in which the concern is with the questions of the meaningfulness or meaninglessness of sentences as raised by modern logic, on the other hand. This latter inquiry is the special field of philosophy.

The philosopher's business is chiefly that of working out the new views of language in the light of the revolutionary distinction between logical constants, i.e. words whose meaning does not depend on their referral to observable facts — words like "and", "or", "if", "not", "all", "some" — and, on the other hand, object-words which get their meaning by referring to observable things. By this kind of technique a sustained effort is made to set aside the insoluble speculations of traditional philosophy about the nature and relations of mind and body — e.g. the old, dualistic ideas of the mental as what is inward and unobservable by contrast with body as the external and observable — which are argued by Ryle to be un-necessary by his pointing out that a distinction which traditionally has been supposed to involve a reference to mentality as something inward — like that between verbs of searching or aiming (e.g. listening and looking) and the corresponding achievement verbs (e.g. hearing, seeing, finding) — also occurs in cases in which the implied mental processes take place without any inwardness as in the distinction between running a race and breasting the tape.

Separations of this kind which, inspired by Russell, are further developed by Ryle, miss the real problem of the relation between mind and body. By contrast a much more fruitful approach is to be found in the tradition of philosophy exemplified in Samuel Alexander's *Space, Time and Deity*, or in Kemp Smith's *Prolegomena to an Idealist Theory of Knowledge*. On this view, which Anderson prefers, natural science and philosophy both "accept as a fact of 'experience' that the mental *is* bodily". Science and philosophy have thus in common a fundamental problem, which the Russell-Ryle methodology seeks to set aside, as to the way in which the develop-ments in body, which we share with the higher animals and which in that sense do not involve the human type of mind, interact with the bodily activities of a specifically human sort which do involve mind. The kind of question which philosophy and the sciences have in common is — to exemplify it rather crudely — whether the higher element of mental activity achieved by human beings as compared with animals (the fact of mankind's search for a coherent world picture) is due to some behavioural or perceptual factor such as the emergence of a grasping hand or of binocular vision, or of the systematic connection of sight with touch as involved in human labour, or of the division of labour as the characteristic feature of human society.

The sciences and philosophy thus have a fundamental problem in common and what distinguishes the work of the philosopher is that he approaches this problem from a different point of view from the natural scientist. The philosopher is concerned with the fact that whether the scientists are studying the emergence of the human mind from the animal mind or are studying the relationship of living matter to inanimate matter, their specialised science, whatever it is — psychology, biology or chemistry — is concerned with *classification and discovering causes*: "what we call *method* or, more exactly, *knowing* method (knowledge of method on the part of the scientist) *is* knowing that any subject we are examining has causes, has genera, as a matter of actual fact". Now it is this latter fact — the preoccupation with the question of what kind, what cause — which defines the area of coincidence between the philosopher's work and that of the scientist. "The primary point is that logical questions arise where any question arises"[8] in the sense that the programme of the scientist — that of explaining in exact detail whether and how life emerges from matter and mind from life — cannot be carried through without raising philosophical questions about what theory of universals and what theory of causality is well founded from a logical point of view. Requiring discussion, both from a systematic point of view and from a historical one, the issues, in regard to which the scientists are obliged to refer to philosophy, have to do with very difficult questions as to the relationship between identity and diversity as it expresses itself in the distinction between the individual and the class of which it is a member and, on the other hand, identity and diversity as it expresses itself in the distinction between the causal relationship a given event has with some of its antecedents and the apparently causal relationship it has with others of its antecedents.

In virtue of holding these views, Anderson has a very different conception of the relationship of philosophy to the sciences from the views on the subject entertained by Russell, by Ryle, and their disciples. Far from philosophy and science being concerned with separate fields, each of them is concerned "with situational reality, with the spatio-temporal field, with things as they, in a single sense, are". What distinguishes them is that philosophy is concerned with the forms of situations, science with their material, but it is only as forms of such material or material of such forms that they (the situations) can be known. But this means that the work of inquiry, if it is to be carried on, must be *at once* scientific and philosophical.

But, this being so, an important consequence seems to follow from Anderson's view which he himself does not make explicit enough — that there is a certain reciprocity between the work of the philosopher and the work of the special scientist. If the latter is not philosophical he will fall into confusion about the nature of classification and causal influence because his view of them will be coloured by the peculiarities of the region of the world which is his special field. If he is concerned with a department where accurate measurement is possible and where experiments can be repeated he will get a different view of what knowing consists in than would be the case if he were concerned with a field of a more biological or historical character in which measurement presents peculiar problems and in which change is the rule rather than recurrence. In the same way if the philosopher is not scientific, if he cuts himself off from the special scientists, his general theories of classification or of discovering causes will go wrong because, being unaware of the ambiguities which the application of these principles to this or that region reveal, the excessive abstraction and generality of his discussions will tend to obscure rather than illumine the problems he is concerned with. Just as the narrow view of the special scientists, owing to their preoccupation with details to the neglect of the whole, requires to be criticised in the light of the generalities of philosophy, so the errors to which philosophy is liable, through an excessive preoccupation with the whole to the neglect of the details, can produce a kind of difficulty which the special scientists are in a position to help with, if they can meet philosophy halfway in a sort of dialogue.

By contrast the view of the relations of philosophy to the sciences in the hierarchical scheme of Russell and Ryle involves a one-sided relationship in which philosophy comments from above on the scientist's description of the world without there being any room for a feedback from the "lower" level which might keep the philosophers right. Instead, this Russellian scheme expects the oversights of the philosophers to be corrected, in their turn, by the supervision of some still more rarified and general discipline which looks down on the philosophers from a still higher level. Their philosophy thus, in the last analysis, seems to involve the knowledge-process in a never-ending regress in which philosophy turns its back on the world and vanishes into the blue.

In order to sharpen the point at issue between Anderson and those he is criticising here, the chief thing required is to do something to clear up the difficulties which he perversely puts in the way of his own thesis by his refusal to work it out in a detailed way. To do this, I propose to argue that Anderson's social view of the relations of philosophy to science is best understood as a different and, I claim, superior way of coping with the same problem as Russell's and Ryle's *de haut en bas* view, namely the problem of the logical paradox implicit in the famous statement, "Epimenides, the Cretan, said that all Cretans are liars". According to the view developed in Russell's theory of types, Epimenides can get out of the logical tangle only by limiting his statement in the sense of specifying what kind of liars the Cretans are, e.g. if he were to say that all Cretans are liars in the sense of their always being unreliable in their first-hand report about things, i.e. in their *talk about the world* then he has cleared himself of the charge of contradiction because in saying that, as a Cretan, he is not talking about the world, but commenting on or talking about their talk about the world. Or again, if he were to say that Cretans are never to be trusted in their comments on their first-hand talk about the world then, once again, he is all right because he himself, as a Cretan, is talking about them in their role as commentators on these first-hand reports about the world, and is therefore not indulging in the talk about talk about the world which he is condemning as always untrustworthy. Of course the same charge can be brought against the Cretans and their talk at still more rarified levels, but Epimenides will always get into the clear by pointing out that he himself is not speaking on that level but on the one above.

The alternative, social way of resolving the paradox is best approached by the comments on Russell of a philosopher who, though in other respects very unlike Anderson, nevertheless is at one with him in acknowledging profound indebtedness both to Samuel Alexander and John Burnet, namely A. D. Ritchie. I quote from his *Essays in Philosophy* some critical comments on Russell:

"Undoubtedly there are logical questions which are purely linguistic. A notable instance is one of Lord Russell's own contributions to the theory of logical types. The sentence 'all assertions made in English are false' apparently fails to say anything. Translate the sentence into French and then it says something. It is capable of being true or false. This shows that the failure to say anything in English is purely linguistic. A linguistic disease requires a linguistic cure and this Lord Russell has provided. Unfortunately his theory has led some writers to produce nightmare speculations about 'meta-languages', on the hypothesis that language cannot discuss or criticise itself. On the contrary, that is what the careful use of language is always doing. Discussion, properly carried out, is simultaneously clarification of fact and of language."[9]

Without saying much more about Ritchie I want to claim that the central idea in what he says advances greatly our understanding of the chief point at issue between Russell's hierarchical solution of the Liar paradox and the social solution which seems to me to be implicit in Anderson. Whereas the Russellian approach holds that the "do-it-yourself" movements, in which Epimenides soliloquises about the qualities of himself and his fellow nationals, is sufficient if we introduce the idea of levels of language to enable him to give vent to *limited* criticisms of his people's (and his own) mendacity, without entangling himself in nonsense, the approach appropriate to Anderson's position — interpreted in Ritchie's terms — shows how if Epimenides, instead of talking solely to himself, enters into a dialogue with a member of another national group and leaves the decision to his foreign interlocutor, the issue of whether all Cretans — himself included — are liars can be settled; not only without his involving himself in talking nonsense, but also in the unlimited sense of "all" which Russell's restrictions rule out. Explicitly put, Ritchie's point is that, whereas the statement "all Cretans are liars" when said by Epimenides, the Cretan, simultaneously affirms and denies itself or, in other words, says nothing in much the same sense as "all statements made in English are false" says nothing, the same general assertion as to the untrustworthy character of all Cretans, if Epimenides lets Socrates the Athenian do the talking, not merely becomes intelligently discussable, but also begins to make sense, in much the same way as "all statements made in English are false" begins to say something and becomes discussable as soon as it is translated into French. Indeed, when the discussion of the matter is left to Socrates, the Athenian, it would not take him long to show the falsity of the statement, understood as an unrestricted generality, that all the Cretans utter nothing but falsehoods all of the time. Such an assertion would be shown by Socrates to be in complete contradiction to the known fact that the survival of Crete as an independent community depends upon the prevalence among the Cretans of a reasonable standard of veracity, both in their dealings with other countries and in their individual dealings with one another.

Moreover, in the course of hearing the question of Cretan

mendacity cleared up by Socrates, Epimenides becomes aware of the general and important fact that there are certain questions about the qualities of any given group which cannot be answered except by reference to what is said in conversation with them by members of some other group. Finally, the hesitations of Epimenides are cleared up by the discovery, made in the course of his conversation with Socrates, that the Athenians, in their turn, are not in a position to discuss intelligibly the question of their own mendacity as a nation, but are dependent for a decision in the matter on the Cretans or some other foreign group in precisely the same way as the Cretans are dependent on them.

Generalising, we may suggest that this social solution depends on a principle which seems altogether to escape Russell, namely, that owing to certain systematic limitations in one's self-perception — e.g. one's inability to observe oneself during sleep — certain essential qualities of oneself, in particular the alternation between consciousness and unconsciousness, are known to one not directly but indirectly, by having one's attention drawn to them by another, e.g. the person who wakes one up. This is a matter to which I shall return at the proper place. For the present it will be sufficient if I illustrate the subject further by showing that some of the other paradoxes of self-reference can be resolved by Ritchie's principles more effectively than on Russell's. Take the paradox of the barber which arises if you "define a barber as one who shaves all those, and those only, who do not shave themselves". Contradictions analogous to those of the Liar arise if one puts the question as to whether the barber shaves himself. Now, according to Russell, the contradiction here, though it can be resolved easily enough, is not resolved on the same principle as enables us to resolve the Liar paradox. The Ritchie approach, however, seems to make possible a social solution parallel to that which works in the case of the Liar. The statement "the barber shaves those, and those only, who do not shave themselves" leads to contradictions only when the barber is a man and not when the barber is a woman. Indeed, an analogous contradiction can be made to arise in the case when it is said that a gynaecologist treats the condition of sufferers who do not seek to cure themselves. The trouble here comes about only when the gynaecologist is a woman.

A more interesting and instructive case is to be found in Russell's other paradox "all rules have exceptions". Russell's solution depends on the hypothesis that language cannot discuss or criticise itself and raises what Ritchie calls "nightmare speculations about meta-languages" — that is to say we can avoid the paradox by drawing the same distinctions as before between rules about things, rules about rules about things, and so on. But, as I have pointed out, Ritchie denies the idea that language cannot discuss or criticise itself.

The problem, common to both theories — Russell's and the one opposed to him — is that of explaining how the paradoxical statement, "all rules have exceptions" may be shown to say something meaningful, and so freed from contradiction. The distinguishing character of a position like that of Ritchie, which is also that of Anderson, is a feature of which the latter constantly reminds us. If we are to understand knowledge, its object has to be seen as a complex situation, interlocked with other complex situations of a different character. Getting knowledge thus has to be described in terms of the social metaphor first found in Plato's *Theaetetus* as involving a debate within the mind in which the rules governing the behaviour of the thing under consideration reveal themselves only in the process of discovering how they are limited and checked by counter rules also inherent in the situation by reason of its being interlocked with other situations. For example, in engineering, the rules governing the strength of materials cannot be worked out in a given case without reference to the weather conditions of the place where the building is to be. Or, again, in social studies, the rules about the way in which an increase of specialisation can increase the wealth of a community, cannot be properly ascertained without reference to the limiting consideration that the extension of specialisation, if carried too far, stultifies and demoralises a community and so tends to be counter-productive. The process of working this out makes it possible to distinguish the sense from the nonsense in the paradoxical proposition "all rules have exceptions".

By contrast, as Anderson never tires of reminding us, the reason why Russell, in order to get rid of the contradiction, has recourse to his hierarchy of distinctions between rules about behaviour of things and rules about these rules, etc., is that, for him, the object confronting us in knowledge is not a complex situation involving simultaneously rules and counter-rules, but consists of a series of separately given facts which, in the process of being co-ordinated, present us with an uncomplicated rule about the behaviour of the thing under consideration, e.g. what we first learn is a straightforward rule like "sugar is always sweet" and the question of the possibility of exceptions to this rule arises only at the higher level where we are discussing rules about rules.

At first sight, it might seem puzzling that Gilbert Ryle, in spite of his considerable differences from Russell, nevertheless makes a point of siding with Russell in reference to the problem of the logical paradoxes, and does not identify with the rival view on the subject to be found in the work of Alexander, Ritchie or Anderson. In the chapter in *The Concept of Mind* on the subject of self-knowledge without privileged access, Ryle seems to be cognisant enough of the possibility of avoiding the endless regress involved in the hierarchical view of self-consciousness and self-criticism by taking, very much as Alexander does, the social view of self-consciousness as constituted by mutual awareness. Why, it may be asked, does Ryle, who is certainly by no means ignorant of the alternative view, given in the *Theaetetus*, of our knowledge of things as involving a kind of internalised debate or dialogue modelled on the experience of arguing with other people, nevertheless come out strongly in favour of the idea, implicit in Russell's treatment of the paradoxes, of self-consciousness or self-criticism as achievable only in solitary retro-spection and at the price of being, in Ryle's own memorable phrase, "always a day late for the fair"? So far as I can see, the fact which, for Ryle, decides the issue in favour of Russell is the new and, as Ryle thinks, revolutionary view of the relation of philosophy to the natural sciences which seems to result from Russell's technical analysis as in the theory of types. If one wants to defend the value of philosophy in twentieth-century Britain, one must not, Ryle thought, make excessive claims for it, but rather encourage it to be content with a subordinate role.

In *The Concept of Mind*, Ryle puts forward some arguments in defence of the Russellian view of self-criticism as involving an endless regress, but the points he makes seem to me to be capable of being answered. A singing master, he says, can criticise a pupil's vocal performance by parodying it while it is still in progress, for example, by raising his own voice in song. But, Ryle goes on, if he wants, in a spirit of self-mockery, to parody his own singing, his vocalised self-criticism cannot, in the same way, coincide in time with his first-order performance but has to take place only after it is finished. What Ryle says, however, is true only if the singing master's self-criticism takes a vocal form. But he can get over this limitation and parody his own singing before it has run its course if he relies on histrionic gestures which will draw the attention of his listeners to the excessive theatricality, for example, of his own on-going performance as a tenor. The famous comedian, George Robey, regularly used the device of simultaneously saying something which, in its context, sounded perfectly innocent, while, at the same time, drawing attention to the *double entendre* by raising his eyebrows.

In support of his position, Ryle produces another example. One can, he says, do a review of a book and one can also write a review of one's own review of the book, but the former, he says, has to be done in a separate article after the latter is published. Ryle's claim here is, however, contradicted in his very next chapter on the subject of 'Observation and Sensation'. He includes, near the beginning, a warning that the analysis he is doing is not adequate to the problem because he is giving the word 'sensation' the meaning it currently has in contemporary discussion, rather than the meaning which it ought to have. Indeed, towards the end of the chapter, he repeats the caveat that his conclusions have to be taken with a grain of salt and modified in the light of what he has not written on the same subject but may write later.

What matters, of course, is the general principle. The defect of Ryle, both in this case and in the former, arises from the fact that, like Russell, he has an excessively simplified view of the scope of our self-knowledge and of the ways we have of expressing it. We do not know the review we are doing only as a set of sentences which we watch ourselves writing. We can also think of it and refer to it as a performance which we expect ourselves to be able to look back to in the future and to congratulate ourselves on or criticise ourselves for retrospectively, as the case may be. In this way we can introduce into our review reflections on the quality of our performance which draw attention to its shortcomings.

The issues raised here are, however, very complicated. It could therefore be pointed out with some justice, in the interest of Ryle's side of the case, that some of the philosophers I am representing as wholly opposed to him, because of ambiguities in their positions, are liable to the very same criticisms as I have been bringing against him. In particular, passages can be quoted from Anderson which seem to exhibit him as holding, in reference to the problem of our self-knowledge, the Rylean doctrine — or something very like it — that we are always a day late for the fair:

"In relation to the position that knowledge is a relation between two different things, my knowing myself presents a difficulty [as to how I am to distinguish the myself who knows from the myself who is known by me] but to one who treats of *acts* of mind, there should be no difficulty. . . . The fact that there are many acts of mind show how it is possible for a man to know his own mind; one act can know another, or any group of others . . . without being required to know itself for, in knowing the mind that calls itself 'I', it does not know all about it, it knows it only as certain particular events or acts."[10]

But here the question has to be put to Anderson as to how this act of mind which, according to him, knows those other acts can itself be made an object of knowledge to itself. It might be thought that the very same regress difficulty, as we found in Ryle as well as Russell, has occurred in Anderson. But whatever the adequacy of Anderson's discussion of the problem of being "always a day late for the fair", of having still on his plate one act of mind which knows the others without being able to know itself — and indeed I have heard distinguished pupils of Anderson say that he simply accepted the regress in his philosophy without being in the least embarrassed by it — the fact of the matter, as I myself understand the problem of self-knowledge, is that this unknown act of mind which knows the other acts of mind itself becomes an object of knowledge to me because these other acts of mind which it knows reciprocally know it. Each act is known to me (the mind which calls itself 'I').

As set forth in the pared-down language of Anderson, the formula suggested here, as a way round the regress difficulty, is perhaps too abstract to convey easily what it means. But its power and value at once seem to me to be put into evidence when one states it in more concrete terms as referring to the inter-relationship of acts of mind to one another as they are held to function in the little known but very stimulating theories of perception as put forward by philosophers like Adam Smith and Ferrier. The acts of mind which are involved in our experience of touching things, acts by which we are aware of the things as hard or soft and having certain palpable shapes without our as yet being properly aware of how they function as acts of mind, nevertheless make the person who does the touching aware, in regard to his visual, auditory and olfactory experience, of the relationship between the eye, the ear, the nose as the respective means or organs of our colour-consciousness, our sound-consciousness, and our smell-consciousness. They do so, on the one hand, as related to the body which touch reveals as existing independently of and outside these sense organs in our own bodies, and, on the other, as qualified by, or as providing a location for, the colours and other qualities known to us as perceived by our sense organs. The important point here is that it is touch, not sight, which is in a position to inform us of the existence, location and function of our eyes because of the impossibility of our discovering through our own visual experience the preconditions of the emergence of that visual experience, e.g. we cannot watch ourselves switch on the light in a completely dark room; the same principle seems to hold for hearing and smell.

But now, what is it that reveals to us the distinction between the finger or whatever organ makes us conscious of tactual feeling, on the one hand, and on the other, the extra-organic body, the existence and nature of which is revealed to us by the organ of touch? Apparently, the knowledge here cannot, in its fullest extent, be acquired by us without some distance-sense like vision which is in a position to tell us what our touch can never tell us, that our experience of the bodies felt — their shape, hardness etc. — arises when they come into contact with our hand or other organ of touch, and that when we cease to feel the bodies through the sensation of their contact with our organ of touch they still continue to exist as objects of our vision even when they are quite beyond our reach. This knowledge of continuing existence out of reach would also doubtless be in some way learned by hearing and smelling as well as some sight. This information that the bodies exist out of reach is no doubt the key fact for the understanding of the distinction between the act of touch and the object of touch. But we have to note also that because the tactual sense is what the old philosophers called a general sense (meaning that our whole bodily surface is tactually sensitive), our hands, as well as co-operating with one another as one complex organ of touch in the exploration of the world, can also work as independent organs of touch which can engage in the tactual explorations of one another in the sense that the left hand can supply us tactually with the knowledge of the relations of our right hand to the bodies whose tactual qualities this latter is revealing to us. There are, however, limitations on the knowledge which our tactual organs of sense (hands) acting separately, can give in regard to one another. That is the reason why the key to the paradoxes of touch is given us in regard to ourselves by our eyes and our other distance-senses and not by touch alone.

I 2

SELF-CONSCIOUSNESS AND MUTUAL CONSCIOUSNESS

It follows from what I have been arguing that, in addition to the strengths, there are also certain weaknesses in Anderson's argument against the position taken up by Russell and Ryle. We can see at once what these weaknesses are by reminding ourselves of the point at issue between the two parties as to whether the relationship between philosophy and the sciences involves a kind of hierarchy, on the lowest level of which the scientists have the special task of discovering the regularities in the facts they observe, while philosophy, looking down from above, comments on the consistency of the scientist's hypotheses, or whether, as Anderson seems to be saying, philosophy and the sciences are engaged in observing the world on the same level and debate as to how the aspects of the world interesting to the philosophers, for example, its pervasive features like causality and generality, are related to the side which interests the scientists, for example the features differentiating one region from another. Anderson, for his part, thinks that the question can be settled in his favour by his drawing attention to the fact that the world is a complex of inseparable interacting tendencies and not, as Russell and Ryle would seem to have it, a collocation of facts which are devoid of intrinsic connections and of which the regularities can be discovered only in a piecemeal manner. But though this point is indeed one of great value for Anderson's position in the sense that he regards the observation of the world by the sciences and philosophy as essentially a debate on the subject of the ambiguities and conflicting tendencies embodied in every situation to be investigated, he nevertheless goes on in the sequel to make difficulties for himself, by taking up positions on the question of our knowledge of minds — our own and other people's — very similar in many respects to the positions taken up by Ryle and Russell. Whereas the relation of philosophy and the sciences is, for Anderson, a dialogue on one level and not a one-sided regressive movement from level to level, he nevertheless, as we have just seen, seems content with a view of self-knowledge which represents it not as a reciprocal affair of the correction of the senses by one another but as a movement in which we never catch up with ourselves, i.e. in which the act of mind or act of sense which knows the other senses itself must always remain unknown.

This tendency in Anderson's philosophy to adopt positions surprisingly similar to the very thinkers — Ryle and Russell — whose positions, in general, he regards as wrong-headed, and entirely repudiates, while at the same time he dissociates himself from the "anti-Ryle" positions of philosophers like Alexander for whom, in general, he professes the utmost respect, becomes very evident when he takes up the topic of our knowledge of other minds, both in itself and in its relation to our knowledge of our own mind. "Behaviourism," he declares, in a comment which might have been made by Ryle, "is to be commended in that it insists on dealing with what is observed and rejecting the 'inner light'. . . . But since the behaviourists do not realise that minds are observed just as other things are."[1] The key to a solution of the problem, according to Anderson, is to be found in the fact that knowledge of mind is obtained as much by observation of other people's minds as by observing one's own. Once this is realised:

"it can no more be contended that, as psychologists, we are interested in other minds only in a secondary and subsidiary way, and that our own minds remain as the essential subject of our inquiries and the test of all the rest, than that, as physiologists, we are primarily concerned with our own bodies and only secondarily with others."[2]

These remarks, no doubt, are all right as far as they go. The difficulty with them is that they do not tell us how observation of other people's behaviour — what they say and what they do — aids us to achieve a knowledge of our own behaviour, as a creature having a mind like theirs, i.e. like those who address us, chide us, comfort us, etc. If Anderson means, that by imitating them, by speaking as they do and by acting towards others as they act towards us, the position he is taking up looks like involving the question of the foundation of our knowledge of ourselves as having minds in an endless and inextricable regress. We learn to behave like creatures having human minds from someone of an older generation, no doubt, who, himself or herself, has learned "the trick" of self-conscious behaviour from some third party who has learned how to be human — from whom, we ultimately do not know, because we seem to have landed in this regress.

Now I do not claim to know Anderson's exact position on the subject, since so much of his philosophy still remains unpublished. But at the same time, it ought to be pointed out that, in his published remarks on Samuel Alexander's theory of the relationship of our knowledge of other minds to our knowledge of our own mind, Anderson concentrates his attention on criticising Alexander for not "rejecting the concept of a subject", for i.e. retaining what Anderson regards as the indefensible idea of "inwardness", of a "private consciousness". At the same time, occupied in denunciations similar to Ryle's of the idea of a person as having a privileged access to a realm of feeling, hidden from other people, Anderson fails to say anything about the fruitful theory evolved by Alexander which avoids the regress of self-knowledge by exhibiting the sense in which it consists in the kind of mutual illumination of each person by the other.

Let us glance at Alexander's treatment of this subject in order to show that it involves the kind of theory, in regard to the knowledge of mind, our own and other people's, which Anderson himself ought to have developed if he was to avoid the regressive idea of mind and make its existence depend on the mutual communication in a kind of debate:

"We are led," Alexander says, "not of course to the enjoyment of ourselves [being Alexander's word for inward or private experience, whether pleasurable or painful] but to noticing ourselves, through intercourse with the others: the knowledge of ourselves and that of others grow up together. Our own individuality stands out for us against a background of other persons. Were we alone in a non-conscious world, we should enjoy ourselves and feel success and disappointment, but we should hardly experience ourselves as individual persons."[3]

Alexander here is repeating what Adam Smith says in his *Theory of Moral Sentiments*. Smith's point is the weighty one that an individual human being, brought up without communication with its own kind, would in some sense be *empirically* aware, i.e. observe his elation in the case of the success of his projects and his disappointment in the case of his failure to get what he wants, but what he cannot at this stage observe, and therefore knows nothing about, is the expression of that elation or disappointment as they manifest themselves in the external bodily reactions to the situation exhibited in his face etc. because of the fact that, not being born with a mirror in his hand, he is not able to observe these parts of himself. On the contrary, what first draws his attention to these outward manifestations of his feelings and teaches him gradually to control his countenance is the fact that, in the observable reactions of the bystanders to the changes in his behaviour, occasioned by success or failure in what he is doing, he is, as Smith points out, provided with a sort of mirror which shows him qualities of himself incapable of being directly observed by him — qualities exhibited not merely in his face, but in his general behaviour. The experience in which one has one's attention drawn to the bodily expressions of one's feelings as well as of one's thoughts by observing the way the other behaves to us, is, Alexander well says, a two-way process — "an experience of sociality", i.e. an experience "of a response on our part to the other being, confirmed by a response on his part to us. The double experience is necessary to sociality; it takes two persons to make friends or two persons to make a quarrel."[4]

But the most important case, surely, for our getting knowledge of our own body as possessing the quality of consciousness, is where we learn from observing others' behaviour to us that we have been asleep, i.e. unconscious. Alexander, I believe, did a notable service in calling attention to the essential part played by others in our learning that we are sometimes conscious, sometimes unconscious; "from the reports of others we learn (as Leibniz observes) that we have continued to exist in sleep and can think of ourselves as existing in the interval, because we in turn have observed others to live in sleep while from their reports they have not been conscious of the interval".[5] Criticising Leibniz, Alexander goes on to suggest that such experiences as Leibniz draws attention to supplement but do not provide the direct consciousness we have of the mental unity of our experience as being broken by gaps which, looking back, we experience as containing nothing.

However, I myself am not impressed by the distinction he draws between the experience of two events *immediately* following one another with nothing in between, and two events experienced as having nothing in between, in the sense of being related by a felt interval in which nothing happens.[6] A better way out of the difficulty could, I think, be found by drawing on the description which Descartes gives of our ordinary experience in the last pages of the sixth Meditation. When we look back from our present to our past what we find is a succession of events which seems unbroken in the sense of each succeeding the other immediately, but which is also experienced as broken in another sense, viz. that when we look back we find relatively coherent systems of events which prepare for and connect with the present we are living through, on the one hand, and, on the other hand, odd events which we call dreams and which punctuate and divide the normal course of things. It is the memory of being wakened by other people out of our dreams which calls our attention to the fact that our bodies have been existing for others and not for ourselves and which gives us awareness of alternation in our lives between being conscious and being unconscious. We learn more about this side of things by comparing the experience of being wakened from a dreamless sleep with that of being wakened from a dream.

As Schelling says, it is the experience of being roused up by others and of observing, in the process, the way they behave towards us in their looks, gestures, etc. which provides us with a mirror showing us, albeit indirectly, the fact of our having been asleep.[7] No doubt the mind has to make a kind of leap here, if it is to become aware of its periods of unconsciousness, but it is an important leap, critical for the emergence of our humanity. Alexander would have done well to have stuck to the mirror theory pioneered by Adam Smith and Leibniz and thereafter taken up by Schelling.

Alexander's account of our knowledge of one another's minds is thus by no means satisfactorily worked out from a logical point of view, and he himself seems to admit this limitation in that he uses the word "assurance" not "knowledge" to describe the way in which we are aware of the other's mind. At the same time, however, his discussion is fruitful in pointing to facts which make possible a more adequate account. In this respect his criticism of the "analogical argument for the existence of other minds" is important. "The analogy of behaviour is not what assures us of the existence of other minds", because "in general the part which the two participants play in the social situation is not the same but different".[8] Before the mutual communication takes place, and when I am a mere spectator of the other, what observation shows me are the differences between the other and myself — the other is, as I observe him, by turns asleep and awake, whereas I never observe myself except as being always awake. What happens when the mutual exchanges begin in the sense of our eyes meeting is that, in a flash, we become aware of one another as each being dependent on the other for the knowledge of the breaks in our consciousness due to sleep or inattention.

Alexander's theory of our consciousness of one another, on the view I am taking of it, rests on a principle which is better stated by

Kemp Smith than it is by himself. We are not and we cannot be, Kemp Smith never tires of repeating, conscious of the foundations of our own consciousness, i.e. of the conditions, physical, psychological, etc., which make possible its emergence. "The mind can unfold its contents in the sunshine of consciousness only because its roots strike deep into a soil that the light does not penetrate."[9] What Alexander adds to the point made by Kemp Smith is the claim that the physical preconditions of our consciousness, of which we are not directly aware, can be brought to our notice indirectly in our experience of the attitude towards us on the part of other people.

The positions taken up here by Alexander and Kemp Smith seem to have had little appeal for Anderson who, on this subject, says: "if we *are* acquainted with our minds, then we may, as Moore puts it, reasonably suppose a similar mind to exist in similar, observed circumstances."[10] Anderson is not too easy to follow here, but it looks as if he has not fully taken Alexander's point about analogy. If, as Alexander says, we are acquainted with our own mind, in the sense, e.g. of observing ourselves working out a theorem in geometry — drawing the figure, putting in the appropriate construction, citing previously proved theorems which we take for granted — then Moore is right in suggesting that when we see somebody else similarly occupied in drawing a geometrical figure, putting in the construction, etc., we are entitled to suppose the existence of another mind similar to our own. But, in accepting Moore's claim that there is an analogy here, Anderson seems to have been unaware of the fact, implicit in Alexander's remarks and subsequently made explicit in some of Sartre's descriptions, that watching ourselves writing a letter is very different from watching another writing a letter. In the case of the other, we see his hesitations, his lapses in attention, his spasms of feeling as they are outwardly expressed in his behaviour and his looks, whereas, in our own case, the corresponding qualities do not appear to be manifested in our own behaviour because of the limitations in principle which make it impossible for us to observe ourselves as we can observe the other — e.g. we cannot vary our standpoint in regard to ourselves in the way that we can in regard to him by altering our distance, and we cannot catch ourselves in a momentary lapse into complete inattention in the same direct way that we can witness this in the other.

The point I have been labouring is that the regress of self-knowledge of which Ryle makes so much and which receives its classic formulation, in modern times, in the Russellian theory of types, was, in traditional philosophy, blocked off by a principle of reciprocity, expounded by Adam Smith, Hegel, etc., and revived in this century by Alexander. Applied to the problem of how we can know our senses with our senses, the reciprocity principle was put by Ferrier in the form "sight pays back every fraction of its debt to its brother-sense touch". Applied in Hegel's *Phenomenology* to the problem of how we are conscious of our own consciousness, the principle takes the shape of the doctrine that self-recognition is inseparable from mutual recognition.

The problems which are resolved by introducing the reciprocity principle seem to have been understood by Russell himself who states them with his usual clarity:

"The visual appearance of a human body to the person to whom it belongs has certain characteristic differences from its visual appearance to others — for example, it can contain neither eyes nor back, and the nose (if made to appear by closing one eye) looks more vast and portentous than to anyone else. We can thus define two classes, one consisting of visual appearance of bodies to their owners, the other of visual appearances related by the laws of perspective to what I see when I 'see you'."[11]

Or, again, Russell raises the problem of the social element in self-consciousness by asking how he knows that "Neurath says so-and-so". Russell answers:

"By seeing certain black marks on a white ground. But this experience must not, according to Neurath and Hempel, be made a ground for my assertion that Neurath says so-and-so. Before I can assert this, I must ascertain the opinion of mankind and especially of my culture circle, as to what Neurath says. But how am I to ascertain it? I go round to all the scientists of my culture circle and say: What does Neurath say on page 364? In reply I hear certain sounds, but this is an experience and therefore does not give any ground for an opinion as to what they said. When A answers, I must go round to B, C, D, and the rest of my culture circle to ascertain what they think A said. And so on throughout an endless regress."[12]

Why does Russell not proceed to elucidate and evaluate the reciprocity principle when he is so evidently cognisant of the complications in the nature of self-consciousness which led Adam Smith and Hegel to formulate it? The reasons behind Russell's failure to follow up this line are worth exploring because of the light they throw on the limitations of the whole school of philosophy connected with Russell. The fact is that he was caught up in, and fascinated by, the fashionable problem of constructing an artificial language, organised on his hierarchical principles, which would provide a touchstone for distinguishing between what was meaningful and what was meaningless in the phraseology of the natural languages. The test for ordinary statements, made in ordinary language, was to be whether or not they could be translated into this technical language, which was to serve as a model.

The circumstance which deflected the interest of Russell and his friends from the ideas of the traditional philosophers about the connection of self-consciousness and mutual consciousness was the difficulty that a principle essential to the modern logic and exemplified in the so-called truth tables — the principle of the relationship of molecular propositions to the atomic propositions which are their constituents — does not apply to a kind of molecular statement in ordinary language, which expresses what Russell calls a "propositional attitude" or what other philosophers would have called "self-consciousness" — as when it is said that somebody knows a certain truth, e.g. Newton's law of gravity. The precise circumstance, as I understand it, which makes these molecular statements in ordinary language about propositional attitudes refractory to the rule which governs the relation, in other cases, of molecular propositions to their constituent atomic propositions, has to do with the fact that whereas the constituent propositions are, in other cases, logically independent of one another, and can have some meaning outside the molecular proposition, the constituent proposition which is vital to molecular propositions expressing propositional attitudes does not seem to be in the same way logically independent of the other constituents — a fact which phenomenologically-minded metaphysicians strive to capture in their slogan "All consciousness is consciousness of . . .". The point is that, whereas in the case of a molecular proposition like "if p, then q", both the statement made in p and the statement made in q can be asserted in separation from one another, things are quite other with the molecular proposition "I know p" in the sense that the "I know" does not have a proper meaning (is incomplete) and conveys nothing if asserted in separation from a statement of what it is that I know. The principle, essential to the construction of the logician's perfect language is that if a proposition p occurs as part of a larger proposition q, i.e. as a constituent in a so-called molecular proposition, the truth-value of q remains unchanged if we substitute for p any proposition having the same truth-value. This means, in Russell's illustration that "the proposition 'if Homer was an Irishman, I'll eat my hat' . . . will remain true if we substitute 'Brian Boru was a Greek'". But now nonsensical results, Russell says, follow if one tries to clarify and analyse ordinary language statements about propositional attitudes by applying to them the same principle of substitution as worked in the case of "if p, I'll eat my hat". The truth of this latter molecular proposition is not affected whether one takes p as speaking about Homer or as speaking about Brian Boru. On the other hand, to follow this principle in the case of "A knows p", it would appear to be the case that the truth of "A knows p" is not in the least affected whether p — the truth A is said to know — is about Newton's law of gravity or about the law of scansion in the metres of Plautus. Thus it is clear that nonsensical results follow if one clarifies ordinary statements about propositional attitudes by applying to them the principle of substitution. "If A believes p and p is true, it does not follow that A believes all true propositions; nor, if p is false, does it follow that A believes all false propositions." Trying to bring the molecular propositions about propositional attitudes under the ordinary rules thus commits logic to the indefensible principle of *falsus in uno, falsus in omnibus* or *verus in uno, verus in omnibus*.[13]

In the event, however, the difficulties of the situation were still further aggravated by the solution of the problem suggested by Russell's brilliant follower, Wittgenstein, and largely accepted by the school as pointing the way ahead, if not as giving the final answer. The needful clarification was effected, according to Wittgenstein, only by the drastic step of abolishing altogether, as a superstition, the traditional idea of the self as a principle of unity which connected one idea with another, where ordinary language speaks of A as believing p, of A as thinking p, of A as saying p — all it means, when the nonsense is winnowed out by the principle of substitution, is that "p" says p, i.e. that a certain utterance is conveying a meaning. The result of his analysis shows, Wittgenstein claims, "that there is no such thing as the soul — the subject, etc. — as it is conceived in contemporary superficial psychology".[14] Fired with an enthusiasm for the programme of reconstructing ordinary language so as to eliminate what seemed to them the nonsensical ideas of interiority, self-identity, etc., the new philosophers turned their backs on the older theories which explained self-consciousness in terms of mutual awareness and in spite of the fact that Wittgenstein himself, and to a lesser extent, Russell, dissociated themselves from the enterprise, the reductionist crusade still continues hopefully in departments of the higher linguistics, schools of artificial intelligence, and institutes for the study of advanced epistemics.

No doubt these exponents of the newly invented disciplines are striving to recreate the spirit of Wittgenstein and Russell in their liveliest and most creative period. But in one way they seem to fall short of this remarkable pair, namely in respect of the fact that Wittgenstein as well as Russell took into account the positions of traditional philosophy in formulating their own innovations. In the present case, one need only draw attention to the very remarkable passage in the *Tractatus Logico-Philosophicus* in which Wittgenstein, defending the disappearance of the conscious self, points to the fact that the eye, i.e. the organ of sight, does not itself occur in the visual field it makes possible, and, using that analogy, goes on to justify his destruction of the conscious self by suggesting to us that it means nothing more than this, that just as the eye is outside the field of vision so the self is outside the field of consciousness which it makes possible.[15]. Now, in the light of all I have been saying, it would appear that Wittgenstein here is on the verge of breaking through to a doctrine very different from his own, and similar to that held by Alexander, by Adam Smith, by Schelling or Hegel or Leibniz, or for that matter by Sartre, or to come nearer home by J. F. Ferrier. The limitation of Wittgenstein is, however, that he did not generalise the principle he had arrived at as these other philosophers do, when they note that touch and the other senses are structured in the same way as sight in regard to the failure of the sense organs to appear in the fields they make possible, or when they discuss the relations between self-consciousness and mutual consciousness so as to bring out the parallel with the intersensorial relations. However, the metaphysical self-doubts of masters of modern logic, like Russell and Wittgenstein — or, for that matter, the late Arthur Prior, author *inter alia* of remarkable works on Scottish theology and Scottish ethics — seem to mean little to the specialists of Cognitive Science.

13

THE OLD LOGIC AND THE NEW

Turning now to the question of the relation of "classes" to "collections" which arose in connection with Russell's alleged paradox of classes that are not members of themselves. The passage in which Russell speaks of the "Chinese philosopher" as having mis-understood the distinction between classes and particulars is important not least because it provides him with one of his main reasons for setting aside the traditional logic. "As the Chinese philosopher pointed out long ago, a dun cow and a bay horse make three things: separately they are each one, and taken together they are another, and therefore three."[1] Let us therefore look more closely into the way Russell and his school set about justifying the distinction between classes and particulars, taking our examples from an old but very good book, R. M. Eaton's *General Logic*, which sets out to defend the Russellian position against its critics. The result of looking into Eaton will, I hope, not only throw light on the point at issue between Russell and Anderson but at the same time suggest that the latter's criticisms seem well founded.

Russell had said "that in the sense in which there are particulars in that sense it is not true to say that there are classes". To explicate and defend this position Eaton proceeds thus — "We can say the class of men is 'large' and a predicate is then affirmed of the class as a single entity; but it does not follow that the men *in* the class are large".[2] The thing to note here is that Eaton is speaking of what he calls the class of all men collectively in the one case and distributively in the other case. In speaking of the class of men as large he means, e.g. that the collection or set of living men is larger than the set of living elephants when the two sets are compared together on a one to one principle. In saying that the members of the class, distributively considered, are not large, he seems to mean, for example, that any member of the class will be found to be less large than a member of the class of elephants when the two members are compared together by an

218

artificial version of the one to one comparison which is achieved by means of rulers divided into feet and inches. The set of individual members is measured against the other set; the individual member, considered artificially, is measured against the member of the other class on the very same principle, except for the difference that while in the one case we measure arithmetically, by what used to be called discrete quantity, we are concerned in the other case with what used to be called continuous quantity, i.e. we measure geometrically. Instead of the unqualified difference between the two as asserted by Eaton, they turn out to be analogous to one another, differing in a certain respect of a very definite sort.

On the view taken here, what Eaton is saying is that what we can say about a collection is quite different from what can be said about the individual member because the first is countable but not the second. But this sharp difference disappears as soon as we reintroduce the distinction between discrete and continuous quantity. Thus Eaton's position would seem to be due to considering that the only kind of quantity that matters is discrete quantity, i.e. what does not have discrete quantity is not countable. No doubt this privileging of discrete quantity against continuous quantity as represented by the arithmetisation of geometry has been responsible for great advances in mathematics, but at present it is not mathematics we are talking about.

So far, in discussing Eaton, we have been concerned with the distinction between speaking collectively or speaking distributively of the members of a class, but we have said nothing so far about the class as such considered as distinct from its members, in either of the two senses. This latter distinction, however, comes into view in the second example offered by Eaton with a view to illustrating and supporting the Russellian thesis. "It may well be true, for example, that 'all that lives dies', and yet the whole class of living creatures might well go on forever."[3] Now, what Eaton seems to be saying here is that while we know by experience that every member of the class of living beings will die, the class of living beings considered as a set might, for all we know from experience, have an uncountable number of members because of the set's always being added to, or might, of course, have a finite number of members in the case where the increase stops. But Eaton seems to have failed to notice that, if our experience entitles us to know that all living things, including those still alive, are going to die, then by the same token experience seems to furnish us with evidence that, in virtue of the operation of the second law of thermodynamics, the set of living beings is also to die out in the sense of having a finite set of members.

So far we have not got beyond the distinction between considering the members of the class collectively and the members of the class distributively, but the question of class as such and its possibility, in contradistinction to its members, begins to make itself felt as soon as we note that even if the set of living things is finite in the sense of their dying out, a certain law still holds good of life, namely this. Wherever life appears it necessarily organises itself on a principle of self-repairment which must eventually wear out. The point is that, roughly speaking, though only God can make a tree, he has to make it according to fixed laws which preclude it from being immortal. Russell and Eaton, it seems, do not like the idea of class taken in the sense that to use Shelley's words: "The one remains, the many change and pass" — that in the midst of all the variations there is a fixed structure of things that e.g. acorns, if they can be got to grow, will be always oaks but never ostriches. This is the kind of thing that appalls the modern thinker who seems to feel offended in his dignity by the very idea of the fixity of things and who, in consequence, cannot see an acorn without feeling there must be some means of turning it into an ostrich.

The weakness of the Russellian system as conceived here — its inability to make sense of propositions like "the one remains, the many change and pass" — has to do with its failure to give an adequate account of facts which would hold good even in a civilisation where everyone was blind, such as that colour is inseparable from visible extension or, to put the same thing in Kemp Smith's more adequate formulation, that shape cannot be seen except through the contrast of two different hues like red and blue as opposed to two different shades of the same colour. Or, as Blanshard put the same point in a Henrietta Hertz Lecture to which Kemp Smith drew my attention long ago, a system of symbols designed by Russell and Whitehead in the interests of accuracy finds no room for the "and" of inseparability as in "this thing is coloured and extended, e.g. white and round", reducing it to the distinction of separables which we find in "this thing is both noisy and smelly", each offending quality can be given without the other by the simple process of holding the nose or stopping the ears.[4] Or — to borrow a similar distinction made by W. E. Johnson,[5] the Whitehead-Russell symbolism obliterates the "and" of conjunction, and the necessary connections it expresses, leaving only the "and" of enumeration whereby the two related things are spoken of as independent and separable from one another. Invented to give us a technical language which would discourse "on what there is" without woolliness, Whitehead-Russell symbolism, in effect, if not in intention, seems to obliterate the terms of natural language in which philosophers like Samuel Alexander and John Anderson could speak about the "pervasive, categorical relationships" which were said to be always themselves operative however the things governed by their operation might alter.

But Eaton, speaking from the Russellian point of view, could here point out that the new system could in principle cope with Johnson's conjunctive "and" without any difficulty, and could for that matter hold its ground against any objections which Blanshard or anyone else — including myself — could bring against it because nothing has been so far said to undermine the distinction, fundamental to the system, namely that between *class-membership* and *class-inclusion*, or in other words between the relationship of the individual member to the class to which it belongs, and of the sub-class to the wider class embracing it. This is the distinction which Russell had in mind when he accused the Chinese philosopher of failing to distinguish between the particulars and the class to which they belong.[6] Established by Peano and Frege in the course of their labours on the foundations of mathematics, the distinction is illustrated and its importance brought out by Eaton himself, when he draws attention to the confusions in Jevons' logic which followed from his failure to make it. Jevons, he says, treats the statement "Iron, copper, aluminium, silver, gold are metals" as if it were speaking about the same relationship as is referred to when one says that "the Great Eastern, the Mauritania, etc. are steamships".[7] Obviously, Eaton expects us to conclude something has gone wrong here.

The point, however, *was not* obvious to the traditional logicians who — as Eaton notes — spoke of the Mauritania or of Socrates as being each a class with one member. The traditional logicians — although they were in the dark as to what they were doing and although the light did not dawn until God let Russell be — explained that, in speaking of Socrates we are speaking of *all individuals identical with Socrates* and added a qualification to the effect that the number of all such individuals does not exceed one on the most exact count. Evidently, however, Eaton goes on, the sentence "all individuals identical with Socrates are men" does not have the same form as the sentence "Socrates is a man", and the fashion set by

Eaton's *General Logic* was very generally followed at the time. I well remember how Angus Sinclair used to distance us from the traditional logic and make us suspicious of its value, by pointing out the strangeness of the convention of meaning by Socrates "all persons who are Socrates".

Eaton, no doubt, might be said to decide the matter "intuitively" but Russell, to his credit, isn't satisfied with intuitive decisions, and instead, uses a mixed method of settling the question partly by a technical definition and partly by what one could call a phenomenological, or as he would have called it, phenomenalist, analysis of what we are speaking about when we use the word Socrates.[8] But now, if we set aside the method of settling the thing by definition because, according to Russell himself, it involves "no knowledge of the real world" and stick to the other method of phenomenological analysis which, according to Russell, involves us in the consideration of an "actual object of sense" meaning by that, no doubt, sense-data, it will be found, I think, that it is not so difficult to begin some justifications of the traditional practices in the matter as against Russell.[9] For this purpose, let us take the case of speaking about Socrates, not when he is a familiar figure, but when we make the acquaintance with him as utter strangers on a first visit to an Athens we know nothing about. Our first intermittent sightings show us only someone with a bald head and a snub nose, roaming the streets trying to buttonhole people so as to involve them in conversations about philosophy. As visitors, we might at first well wonder if Athens contained more than one person with these indistinguishable characteristics, baldness, snubness of nose etc., and had the knack of diverting casual conversations into metaphysical channels. In principle, the situation would not be very different from that in which our sightings were of some shabbily dressed man, pale faced, suffering apparently from some psychiatric disorder who went about picking up bits of paper. Is there only one such person in the city or does he have a double? In the case of the picker-up of paper, we may never get an answer to our question, but in the case of Socrates we can establish that there is only one of him by finding out in conversation with other people what happens, off our perceptual stage, so to speak, but within their range of perception, to account for the various sightings of the bald-headed philosopher. But the information I would thereby get to the effect that there is "at least one" such individual and "at most one" such individual in Athens, is a case of *de facto* corrigible information, and does not preclude the

222

possibility of there being, in Athens, a double of Socrates, even to the extent of possesing the same name, who, as regards his present qualities, is indistinguishable from the other, although, no doubt, he has a different history and origin. No doubt, this traditional view of Socrates' individuality will not do for Russell holding, as he does, the more specialised view associated with Peano and Frege because it ties up so very neatly with the technical (and no doubt valuable) theories of the foundations of mathematics. Still, it is strange to find that someone who takes so seriously the idea of the unique individuality of everything, in the technical meaning put on the term by theorists of mathematics, should be the very man who, faced with the claim about unique individuality in the ordinary sense — like Huyghens' cry when the news came from Sweden in 1650, "My one and only René, there will never be another Descartes" — would automatically reach for his joke-book.

14

PLATO AND HEGEL

My central topic in this part of the book has been a discussion of the issue between the hierarchical view and the reciprocal view of self-knowledge as it has developed in twentieth-century Britain. I want to try now to widen my horizons so as to free the subject from the limitations of a provincialism in time, by saying a word about the evolution of this same problem in previous centuries. For this purpose I want to draw on a forgotten book which deserves to be better remembered — *The Political Philosophies of Plato and Hegel* by M. B. Foster.[1]

The argument of Plato's *Republic*, it is pointed out by Foster, is a good example of the way in which an over-simplified analysis of a complex can lead to a vicious regress. In order to elucidate the nature of government, Plato contrasts what he calls the first city (i.e. a small independent country which has kept itself going by evolving a simplified version of the division of labour carried on by various kinds of producers — artisans, agriculturalists, merchants — without there being any regular government by professional officials to supervise the transactions of the society) with a developed city which, as well as containing the primary producers, contains "non-productive" labourers to supervise them and in which a government has been set up to organise the division of labour and to prevent abuses. But now, just as the primary producers in both cities are specialists who work on the one man one job principle, so also the government officials in the second or developed city are to be specialists whose work is organised according to a peculiar version of the one man one job plan.

It is important to get clear the nature of the Platonic version of the division of labour because it is essential for our understanding of the limitations of the ideal state as sketched in the *Republic*. On the one hand there is a class of various kinds of producers whose special work is that of carrying forward the material and economic side of the small country. In this role, they have the fullest opportunity to develop the

side of human nature which finds its satisfactions (or its disappointments) in the mastery of one of the crafts connected with providing
food, clothing or housing, in the making of money, and in the
bettering of their position in relation to their competitors in what is
a sort of free market, in the founding of a family, the bringing up of
their children as well as exercising their free choice in personal
relations and hobbies and pastimes. By contrast, in order to increase
their efficiency in the practical work of the country, they are entirely
shut out from its intellectual life which is left in the hands of the other
class, and are therefore debarred from developing the side of their
natures which finds its satisfactions (or disappointments) in the
understanding of the way things work both in the field of the natural
sciences and the sciences of law and morals. In the same way the class
which has the responsibility for the intellectual side of the country's
life both in the matter of the general theory of things, in physics and
politics etc., have to conform, as regards the material and bodily side
of their existence, to a sort of quasi-monastic rule. They are
forbidden to own property or make money or better their position.
At the same time they dine in messes, are forbidden the satisfactions,
or otherwise, of family life and their relations to the opposite sex are
strictly regulated by eugenic principles which prescribe the times of
breeding, select the partners and leave nothing to personal choice.

Whereas the workers of the other class are participants in a relatively free market in which choices are allowed, the intellectual class
(or guardians, as Plato calls them), are organised according to a sort
of scientific socialism in which their material well-being is not under
their control, but in which everything necessary to it, according to
the ideas of the system, is provided by the State. As in the religious
foundations of the Middle Ages, the organisation of which owed
something to Platonic principles, the purpose of this very strict
regimentation on the material side was to free the intellectual and
spiritual life of the guardians in order to enable them to master the
knowledge necessary to permit them to supervise efficiently the life
of the State as a whole. Their primary business, no doubt, is to
administer the laws applicable to the productive side of the economy
so as to settle the disputes arising out of the competition and
bargaining of the producers as well as out of the complications of
their family life. But in order to understand as well as apply the laws,
the guardians were expected to be far more than lawyers and their
social life was occupied in a vast programme of general studies from
astronomy to music and philosophy organised around the central

idea of man as a political being. No doubt this rigorous course of studies involved a great deal of self-denial but the compensation was that it allowed the guardians to develop the spiritual side of their nature and to enjoy the intellectual satisfactions from which the primary producers were shut out.

As M. B. Foster shows, the defects of this scheme are very justly summed up in Hegel's dictum that Plato's Republic lacks freedom. What Hegel means by this is that the one-sided development of human nature which Plato envisages mutilates the personality in the sense of denying to the one class the satisfactions of curiosity about intellectual matters, and to the other class the satisfaction of being free to satisfy their physical needs in their own way. What is really objectionable about these defects, from a rational point of view, is, according to Hegel, that they introduce a contradiction into the Platonic idea of the state in virtue of which it turns out to be by no means the perfect arrangement of things which Plato intended. Not only does this defect of subjective freedom introduce necessarily into the workings of the Platonic community difficulties and complications which he did not allow for, but, what is worse still, his guardians, because of the restricted role he allocates to them, are, in the nature of things, incompetent to deal with the full range of the problems they will have to face. The role of the guardians is primarily to regulate the productive and lower sector by achieving a just settlement of the disputes arising out of the material production, etc., but what of the disputes which, in consequence of the built-in limitations of human nature, may arise among the guardians themselves in the course of their communal study of the sciences? In addition, their own experience of living under a regimented scheme in which their material needs are catered for, without their doing anything about it, is liable to create in them blind spots as to the nature of the competitive system of economics under which the primary producers operate. Consistently with Plato's principles of specialisation it would be necessary for settling the disputes which arise among the guardians to introduce a higher tier of super-guardians to supervise the supervisors of the primary economy and its producers. Plato's scheme thus involves us in an endless regress which is fatal to the claims of consistency and clarity which he made on its behalf.

The natural way out of this difficulty, according to Hegel, is to abolish the hierarchy, and with it the endless regress it involves, in favour of a reciprocal scheme. On the one hand the lower level producers, without ceasing to be primarily occupied with the practical crafts, are now admitted to the intellectual life of the community by being given a certain amount of general education. They thus not merely enjoy the intellectual satisfactions which were denied them before, but at the same time they are put in a position to criticise the quality of the supervision carried out by the guardians and to correct them in respect of matters which are outside their direct experience. On the other side, the monastic regimentation of the guardians is abolished, and, without their ceasing to be primarily occupied as before in the understanding of the intellectual principles of human nature, both in respect of the working of human society and man's relations to the rest of the universe, they are now in a position to participate, to a certain extent, in the competitive economy and to exercise their subjective freedom in bettering their position, founding families and regulating their private life according to their own choice. The society, instead of being a hierarchy, now consists in the mutual illumination of a debate in which each side criticises the other.

Following Hegel's lead, Foster points out that this development from the hierarchical scheme of Plato to the reciprocal scheme of Hegel, is not just a matter of intra-mural professorial theorising, but in a certain way sums up the results of the historical experiences which have led Western man from the slave-owning states of classical civilisation to the free states of a modern civilisation, the coming of age of which was signalled by the French Revolution. No doubt the brief indications, which we get in Foster, of the philosophical revolution through which these political developments became conscious of themselves is in itself not very illuminating, but it strikes me that, if he had cast his net more widely, the scheme he suggests would have made sense. For example, to speak of the movement of philosophical ideas in Scotland alone, the two sides of the Hegelian criticism of Plato are prepared for by George Buchanan's defence of the presbyterian revolution in his *De Jure Regni* (1579) and David Hume's remarks in his *Essays* on the significance of the rise of the study of economics. In the slave-owning states of the ancient world, the intellectual leaders were uninterested in the facts of economics and that is the reason for the instability of the classical states as opposed to the modern states in which governments have been conscious of the importance of the science of economics. Dealing with the other factor of the spread of general education to the populace as a whole, Buchanan indicates the other side of the revolution by remarking that the ability of the ruling classes to govern well will be decisively strengthened if they open themselves to the criticisms of the people they govern. The latter, no doubt, are, taken individually, very ignorant of these matters, but if they get together in a representative assembly, the individuals involved will be able to criticise and, to some extent, remove one another's blind spots, and out of their individual ignorances there will emerge a public opinion knowledgeable enough to draw attention to limitations in the outlook of the ruling class.

What matters to us about Foster's account is that the points he makes in reference to the political philosophies of Plato and Hegel show the fundamental point at issue between them to be the same in principle as that which we have seen studying in reference to the respective views of Russell and of Anderson on the relations of philosophy to the special sciences. For Russell, the sciences seem to be, each of them, confined to a department of experience, and to leave logical questions, so far as they are troublesome in their studies, to be settled by an endless hierarchy of philosophical supervisors who are cut off from participation in the first-hand experience of nature. By contrast, Anderson views both the sciences and philosophy as activities conducted on the same level which are both aware of experience as presenting us with a world which exhibits a kind of unity in variety, each region having its own marked peculiarities and yet united with the others by factors pervading the whole. Philosophy and the sciences are equally cognisant of both sides, differing only in the fact that the one group occupies itself with the common elements more than with the regional peculiarities, while the other party does just the reverse.

A "social" conception of knowledge — according to which science and philosophy, individual selves, and our senses, each, at their own levels, reciprocally illuminate one another — can also, in the light of Foster's historical argument (as well as Hume's and Buchanan's), be seen as closer to the spirit of a freely ordered society than is the scientism of Russell and company.

15

FROM ATOMIC TO MOLECULAR
PROPOSITIONS

In order to make clearer the point at issue between the two groups of philosophers who are under discussion — on the one hand the developing movement of modern thought from Russell and Moore by way of Gilbert Ryle, and on the other hand the group of traditionally-minded thinkers of the twentieth century like Samuel Alexander, John Anderson and Kemp Smith, G. F. Stout and others — let us note certain important matters on which the two sides agree.

Anderson, for example, does not demur when his critic Ryle reminds him that they are at one in rejecting the *a priori* metaphysical arguments for the existence of a transcendental realm as employed by C. A. Campbell, the Glasgow idealist mentioned by Ryle. For Ryle as representative of the one group and Anderson as representat-tive of the other, knowledge of the world depends solely on observation and experience, non-empirical arguments (i.e. rational arguments such as Campbell uses) being outlawed by both as giving no information about matter of fact and existence of a transcendental sort. But on the basis of this preliminary agreement they go on to differ very sharply as to the nature of observation and experience and how they give rise to knowledge. Ryle, for his part, is attracted by Russell's theory that all we get or can get from experience and observation properly speaking is a series of reports on particular things, i.e. individuals and their qualities and relations to one another. This is the lowest level of knowledge out of which the kind of knowledge claims we make in ordinary everyday language evolve as the result of a processing of the original data of sense in which there is a kind of upward movement through a hierarchy of intellectual levels. The second level involves what one might call the work of sub-editing, in which the original reports are compared in order to detect incompatibilities and a theory of what is really happening to the individuals is built up by rejecting some of the evidence as false. The third level involves a kind of editorial stage in which the story built up and accepted about the individuals is generalised in comparisons which draw upon the records of the past and in this way scientific laws come into being in the form of general hypotheses which, of course, await experimental testing and which may have to be revised or even totally rejected.

Anderson, and those who think like him, hold the contrasting opinion that the data originally provided by observation and experience contain far more than reports about individual things and their qualities and relations. The detection of incompatibilities in which realities are distinguished from mere appearances and illusions also form part of what happens at the original level. So, too, generalisation also is taking place at this fundamental perceptual level because Anderson and his friends follow Kant's view that the perception of things is impossible without being aware of their causal connections.

According to Ryle in the article he contributed to the *Australian Journal of Philosophy* in 1951, Anderson's views about the nature of knowledge, in so far as they differ from Russell's, are both out of date and false. Indeed the charge seems to be that if Anderson had read and properly understood Russell, he would give up his distinctive theory of knowledge, or at least the parts of it where it approximates to the kind of position held by Alexander or Kemp Smith. Let us, therefore, in order to assess the justice of what Ryle says, look carefully into the appropriate places in Russell's *Inquiry into Meaning and Truth*.

As the result of his dealings with the Liar paradox, it becomes clear, Russell says, that the arguments for the necessity of a hierarchy of languages are overwhelming. "The hierarchy," Russell goes on, "must extend upwards indefinitely, but not downwards, since, if it did, language could never get started. There must, therefore, be a language of the lowest type" which Russell sets out to describe in one of its possible forms, and which he calls the object-language.[1]

The difference between the object-language, i.e. talking about objects, and the second-level language, i.e. talking about talking about objects, Russell goes on, is that we could express in the object-language, given sufficient capacity, every non-linguistic occurrence, for instance occurrences such as "while John was putting the horse in the cart the bull rushed out and I ran away" or "as the curtain was falling there was a stampede". There are, he goes on, some differences of opinion as to whether it is possible to express in the object-language such observable facts as desires, beliefs and doubts. However, what is certain, Russell concludes, is that the object-language does not contain the words "true" or "false", or logical words such as "not", "or", "some", and "all".[2] As mentioned before, what we get at the lowest level is a series of reports of occurrences, while at the second level the mind begins to reflect critically on the reports in order to detect incompatibilities, etc.

The difficulties of the position which Russell takes up here begin to be evident as soon as he tries to explain it in some detail. The doctrine of a hierarchy of languages, he allows, obliges us to revise ordinary language in a way which puzzles common sense:

"When I say that we make assertions in the object-language about non-linguistic occurrences like 'the bull rushed out', I must guard against a misunderstanding, for the word 'assert' is ambiguous. It is used sometimes as the antithesis of denial, but in that sense it cannot be used in the object-language. . . . An assertion which is the antithesis of denial belongs to the second language; the assertion which belongs to the primary language has no antithesis."[3]

But, as Russell sees, common sense, as well as the kind of philosophers who profess to represent common sense, find something very puzzling about this kind of assertion in the object-language which has no antithesis. Normally, it would seem, that which is asserted could be denied, but this rule has to be broken to get the hierarchy of languages started. To silence the objections of common sense to the use of assertion in this unfamiliar sense, Russell explains his position with some care on pages 127-129, and completes the theory outlined there in his second chapter, pages 328-336. What happens when we learn a new word, e.g. when a small child acquires the use of a word like "book"? The important point about the answer given by Russell is that although "W" (a "whole", for example, "book") is in fact the name of a certain bundle of qualities, we do not know when we give the name *what* qualities constitute W. That is to say we must suppose that we can perceive, name, and recognise a whole without knowing what are its constituents. In that case, the datum which appears as a subject in our judgement of perception is a complex whole, of which we do not necessarily perceive the complexity. A judgement of perception is always a judgement of analysis, but not an analytic judgement. It says: "'The whole W, and the quality Q, are related as whole-and-part', where W and Q are independently given."[4]

In the course of this explanation by Russell of how a new word is learned, a further difficulty is brought up by this claim that W and Q can be given to our perception independently of one another. Let us, like Russell, abridge the difficulty by agreeing that we can attend to, that is single out, recognise and name a book given in perception without noticing its peculiar qualities (i.e. without having a knowledge of its details). The question at once arises as to whether Russell is right in his supposition that in another set of acts of attention we can focus on the colour of the book, somehow distinguishing it from the shape and other qualities. Seriously facing up to this question in his final chapter, Russell, we find, gives the same kind of superficial answer as was given by Condillac, and not the much more profound answer given by Hume in his discussion of abstraction.[5]

What Russell does here is to go back to his speculation as to the kind of analysis made by the child who is learning to spell. Words are composed of distinctive letters which can be separately named and, in the course of time, come to be named by the child when he has learned to spell. Now Russell uses this example to explain how it is possible to perceive the whole without noticing the parts, or to perceive a part without noticing the whole. He does the first by perceiving the word as a sort of distinctive shape, and he can do the second, which consists in perceiving one letter without perceiving the other letters which compose the word, by the simple enough process of covering over the other letters, leaving the letter in which he is interested visible.

Russell thinks that he has cleared up the entire difficulty of perception of the whole and the perception of a quality by using the example of looking at a printed word on paper, but the kind of contradiction he is caught up in soon becomes evident when we read his detailed description of the whole process:

"A child who is being taught, by modern methods to read the word 'CAT', learns to make, in succession, the sounds 'k', 'a', 't'. (I mean the sounds these letters stand for, not the names of the letters.) At first, the interval between the sounds is too long for the child to be conscious of their succession as forming a whole, but at last, as the rapidity increases, there comes a moment when the child is aware of having said the word 'cat'. In that moment, the child is aware of the word as a whole composed of parts. Before that he was not aware of the whole; when he can read fluently he ceases to be aware of the parts; but in the first moment of understanding, whole and parts are equally present in consciousness. What the child is aware of in this moment cannot be expressed without such propositions as: the sound 'k' is part of the sound 'cat'."[6]

FROM ATOMIC TO MOLECULAR PROPOSITIONS

Now in this account of the mental analysis in which the child comes to learn that the sound "cat" has three elements, "k", "a", "t", Russell seems to have entirely forgotten the difference between vowels and consonants, in the case of words written down, and in the case of spoken words. The fact of the matter, as the ancient grammarians knew, is that "k", considered as part of the spoken word, is inaudible and unpronounceable when we take it by itself. Whereas in the case of the written word "cat", it is possible to see it as a whole, or to see it part by part, because the letter "k" remains visible when it is considered in isolation from the other letters, it is quite impossible to isolate the sound "k" from the sound "cat" by a process analogous to that of seeing the "k" in the printed word without seeing the other letters. As the older philosophers — Hume and Plato among them — were aware, the analysis of the sound "cat", which enables us to be aware of the "k" as a distinguishable but inseparable part of the complex, is achieved by a comparison which notes the resemblance and difference between three such sounds as "cat", "bat", "cot" — a process which enables one to be aware of "cat" as like "bat" in one way, and like "cot" in another way in point of sound. The point here is well discussed in the passage in Hume on the distinctions of reason (i.e. abstraction) which made such a profound impression on Husserl, and which leads him in *Logical Investigations*, part 2, chapter 2, on the subject of abstraction, to note the superior value of the Humean theory, that abstraction involves comparison, to the more common theory followed here by Russell, that abstraction is accomplished by shifts of attention.

But might not Russell's error be taken to be an accidental slip in regard to a factual matter which does not affect the logical doctrine he is expounding — the hierarchy of languages? Not a bit of it. The damage this slip inflicts on his ideas about the hierarchy becomes evident as soon as we recognise that in noting "cat" to be like "bat" in one way, and like "cot" in another way, we have already introduced along with the notion of identity in kind or likeness in a certain respect, the notion of difference in kind or unlikeliness in another respect, and to have done this is tantamount to having introduced the word "not" at the lowest level, that of the object-language. The result is the ruin, as it seems to me, of his paradoxical idea that there are two kinds of assertion — a familiar kind which is inseparable from its antithesis, denial, and another technical kind of assertion understood by logicians, but not by other people, which is disconnected from denial. The rule governing the hierarchy of ways of talking — that "not" occurs only in the second-level language and not in the object-language — has taken a big knock.

Russell, however, is aware in his own way of the difficulty which he tries to get round by a pragmatic move. He admits that the consonant "k" is an abstraction in the sense of its being audible not in isolation but only in combination with some spoken vowel which we distinguish from it by the complicated comparisons noted above. The fact that it is an abstraction, however, is immaterial, since, in practice, once the abstraction has been made, we can forget about it, and treat the "k" as if it were a concrete, separable thing.

He discusses the topic in connection with our experience of colour, admitting that this latter is also an abstraction:

"Since we can distinguish similarity in colour from similarity in other respects (e.g. shape), we do not avoid the necessity of a certain degree of abstraction in arriving at what is meant by 'yellow'. We cannot see colour without shape, or shape without colour; but we can perceive the difference between a yellow circle and a yellow triangle, and the similarity between a yellow circle and a red circle. It would seem therefore, that sensible predicates such as 'yellow', 'red', 'loud', 'hard', are derived from the perception of kinds of similarity."[7]

Clearly, therefore, Russell is aware that abstraction through comparison is involved in hearing as well as in seeing.

In practice, however, we can, Russell says, ignore the comparison. "Perhaps, indeed what has been said about the comparison applies only in the *learning* of the word 'yellow'; it may be that, when learnt, it is truly a predicate."[8] In using the word predicate, Russell means that what the word applies to can be treated for all practical purposes as a simple independent quality capable of existing in isolation. In making this assertion, Russell seems to be perfectly confident of being right, and the reason for the words of hesitation he uses in the sentence "it may be" is not that he is unsure of himself, but that he is leaving the investigation of the learning process to the psychologists, and confining himself to the logic.

But now consider how Russell goes about the business of justifying his confidence in his doctrine. When we say:

"'this is yellow', the meaning seems to be 'this has colour-similarity to that' . . . the object called 'that' is yellow by definition, and colour-similarity is a dual relation which can be perceived. It will be observed that colour-similarity is a symmetrical relation. That is the reason which makes it possible to treat 'yellow' as a predicate and to ignore comparison."[9]

The word "yellow" thus refers to a perceived object which is simple, ultimate and unanalysable, and which, in the cases where perception suggests an exact match, may be, Russell thinks, intelligibly enough, spoken of as existing in two places at the same time — as being, in fact, something like one of the "eternal objects" spoken of by Whitehead.

Now the precise meaning, if there is one, of what Russell is saying need not concern us just now. What I want to do rather is to draw attention to the fact that in speaking here of colour-similarity as a symmetrical relation, Russell seems to be contradicting a well-known doctrine of his own which is still a topic of discussion in articles in philosophical journals, namely, that sometimes colour-similarity is *not* a symmetrical relationship.[10] Distinguishing carefully between two sorts of experienced colour-similarity, Russell is making the claim that colour-similarity is a symmetrical relationship when one is looking at two differently situated patches of yellow which are an exact match. But note that for Russell colour-similarity cannot be a symmetrical relationship where one is seeing, not colours which are an exact match, but several different shades of the same colour — which we could call A, B, C. A is visually indistinguishable from B, and B is visually indistinguishable from C, but at the same time, if A and C are compared together, leaving out of account the intermediate shade B, they are seen to be clearly distinguishable. If A, B and C were, in Russell's view, all cases of an exactly matching yellow, then the relationship of each to the others would be symmetrical, but when we are dealing with shades, the symmetricality disappears.

Russell thus makes it easy for himself to ignore the comparisons and treat what is called "yellow" as a simple independent object of perception only because, as he tells us at the beginning of this same paragraph, he is going to simplify his problem by ignoring the fact that there are many shades of yellow, and by discussing an artificial situation, in which only one sort of yellow could be seen, unaltered in hue wherever it appeared, and being, so to speak, a sort of constant (hence "eternal object") which reappears unchanged.

There is obviously something very unsatisfactory about Russell's procedure here. Having started off on a sort of *terra firma*, in which he explains how we make the abstractions which enable us to give colour-words their meaning, he moves into a realm of "a light which never was on land or sea" when he begins talking about a world of colours consisting of these unchanging eternal objects. One naturally wants to ask him questions. But when one puts them to his text, it suddenly reveals a testiness quite unlike the even flow of detached wit which is his normal way of expressing himself. "This question," he says in a footnote to the passage, "has no substance. The object is to construct a minimum vocabulary." Brushing aside the objection that he should say more about how we know the meaning of words, Russell tells us that the only thing that matters is the construction of the object-language, and the languages of a higher order. As happens so often, the very idea of asking for a foundation for logic causes irritation. As Arnold says, "Others abide our question, thou art free."

Russell's curious behaviour here suggests that he is aware of getting into difficulties. What these difficulties are, becomes clear enough the next time he turns to the question of our knowledge of colours:

"We certainly know — though it is difficult to say how we know — that two different colours cannot co-exist in the same place in one visual field. . . . More simply: 'this is red' and 'this is blue' are incompatible. The incompatibility is not logical. Red and blue are no more *logically* incompatible than red and round. Nor is the incompatibility a generalisation from experience. I do not think I can *prove* that it is not a generalisation from experience, but I think this is so obvious that no one, nowadays, would deny it."[11]

I find something extraordinary about this claim to the effect that "red and blue are no more *logically* incompatible than red and round". I think I know what is meant by saying that red and round are not logically incompatible. What is being said is that a red patch of colour which is round may be altered so as to be a square without alteration to the colour. But red and blue are a different matter altogether. In seeing the red patch, whether its outline is round or square, we see it as standing out against a background of some other colour, e.g. blue or yellow. This colour contrast is a condition of our seeing the red shape, in the sense that if the background were re-coloured, so as to become itself red, or rather, to make the thing a little more realistic, various shades of red, approximating to that of the red shape originally seen, then the outline, square or round, would become difficult to see, or rather disappear altogether. Instead

236

of seeing a shape, we would see an interrelationship of shades of colour which obeyed the rule laid down by Russell himself when he noticed that the shade A in one place was visually indistinguishable from shade B, or shade B was visually indistinguishable from shade C, but that the shade at A and the shade at C were visually distinguishable. What this means is that the perception of distinct outline has gone in the sense that though we know that a certain shade occupies a certain area, we cannot say exactly where the area ends in relation to the shading in the adjacent area.

I have been illustrating the point by reference to vague memories and imaginings of what might be experienced, but the knowledge we can get can hardly be said to be a generalisation from experience. It seems to be some kind of necessity that we cannot see the red shape with its definite locatable boundaries except in contrast to some other colour — blue in contrast to red. Where the blue is replaced by another shade of red the outline disappears. To this, Russell might reply by saying that although the *outline* disappears, the *red* itself does not. A quotation from Kemp Smith helps us to see what would be misguided about such a response:

"The fundamental fact of [visual] experience, it may be noted, is not colour, but colours. Had there been but one colour, we would not have required a special word for it; the visible and the coloured would have coincided, and the differences of shape would not have been possible visual experiences."[12]

Following out this line, Kemp Smith qualifies the common assertion that colours are indefinable. Red, he says, is defined as what shows up against both orange and purple in respect of defining outline, but does not show up as such against another shade of red. All this is, of course, something which experience shows, but there is also an element of necessity in it. Apparently it could not be otherwise. That Russell does not see this point seems to be due to certain limitations in his notion of necessity, and therefore in his notions of logic.

A comparison of Russell's account of the foundations of common sense with what Kemp Smith, Alexander, and the other philosophers of that group say on the same subject, suggests the criticism that the difficulties he gets into, not only on the present topic of our knowledge of colours and shapes, but also over the rest of the field, are due to the very sharp separation he introduces between the primary object-language and the hierarchy of more elevated ways of talking, which brings into play the so-called logical words. Taken by itself, Russell's description of the way in which we learn to speak about things in the object-language by first being aware of the things as undifferentiated wholes, and then proceeding, by means of an analysis by comparisons, to make explicit to ourselves their previously unknown detail, i.e. their qualities of colour, shape, hardness, etc., goes about the problem in the right way, and contains the promise of leading to the desired clarification of the obscurities. The objection to his procedures is simply that, in so far as they do really throw light on how the learning is done, he is already envisaging his subject — the learner — as engaging in operations requiring the logical words the introduction of which is supposed to be reserved for the next stage. Insofar as the qualities of the thing which our language-learner now begins to single out and to name are distinguished from one another, and from the thing whose qualities they are, by means of the process of noting resemblances and differences, in certain respects the language that is being used already involves denials as well as assertions, and at the same time also involves the knowledge of some general facts. In order to learn the kind of fact of which Russell speaks — that Q, the quality, is part of W, the whole thing — the language-learner is already obliged to make himself cognisant of the general fact that the experience of colours is, in a variety of complicated senses, inseparable from the experience of shape or extension, while at the same time, the knowledge of negativity simultaneously comes on the scene as a result of his having to grasp the fact of the colour as not merely inseparable from the extension aspect, but also as distinguishable from it.

The most peculiar and striking feature of Russell's philosophy is that he seems prepared to admit the truth of this part of the account, which contradicts his principles by introducing logical operations before they ought to be introduced, but yet, at the same time, seeks to save the consistency of his philosophy by declaring that the learning-process does not matter to him. What he is concerned with is really, he seems to claim, not so much the foundations of common sense, but the scientific attitude which arises on the basis of common sense, the foundations of which can henceforth be neglected. As the result of this deliberate separation, we get two different accounts of the rise of knowledge. On the one hand we get a description of the way in which ordinary language is acquired, which, so far as it goes, is an illuminating enough account of the foundations of knowledge, and is in line with what the philosophers of the school Russell opposes say on the same subject. On the other hand, the subsequent move from the level of common sense to the level where the technical language of science is supposed to be mastered, is carried out by means of the elaborate theory of a hierarchy of languages which, as I argued earlier, is the result of a half-truth, and which, as Russell worked it out, makes the scientific mind look like something out of Swift's Laputa.

Russell's defects, however, are balanced by his qualities, not least of which is that his work enables us to see what the English-speaking world of thinking has taken so long to see — the point of Sir William Hamilton's remark that "a mathematician in contingent matter is like an owl in daylight". To get a prime example of the kind of thing Hamilton was alluding to, one need do no more than note how, in his discussion of colour, Russell takes it for granted that it is normal for a shade of yellow to exist in different places at the same time in a form so much an exact match that each is substitutable for the others without any noticeable difference, as if their relations were analogous to that of a = b. By contrast, his method of interpretation makes it a kind of anomaly that, in the case of adjacent shades of yellow, A, B, and C, the first can be indistinguishable from the second, and the second indistinguishable from the third, while the first is nevertheless plainly different from the third. But as is clear from the early and revealing article on 'The Relation of Universals and Particulars' the facts of experience, are, so to speak, "rigged", so as to enable Russell to treat of the qualitative identities and differences of hue — yellow, red, etc. — as if they could be stated in what look like equations with "=" or "≠".[13] But in everyday experience, surely, the hues behave very much in the same way as the shades.

Does the tie match the shirt? It may seem so in the artificial light within the shop, but one takes them to the daylight of the door just in case. As Hume knew, blue and green are more like one another than they are like scarlet, but become different from one another when compared to bluey-green, while scarlet itself is like green when they are compared to the sound of middle C. So too Hume makes the point, slurred over by Russell, that a "gap" in a graduated sequence of shades of blue finds visual expression in a somewhat sharper spatial demarcation of one shade and the next than occurs in reference to the other shades. Cézanne also was on to the same fact in his reported remark, made so much of by Sartre and Merleau-Ponty, that colour and shape are one, and Cézanne is not the only artist to have something to say on the subject which could, with advantage, be taken notice of by, among philosophers, Russell's admirers — and not only by them. For example, two surfaces which the layman would pronounce as uniformly red and of an exact match would appear to the artistic eye as non-uniform and in many respects different in lighting and shading, and that not because — as I once heard Professor Grice say — of some physical difference in the painter's optical physiology, but because of a painter's wider experience in looking at and handling colours. But we do not need to go to painters. A dressmaker is well aware of the distinction — aimed at but missed by Russell — between the measurable and the immeasurable aspects of objects of visual experience, when she is able to create a dress which fits her subject's ample form without, however, making her look large. Russell's equations are thus adequate, up to a point, for the description of the tangible side of things, but not for the way things look — a fact which not only brings out what is true in the irascible Hamilton's "So much for mathematical logic, so much for the Cambridge philosophy!", but also serves to remind us of the still more important fact that there is more to seeing than seeing itself, that touch has a part to play even in the recognition of colours.[14]

The lesson to be learned from the flaw in Russell's philosophy is reinforced by consideration of the contributions of those of his contemporaries who, like Kemp Smith and Anderson, sought to check his growing influence. In so far as their theories improve on the corresponding thing in Russell, it is because they, unlike him, bring together the logical operations and the object-language which he kept apart. In so far as, on the other hand, their philosophies — as was certainly the case with Kemp Smith and Anderson — fail to achieve a full and systematic development, and peter out in hesitations, silences, and loose ends, it is because, in working out their positions as professional philosophers, they are too much affected by the separatist spirit of which Russell, indeed, was the chief proponent in Britain, but which made its mark on a whole generation of thinkers, whatever their positions. Kemp Smith's analysis of the role of abstract thinking in visual perception, for all its excellence, suffers considerably from the fact that, in a spirit of professionalism, he keeps out of it the whole question of the relationship of touch to sight and the other senses, as if it had nothing to do with them.

By contrast, the eighteenth-century philosophers took a much more all-in view of the relation of the senses to one another, and Bishop Berkeley, who led the way here, insisted on the importance of the co-operation of sight with touch, not only in reference to the more peripheral and specialised topic of the perception of distance from the eye (a question which is really to do with the theory of measurement) but also on the fundamental topic, central to any philosophy of mind, of the way in which our control of our attention is inseparable from the use of touch and manipulation to aid the processes of vision or of the other distance-senses. To attend to something, e.g. a book one is asked to read, it is not enough to keep one's eyes fixed on the page where it has opened, because of the tendency of the attention to wander. To keep one's mind on the book, or whatever object one is looking at with a view to studying it, Berkeley says, it is necessary to take account of the fact that the attention is a flighty thing which, though briefly held by any new feature presented to the senses, quickly loses interest in it.[15] To keep up our interest in the book, or whatever else we are studying, one has, therefore, always to keep presenting it to vision in a new light by flicking over the pages, or, if the object is some work of art, altering the background against which one sees it by changing one's position. What keeps the process going, of course, is the hope that, sooner or later, in paging through the book, one's glance will light on a phrase which suddenly challenges one's interests.

These pages of Kemp Smith on the common sense of colour-perception would have benefited considerably by taking into account the co-operation of sight with touch, not only because Berkeley is reminding us of what common sense really is, in its original and Aristotelian signification, but also because the treatment of touch in connection with sight would have enabled questions to be asked about the way the experience of paint affects the way in which we think about colour. One does not only look at the colour of solid things, but one also has experience of coloured fluids. In this way, the follow-up of the opening made by Berkeley could lead to a theory of colour which does not leave out of sight the fact that blue and yellow make green, as if it were altogether irrelevant to the philosophy of the subject.

16

THE PROBLEM OF CAUSALITY

Let us turn now to Russell's denial that experience can found generalisations:

"Propositions containing 'all' or 'none' can be disproved by empirical data, but not proved except in logic and mathematics. We can prove 'all primes except two are odd' because this follows from definitions; but we cannot prove 'all men are mortal' [a proposition about experience] because we cannot prove that we have overlooked no one."[1]

Made familiar first by Russell and his group, then by Ryle, and achieving the status of a popular orthodoxy since Popper, the doctrine of the impossibility of establishing general truths by experience had been in the early years of the century under powerful attack from a whole generation of philosophers of a different way of thinking from Russell — Alexander, Whitehead, Kemp Smith, Stout and Anderson, to mention no others. Their ideas on the subject find forcible and compressed expression in Anderson's view — a view denied by both Russell and Ryle — that the world as given to experience is not a set of separable facts but a complex "situation or domain" constituted by interlocking movements which impinge on one another. It is in the light of this view of things that these philosophers try to justify their thesis that experience enables us to grasp the inevitability of man's death, considered as an animal. It is a fact of experience, Kemp Smith used to say in his lectures, that "it is in the nature of the organism to wear out" or in other words that living is in some sense experienced as inseparable from dying. Taken by itself, this statement seems to me insufficiently illuminating, and to get the full force of it, one must analyse it so as to take into account the fact of everyday experience that, by comparison with inanimate bodies, animate ones are in a certain way self-repairing — a broken leg will mend itself, a broken bar of metal will not. To put the matter concretely, observation shows that both in reference to oneself and to other people life begins to ebb unless the expenditure of energy put out in the daily round is compensated for by self-renewal through eating and sleeping. Moreover, if we compare ourselves with our companions, taking into account the various ages — youth, middle age and senescence — we have constant evidence of the self-renewal process as having its limits, i.e. of the impossibility of in the long run repairing the wear and tear.[2]

Greatly influenced by Hume's view of causality — especially in the simplified version of the *Enquiry* — Russell and the philosophers who, like Ryle, in this respect carry forward the movement he initiated, are entirely out of sympathy with the doctrine found in Alexander and used by him to support his ideas of our knowledge of our own deaths, namely that our grasp of causal connection is founded on experience.[3] How is it possible, Russell asks, to found on present experience, and the records of memory, generalisations like "all men are mortal", or, for that matter, the very principle of causality itself — "every change has a cause" — which lay down the law about things which have not been experienced yet? The claim of our being able actually to experience the necessary connection between two states of affairs clearly does not apply in the case of a causal relation where in the nature of the case we are dealing with — states of affairs which are successive — the second billiard ball begins to move on the impact of the first which then stops. Perhaps the claim to experience necessary connection might be upheld in the case of our claim to know the inseparability of our experience of visual shape from our experience of colours, but that is only because in this latter case the two states of affairs are simultaneously given to our vision, and hence the one state of affairs is not experienced as over and done with before the other state of affairs begins, as happens in the case of the movement of the billiard balls. Nor — as Russell points out in a famous example — does it meet the case to try to reverse the claim by pointing out that the perception of causality consists in our *expectation* of a certain event as being followed by the same kind of event previously experienced as invariably following it. Because the chicken is invariably fed at dawn, it no doubt expects to be fed as soon as the sun rises. But its association of the two events is far from affording it an actual experience of their causal connection in view of the fact that one fine day the chicken's belief may be falsified by the experience of having its neck wrung by the man who invariably fed it in the past. In any case, as Russell also points out, this kind of custom-bred expectation cannot possibly afford us knowledge of a causal connection because the idea of causal connection is the idea of a rule which claims that the relation between a certain state of affairs and another state of affairs holds for all cases whatsoever.

It is on this issue of finding a meaning for the "all" that Russell breaks entirely with the associationist view on the subject of "all" in favour of the views of the so-called logical empiricists — familiar to us in the form of logical positivism. "All" has to be reclassified as a logical word like "not" or "if", etc., that is to say, as one of the words which do not refer to what is experienced in the direct way in which words like "red", "blue", "hard", "soft" do refer to what is given in experience, and the meaning of which might, roughly speaking, be said to be known to us innately or by instinct. The origin of generalisation is thus explained in parallel with the way in which the origin of negation is explained — in terms of the theory that ordinary speech is a hierarchy of ways of talking, each successive stage of which, after the first, introduces a logical operation unavailable at the previous stage. The starting point, as I explained at some length earlier, is an object-language in which atomic propositions about facts given in experience — e.g. "this is red" or, more accurately, "red here now" — are asserted without one's being, at that stage, in a position to deny them. (Ryle seems to call this kind of thing "unstudied utterance", meaning by that, I think, pre-reflective utterance.) This is followed by a second stage in which "molecular" propositions are manufactured by conjoining ("and") or disjoining ("or") along with negation in so far as comparison of the relations between the atomic facts shows the negation of one of them to be necessary. That is to say, the move from the first, unstudied, level to the second level is a move from a level on which we find ourselves asserting "this is red", "this is hard", as if these facts were independent of one another, to a higher stage in which we find ourselves asserting, "this is red but not hard", "this is red or hard", "this is red and hard" according to the results of our comparisons.

At this second stage, we may recall, the mind in Russell's view of it is engaged in experimental structuring by the application of the logical words to the unrelated sense-data encountered in the process of turning its attention to a hitherto unexplored and undifferentiated part of an otherwise already known familiar environment, e.g. an unfamiliar corner of an in other respects familiar room. The subject, in formulating to himself the molecular propositions "red and hard", "red but not hard", "red or hard", is trying to interpret his unco-ordinated impressions in such a way as to first differentiate, if necessary, what is illusory and what is veridical in them, and having done that, to form some hypothesis which further experience will test as to what really is contained in the hitherto unexplored part — one thing or two things or nothing at all but a gap through which the background wallpaper is seen.

On the basis of the move from the first to the second stage the mind next moves upward to the third stage of generalising its ideas by substituting the logical words "something" or "everything" for the singularities previously dealt with in the process of discovering that the unexplored corner is filled with this red, hard thing. That is to say instead of saying to itself "this is red and hard" the mind says to itself "something is red and hard", or else, by another substitution giving a different hypothesis, says "everything is red and hard", moving on from that to a still greater generality in which it formulates to itself the proposition "everything is something", i.e., "everything has some characteristic". Formulated in this way as hypotheses, they now can be tested by further observation and experiment which, as said before, can refute them, but can never fully establish them in all their generality.

In expounding this doctrine, I am drawing on Russell's explanations of it while trying to fill the gaps which he seems to leave. The crucial passages are, for his doctrine of atomic forms pp. 95-99 of his *An Inquiry into Meaning and Truth*, for the moving from atomic forms to molecular, pp. 63-64, and for the movement from molecularity to generality, pp. 262-266. Any reader who is curious will find more enthusiastic accounts of the doctrine from thinkers — e.g. Professor Dummet in his book on Frege — who seem to regard the move from "John loves Jane" to "everybody loves somebody" as a philosophical advance comparable to that made in Plato's *Theaetetus*. I myself take a more sceptical view of its value as a permanent contribution to philosophy.

The objection I am going to make against this move from the second stage, that of molecularity, to the third stage, that of generality, is the same in principle as the criticism I previously made against the move from the primary language or object-language of atomic forms to the second language level of molecular propositions. Just as Russell's view of negation as occurring not at the primary level of the object-language but at the secondary level of talking about the object-language (the introduction of words like "not", "if", "or" arises at this level, as the examples he shows very strongly suggest, from his refusing speculations as to how the distinctions between vowel and consonant arise at the pre-literate stage of spoken language, and from his taking for granted a situation in which human beings grow up in a world where letters have been invented and languages are written) so a similarly positivistic dislike of launching out at the speculations about first beginnings is what leads him to the view that generalisations — that is to say, thinking about causality (introducing the logical word "all") — can arise only at the third level of talking about talking about the object-language (i.e. talking about molecular propositions). In his speculations about the origins of the idea of generalisation Russell fixes his attention on the level of social life on which man has succeeded in making instruments for accurate measurement, and is well on the way to making telescopes, sextants, etc. The way to understand what philosophers like Kant and those who follow him, e.g. Samuel Alexander, mean, by their claim that generalities are discovered in experience, is to raise speculative questions about how the stage of life which has not invented measuring instruments discovers the idea of the repetition of time and space equalities which their invention presupposes. Just as Russell and Moore, in their discussion of the equally fundamental question of the nature of our experience of colours, their relation to one another and to our experience of shape, speak as if our original source of this law of knowledge were the colour charts used by firms selling paints, so their discussion of our understanding of the nature of time takes it for granted that we are born and grow up in a world which possesses a ready-made supply of mechanical clocks.

What I have called — crudely enough — Russell's "atomism" is, on the present view, due to the fact that, accepting as ready-made the distinctions taken for granted by civilisation, he fails to do justice to the preliminary problem of distinguishing between inseparables — i.e. the problem of abstraction which has to be solved by mankind as a condition of this civilisation. This sort of oversight, as I see it, which has been already exemplified in regard to his discussion of the foundations of our knowledge of the distinction between colours and shapes, reappears in another form in the way he deals with our knowledge of the distinctions which, as will emerge later, are fundamental to our commonsense notion of causal connection, i.e. the distinction between place and time.

He introduces the subject in this way: what would commonly be called a thing is nothing but a collection of qualities — redness, hardness, etc., "wherever there is for common sense a 'thing' having the quality C, we should say, instead, that C exists in this place and that the 'thing' is to be replaced by a collection of qualities existing in the place in question".[4]

To be aware of a set of qualities as constituting one thing, in the ordinary sense, it is thus, for Russell, essential for us to know that they are in one and the same place. The importance of the knowledge of their place arises from the fact that the qualities in question — what he calls redness, hardness, etc. — are for him the same kind of thing that his one-time collaborator, Whitehead, calls "an eternal object". The idea here is that the visually given object which we would call redness — in the cases where there is an exact match of shade (so far as such a thing is possible) — can be described by us only in terms which speak of the same red (or whatever the quality is) existing in different places. The place of the qualities has therefore to be fixed by us before we can speak in the ordinary sense of one thing. But to do this Russell relies upon the scientific equipment of advanced civilisation:

"If I start from Greenwich with a good chronometer, or with a receiving set on which I receive a daily message at noon G.M.T., I can determine my latitude and longitude by observation. Similarly I can measure altitude. Thus I can determine three co-ordinates which uniquely determine my position relative to Greenwich. . . ."

Russell himself goes on for nearly another page explaining the way we can distinguish accurately the place where one set of qualities occurs from another place where a supposedly identical set of qualities occur — meaning, I take it, by identical set of qualities, e.g. two instances of the same make of car — on the assumption that we can distinguish the place relations by the elaborate measurements of science, without ever committing himself to the speculative question of how the accurate knowledge of science arises out of the ordinary knowledge got by the senses without the aid of instruments.[5]

Of course the time requires to be known as well as the place because of the principle which Russell is trying to elucidate for us that two things cannot be in the same place at the same time. He therefore involves himself in an analogous discussion in respect of time. "What we want is a class of events having a temporal uniqueness analogous to the spatial uniqueness of latitude, longitude and altitude."[6] Illustrating what he means, a few lines earlier, Russell explains our knowledge of time as being a knowledge of succession. For this purpose:

"we desire to find empirical objects such that, in regard to them, time shall be serial. That is to say we desire to find a class definable in terms of observable objects such that if x, y and z are members of the class, we shall have the rules that (1) x does not precede x, and (2) if x precedes y, and y precedes z, then x precedes z; (3) if x and y are different, either x precedes y or y precedes x."

Now we can get this kind of knowledge, he says, "if we can get the date and time of day as determined by an observatory". Russell hesitates here because observatories can make mistakes, but after two pages of not very clear reflections on the difficulty, he returns to the idea:

"So long as we are not in search of logical certainty, we can arrive at what is empirically sufficient by the means which we formerly rejected, e.g. memory and the second law of thermodynamics. Not all the causal laws with which we are acquainted are reversible, and those that are not afford means of dating. It is easy to construct a clock, which in addition to exhibiting hours and minutes will every day exhibit a number greater by one than that exhibited on the previous day."[7]

We seem thus to have to return to the observatory.

So far as the topic we are entering on is concerned, the foundations of our knowledge of causal connection, Russell now proceeds to congratulate himself on the results of the analysis. We have, he says, "reduced to the empirical level, certain properties of spatial-temporal relations which threatened to be synthetic *a priori* general truths". What he means here is that his analysis has rescued Hume's sceptical analysis of causality from the criticisms made by Kant and followed by Alexander and the rest of the philosophers opposed to Russell, namely that our natural knowledge of causality, involved as it is in the perception of things as moving, makes knowledge of place inseparably connected with knowledge of time. This is the fact, as Alexander points out, to be followed by Kemp Smith and Anderson, which Kant is trying to describe with the help of the term "synthetic *a priori*" and which Russell wants to get rid of. The result of Russell's analysis thus poses in a new form the old question which divided Kant and Hume, as to whether or not the experience of change is inseparable from the experience of causality.

The meaning and well-foundedness of the Kantian view, so emphatically rejected by Russell, of time-experience as essentially involving the experience of the movement of something in contrast to a relatively fixed background-point, was given new life for Alexander's and Kemp Smith's generation by an item in late nineteenth and early twentieth-century philosophy which is altogether neglected in modern discussions in the English language, but which Russell himself, in the passage we are discussing, calls attention to — namely Bergson's objections to the Humean doctrine taken over by Russell, that in its fundamental form time-experience is an experience of unrelated succession and is not to be taken as involving space-experience and movement against a background. The idea and impression of time, Hume had said, are typically given in the experience of hearing five notes on a flute played one after the other. The choice of the flute is quite deliberate on Hume's part because according to what he says in his *Dissertation on the Passions*: if the notes were played on a stringed instrument, the continuing vibration of the previously heard notes would interfere with the hearing of the note next heard by reason of their being in effect *internally* related to it, whereas in the case of the notes played on a flute, there would be, in Hume's view, no carry-over, and each new note would be heard separately from its predecessors by reason of its being *externally* related to them.[8]

The fact, supposed to be illustrated by the case of the flute, is Hume's evidence that time is actually experienced as a succession of unrelated sensations. This decisively discounts the Kantian counterclaim that the succession of heard sounds is in some way experienced as bound together by reason of its relation to the continuing thing, whatever it is, perceived along with it. The spatialising of time in the sense of perception of a permanent in contrast to the succession is, Hume admits, required in the case where we actually measure time.[9] But, as the flute experience shows, the primary experience of time involves mere succession, and so, although it is thus true for Hume that an empirical object cannot be experienced as enduring except in contrast to a succession, a succession, according to Hume, can be experienced by itself and does not require to be experienced in contrast with a permanent. The Kantian point that the permanent and the successive — the stationary and the moving — are not experienced except in contrast to one another is thus set aside by Hume long before Kant wrote his *Critique of Pure Reason*.

Hume's views on the subject were, however, powerfully challenged by Bergson in the book translated under the title of *Time and Free Will*, which for that reason impressed admirers of Kant like Kemp Smith and Alexander. We must, said Bergson, distinguish between the two ways of hearing five notes played on the flute. They can be heard as a kind of rhythm, like the postman's knock of "rat-tat-tat", i.e. as internally related, the final sound being heard differently according to differences in the preceding sounds; or the sounds can be heard as externally related and as having nothing to do with one another. But this latter experience involves a kind of measurement in which, simultaneously with the process of hearing the sounds, we look at our hand and tick off the notes — one, two, three, four, five — by successively moving finger after finger. The experience of the notes as internally related (the former case) involves a sort of aesthetic view — a musical experience. But the latter case where the sounds are counted with the help of the visible hand, is the time-experience presupposed by the scientific view of things which thus proceeds, not according to the description of it given by Hume, but according to Kant's description of it. In other words, time-experience in this primary way involves the *a priori* synthesis which Russell sought to deny — that the experience of succession is inseparable from the experience of the stationary.[10]

Under the influence of Bergson, Kantian commentators like Kemp Smith revitalised the discussion of the analogies in the *Critique of Pure Reason*, in which Kant seeks to correct Hume's oversights in regard to causality. Reformulated by Kemp Smith so as to do justice to what is best in Kant's rather confused account, the proof, Kemp Smith affirms, ought to have proceeded in the following manner: "Time is conceived only as motion" — this is the point which Kant had originally not made clear — "and motion is perceived only against a permanent background in space. By the permanent," Kemp Smith goes on, "is not meant the immovable, but only that which is uniform and unchanging in its motions. The uniform motions of the heavenly bodies constitute our ultimate standard of time."[11]

The value of Kant's discussion here is that it shows how experience involves our doing what Russell and Mill, following Hume, deny it can do — grasping the truth of a general proposition about a necessary perception to the effect that the movement of a thing cannot be perceived except against the background of a relatively fixed point.

The complications of the point at issue here are made pretty plain if Hume's remarks on the subject are combined with what Berkeley says on the same theme. Pointing out that one cannot see a visible object change place except in relation to some other visible object, Berkeley makes explicit the paradoxical principle that if the second visible object disappears, then the object which remains is no longer seen to be changing places; the experience of the eye's movement in following this solitary visible object might constitute some evidence for its movement, but because our experience of these eye movements is non-visual and kinaesthetic, they are legitimately enough ruled out by Berkeley who is simply speaking about sight and what it can do. Hume, for his part, does not say anything about the facts Berkeley calls attention to here, possibly taking them for granted, but he does add a further point, not, I think, mentioned by Berkeley, but essential to the position he is maintaining. If this kind of experience of the two bodies moving in reference to one another is to convey to us the idea of endurance or lastingness as well as of change, the bodies seen must in other respects retain their character — their colour, size, etc. — throughout the experience of their change of place in reference to one another.

The analyses of the British empiricists in reference to this subject, in spite of being unsystematic, are very valuable, and their weakness is for the most part, I think, simply due to the fact that they do not put down on paper all they know. However, we can, I think, make clear the point on which Hume goes astray in comparison with Kant if we note Hume's close relationship to Locke. Rejecting Aristotle's view that the fundamental thing about time-experience is the experience of movement, which the measurement of time requires, Locke goes on to speak as if the basic time-experience was the experience of an unrelated succession of sensations such as Hume tried to exemplify with the five notes on a flute. The position of Locke and Hume was, of course, for a long time very influential and the great impact made by Bergson seems to me in large part due to the fact that he overthrew the atomism of the empiricists and prepared the way for a new understanding of what Kant was getting at with his "synthetic *a priori*".

So far we have been following up Kemp Smith's account of the discussion of substance in Kant which forms the introduction to his discussion of causality. It is in regard to the latter, of course, that the crucial question arises as to whether Kant really did answer Hume. The point about substance no doubt constitutes a considerable advance or clarification of the problem, but there is a great difference amongst philosophers as to whether what Kant says about causality really does refute Hume's position. Russell clearly is sceptical on the point, whereas Kemp Smith is a believer in the value of Kant's contribution. Let us see how his view of Kant works out.

Carrying on from where the analysis of the perception of substance stops, Kant, as expounded by Kemp Smith, finds the answer to the Humean scepticism about causality in an experience fundamental to all movement — the perception of a distinction, said by Kemp Smith to be missed by Hume — between subjective succession and objective succession. Take the experience of standing on a river bank whence one sees a ship proceeding downstream by contrast with some object on the further bank which one sees as directly opposite to oneself. Because the ship is too big to have all the parts of the side of it which faces one taken in by oneself simultaneously at one glance, what one actually sees is a reversible sequence of the ship's parts, in which, in alternating succession, first the stern presents itself to one against the rearward portions of the background on the other side, and then the bow of the ship presents itself against the parts of the background which are seen as one looks downstream. At the same time, simultaneously with this perception of the alternating succession of the front and rear of the ship, one finds that every time one looks at the background object on the other side, it has changed, so that the object which we now see the stern passing is the same object which we remember seeing the bow passing the last time we looked. The crucial question for Kant, of course, is how common sense works out its ordinary description of what is happening to the ship, on the basis of these very complicated and confusing data given in the original experience. And it is here of course that the distinction between what is subjective and what is objective in the succession is introduced as the solution to the problem. According to Kant, the spectator is aware of the alternating succession of now bow, now stern, as due to the movements of his eyes and shifts of his attention, just as at the same time he is aware of the irreversible elements in the succession which he sees as being unaffected by the movement of his eyes, and due to something, whatever it is, not in him and his eye movements as perceived, but in the ship in its relation to the movements of the river, etc. so far as they go on independently of himself and his perceptions.

The really important thing Kant does here, Kemp Smith says, is to draw attention to the "fairly obvious fact" that, "while in certain cases, the order of our perceptions is subjectively initiated, in other cases we apprehend the subjective order of our experiences as corresponding to, and explicable only through, the objective sequence of events".[12] Consciousness of this distinction between subjective and objective sequence, Kemp Smith goes on, is a "necessary presupposition of all awareness", and this awareness, in which we make the fundamental distinction between appearance and reality in what we perceive, as the achievement of common sense requires, presupposes this knowledge of how far the movements of our eyes alter what is given in perception.[13] In this way some sort of knowledge of causes is embedded in our experience of the world right from the start.

Without saying any more about the essential role causal knowledge plays in our conception of the world, on Kant's view of things, Kemp Smith, in order to convince us of the truth of "Kant's answer to Hume", simply refers us to the authority of G. F. Stout's *Manual of Psychology*:

"Unless we assume from the outset that the primitive mind treats a perceived change which challenges its interests and attention, not as something self-existent in isolation, but as something conditioned by and conditioning other changes, it seems hopeless to attempt to show how this causal point of view could have arisen. . . . There is good reason for denying that customary repetition is even required to furnish a first occasion or opportunity for the first emergence of apprehension of causal relations."[14]

The point Kant drew attention to, namely the changes effected in the scene before us, as the result of our moving our head, refutes Hume's claim that our knowledge of one sort of event as causally connected with an antecedent event is always acquired through repeated experience, and is not revealed immediately to us.

Kemp Smith speaks in his *Commentary* as if Hume knew nothing about the Kantian distinction between subjective and objective succession, but the actual text of the *Treatise of Human Nature* tells a different story. "We remark a connection betwixt two kinds of objects in their past appearance to the senses, but are not able to observe this connection to be perfectly constant, since the turning about of our head or the shutting of our eyes is able to break it."[15] Indeed, Hume brings out far more emphatically than Kant the existence of this experience of the way in which changes in our organs of perception produce changes in what we perceive by their means. "When we press one eye with a finger, we immediately perceive all the objects to become double, and one half of them to be removed from their common or natural position."[16] Indeed, as we shall see, Hume had considered experiences of this kind very carefully, and it is therefore perfectly fair, as well as reasonable in itself, to raise the question as to why it did not occur to him that this kind of casual experience where our sense organs are in question might be immediately known, and is not one of these cases where the knowledge of a connection between events dawns on us only in the light of a repeated experience.

As a matter of fact, a question of this sort was raised about Hume in Thomas Brown's *Inquiry into the Relation of Cause and Effect*, in the course of a section which is well worth looking at because of the light it casts on the dark places in the treatment of the subject by Kant and his modern commentators. Hume, Brown points out, actually admits the fact that sometimes the causal connection between two events reveals itself immediately and he then endeavours to reconcile this peculiar fact with his theory that causal connection in general is not discovered in a single experience. "'Tis certain, that not only in philosophy, but even in common life, we may attain — Hume admits — the knowledge of a particular cause merely by one experiment provided it be made with judgement, and after a careful removal of all foreign and superfluous circumstances."[17]

Pointing out, quite rightly, that Hume's attempt to explain away this awkward fact falls short of his usual high standard of argument, Brown describes a variety of cases in which what Hume calls a single experiment affords us the basis for the knowledge of a causal connection. I take a sweet in my hand, and, popping it into my mouth, feel the distinctive taste, or again, I pick up a flower, and bringing it towards my nose, at once discover that it is the source of the disagreeable odour, or again, I bring my hand in contact with a flame and feel the pain, or I put a watch to my ear and know it to be the cause of the ticking I hear. In all these cases I am supposedly aware in my perception that nothing else is happening to me which was not happening before except this one sequence of events. Why should it not afford evidence of a direct experience of causality?[18]

Brown does not, so far as I remember, discuss the case of sight, but it can be brought into line with what he says about hearing, smelling, etc., if we think of the experience we have when, entering our house in the dark, we switch on the light. Now, to bring out the common element which connects Brown's description of the immediate perception of causal connection with the description Kant gives, it is necessary to call attention to a circumstance common to the situations described by both thinkers, but not, so far as I know, noticed by either. The important point is that touch not merely reveals to me the existence of the sweet, or the flower, or the watch, or the light switch, but it also reveals to me the existence of the sense organs which enter into the experience — the nose, the ears, the eyes, the mouth. I can cut off the experience of seeing by putting my hand over my eyes, and I can do the same thing in the same direct way in regard to the ears and the nose. The sense of taste in the mouth can also be discovered with the hand in a more roundabout method of experiment. Indeed the fact would seem to be that it is experiences got with the help of the hand which let us know what we see with the eyes, hear with the ears, smell with the nose, etc.

So far I have been engaged in refining upon Brown's positions and correcting them in the light of some subsequent members of the same school, especially Ferrier.[19] What has been done in these cases is that touch has enabled us to distinguish sharply between the organs of sense considered as tangible objects to us and the respective qualities — smell, sound, colour, etc. — which are experienced in the tangible bodies affecting the organs, e.g. the flower or the watch.

The introduction of these distinctions into Brown soon makes clear the sense in which he was, from another point of view, concerned with the same kind of problem as was raised by Kant when he drew the distinction between subjective and objective succession, i.e. between the changes in the things we perceive which are due to the movements of our eyes, and to the changes which occur independently of our sense organs. In the case of Kant's seeing, touch is what ultimately provides us with a means of knowing whether movement seen has its source in our eyes, or has its source in something that has happened to the thing we are looking at, as a result of some cause independent of ourselves. So too, touch is essential to our knowing whether some peculiarity in the sound we are listening to is due to our ears or to something quite independent of us, and connected with the body which makes the sound. The same distinctions could be drawn in regard to smelling and even tasting.

But let us now, having studied carefully the criticisms of Hume's theory of causality which result from calling upon Brown to fill up the gaps in Kant, and upon Kant to do the same with Brown, turn back to Hume's text in order to see what reply he can make to his critics. This exercise will have the advantage of drawing our attention to what seems to me a very remarkable section of the *Treatise* — book I, part IV, section IV, "Of the Modern Philosophy" — in which Hume, in a bold undertaking unparalleled in eighteenth-century philosophy, enters on a critique of the eighteenth-century's favourite avenue of sense, namely touch. My analysis, put in motion in order to unite Brown's and Kant's answer to Hume on causality, depends on the idea, very widespread in the eighteenth century (e.g. Berkeley and Reid), that, unlike the other senses, touch is illusion-free. But according to Hume this is not the case, and in fact the distinctions between subjective succession and objective succession arise in connection with certain paradoxes of tactual experiences which are in a certain way analogous to the paradoxes of visual experience. It is not true, says Hume, that the impressions of touch present us with the solidity and externality to ourselves of the bodies touched in a straightforward way, since "tho' solidity continues always invariably the same, the impressions of touch change every moment upon us; which is a clear proof that the latter are not representations of the former".[20] What Hume means here is that the tactual experience as the result of which we would judge an object placed in our hand when we were blindfolded to be a solid cube, fixed in shape, consists of a succession of shifting feels, as our fingers run over the body in the process of ascertaining the shape. Touch thus presents problems altogether analogous to those of the visual experience in which a coin held up before our eyes grows visibly smaller in contrast to the fixed background according as we stretch forward the hand that holds it until the arm is fully extended. In this case too, the visual impressions which are of a changing size do not represent the size of the object which is affirmed to exist by common sense as unchanged.

This passage, and the context it occurs in, are little studied by the commentators on the *Treatise*. But its importance for Hume himself may be gauged by the fact that the paragraph immediately following the sentence I have just quoted presents us with one of the most forthright and memorable affirmations ever made of the difficulty of connecting causality with the problem of a perception of the external world in the way in which Kant tried to do with his distinction between objective and subjective succession:

"Thus there is a direct and total opposition betwixt our reason and our senses; or, more properly speaking, betwixt those conclusions we form from cause and effect, and those that persuade us of the continued and independent existence of body. When we reason from cause and effect, we conclude that neither colour, sound, taste nor smell have a continued and independent existence. When we exclude these sensible qualities, there remains nothing in the universe which has such an existence."[21]

This because touch and the experience of solid shape, which at the time the *Treatise* was published, were generally held to constitute an experience of independently existing matter, have been shown, in the argument of the chapter which ends with this paragraph, to be just as much vitiated by illusions as the other avenues of sense.

Hume, in my opinion, argues this matter out very efficiently, but the very thoroughness of his analysis points to certain facts in the light of which we can meet his sceptical conclusions and so give new force to the criticisms of his theory of causality which he is trying to answer here. Reading the whole of what Hume says we see that he is concerned with the contrast between what we know about a body by touching it or holding it in our hand — the experience of touch from the inside — and what we can learn by observing the same hand in its dealing with the object it is touching or holding, i.e. the same experience considered, so to speak, from the outside. This is what Hume is referring to when he says, "'Tis easy to observe that tho' bodies are felt by means of their solidity, yet the feeling is a quite different thing from the solidity; and that they have not the least resemblance to each other".[22] Now, when Hume uses the word "observe" here — as above, or as in "observes that hand to be supported by the table" — the word has to do with a visual experience. He is watching the hand touch the object so as to contrast the visual experience of what it is doing in relation to the object, with the feeling we have tactually of the same relationship of the hand to the object. Hume is not at his clearest here, but the point of contrast he is making between the two avenues of knowledge we have of the same fact — hand in relation to object — draws attention to a feature of the situation which is sometimes mentioned in modern phenomenology, that while the visual side of the experience shows clearly two things engaged with one another (hand and object), the tactual information given to us does not exhibit the hand as properly separable from the object it handles, but shows only one, as Hume calls it, simple (i.e. inseparable) thing. At first sight perhaps appearing a sort of questionable paradox, this latter claim can be shown by a little reflection to rest on a well enough founded point of logic. The tactual experience itself cannot possibly tell us about the relation of hand to object touched, as common sense knows it, i.e. it cannot possibly tell us that the object touched continues to exist when it is no longer felt or even continues to exist when it is out of reach of any of our tactual organs. This fact of common sense which is presupposed in all our touching cannot itself be known to us by touch, but only by vision, or perhaps by some of the other distance senses.

We are now in a position to suggest a clarification of Kant's view of causality which will remove some objections to it by giving it a more systematic form. The point he was making was that in order to give a consistent description of what we perceive, it is necessary to allow that we have a perception of causality from the start. But it is very important for evaluating his view to see that the causality he introduces operates in perception in so far as perception involves the comparison of the sense avenues with one another. Whether or not there is anything about this point in Kant I don't know, but it emerges clearly enough as a generalisation when one notes what his position has in common with the discussions of the same topic which we find in Hume or in Thomas Brown, and later in Ferrier. Knowledge of causality would, on this view, be one of the things which we know, not by one sense alone, but by comparing the various senses with one another so as to reveal facts which we could not discover in any of them taken separately. In this sense causal knowledge might be called a kind of common sense knowledge, taking "common sense" in the signification given it by Aristotle.

This idea that our grasp of causality requires the co-operation of two senses — sight and touch — may be further illustrated by reference to the distinctive kind of theory of causal perception which is found originally in Maine de Biran, and more recently, Whitehead. In the experience of making efforts in the face of resistance as described in the chapter on "pushing and pulling" in Fraser Cowley's *Critique of British Empiricism*, we are said to have a direct knowledge of the causal connection of two counter-movements.[23] Properly speaking, however, what we are experiencing here is the mutual influence of opposing forces which are inseparably locked together to such an extent that their separate nature is not given to us, i.e. they cannot be properly differentiated. To achieve, in this situation, a knowledge of causality in the proper sense there has to be a climax in which, as in the case of pushing a heavy object, the latter is suddenly dislodged and put into motion, while the counter-movement of my pushing ceases. Clearly, however, the touch-experience involved in the pushing cannot give us the information about this crisis in which the body pushed breaks contact with us and our own movement stops. To get facts of this kind we have to supplement what we know by touch with using our eyes and getting visual information about what is happening. Take away the visual aspect of the experience, and we lose the knowledge of the separability of the two items which are locked in the opposition. It therefore seems to be inaccurate to claim, as these theorists do, that the essence of the causal experience is the experience through "active touch" of effort in the face of resistance; the co-operation of sight seems to be also required. In principle, therefore, this theory would seem to be concerned with the same kind of point which Kant makes, though envisaged from a different and narrower point of view.

Since the kind of causal experience which has been under discussion here has been chiefly concerned with one's knowledge of one's influence on the things one perceives, or of their influence on one another independently of one's perception of them, it will be as well to end by saying something about causality as it occurs in the social fact of people's influence on one another. This extension of the theory depends upon the fact that our experience of other people's reactions to what we are doing can serve us as a kind of sixth sense which teaches us things about ourselves incapable of being directly given to us in our ordinary self-observation. I have already explained this point in discussing Alexander in a previous chapter but the situation we are concerned with here is best summed up in Hume's saying, "The minds of men are mirrors to one another".[24] Following up Hume's lead, Adam Smith explains the mode of operation of this mutual knowledge and its causal effects in a passage which deserves to be as famous as that of Hume:

"Were it possible that a human creature could grow up to manhood in some solitary place, without any communication with his own species, he could no more think of his own character, of the propriety or demerit of his own sentiments or conduct, of the beauty or deformity of his own mind, than of the beauty or deformity of his own face. All these are objects which he cannot easily see, which naturally he does not look at, and with regard to which he is provided with no mirror which can present them to his view. Bring him into society, and he is immediately provided with the mirror which he wanted before. It is placed in the countenance or behaviour of those he lives with, which always mark when they enter into, and when they disapprove of, his sentiments; and it is here that he first views the propriety and impropriety of his own passions, the beauty and deformity of his own mind."[25]

Common sense, in its meaning as knowledge which results from the pooling of information received through one's different senses — sight, touch, hearing, etc. — is stretched in its significance so as to mean common sense achievable through mutual communication with somebody else.

Breaking off the argument abruptly, I want, by way of finishing, to put on record that the object of this exercise has not been to deny merit to Russell, to Moore or to Ryle, all of whom have, by their writings, given me a great deal of stimulus as well as entertainment. What I am arguing, rather, is that they have been somewhat overvalued — and not just by the circles close to them. To see what I am driving at here one need not do more than look at the titles of the chief works produced by the group — *Principia Ethica, Principia Mathematica*. Ampère may well have deserved to be called "the Newton of electricity" — as Clerk Maxwell mentions — but Moore and Russell, despite their merits, are very far from being the Newtons of anything.

But while the value of Russell's work — outside the particular tradition of academic learning of which he was such a luminary — is thus limited, I am very conscious of having left it vague as to where these limits are. In particular, I have said nothing here about the important dispute between Ryle and Anderson as to the value of Russell's ideas about geometry. But I have made three points of substance in regard to British philosophy. First, what I have called Reid's programme for an Aristotelian analysis of the foundations of common sense, ordinary language, etc., seems to me to offer a fruitful alternative to Russell's non-Aristotelian analysis of the foundations of common sense, etc., in the sense that Reid's idea of the inter-sensorial foundations of common sense — as exemplified in Berkeley's doctrine of the inseparability of touch from sight in the theory of vision, or in Plato's and Aristotle's questions as to how we are aware of the relations of sight with hearing, or with taste — appear to me to open the way for an intelligible discussion of what in Russell's theory of common sense it is difficult to give a meaning to, namely the *a priori* elements in our knowledge. Secondly, the connection thus brought into view between twentieth-century philosophy in Britain and the eighteenth and early nineteenth-century argument between the common sense of the North and the utilitarianism of the South, not only makes it possible to do belated justice to the forgotten merits of the group of twentieth-century philosophers, in Scotland and out of it, who upheld the values of speculative metaphysics in the face of the positivistic commitments of Russell, but also, by drawing attention to the life-long argument of the poet MacDiarmid with himself on the question of metaphysics or positivism, as well as to his remarks about the philistinism of Russell and Whitehead where poetry was concerned, opens the way to a better understanding of the close relations of literature to philosophy than has of late years been common in Britain. Finally, by tracing back the debate among the academics and literary men, in Scotland at least, to its source in the bitter arguments over the changes in the curriculum, whether it should be organised on utilitarian or non-utilitarian lines, I have, I hope, done something to correct the illusion which, though by no means so common as it once was among philosophers, is still very much alive among social historians, namely that the great traditional debate about philosophy is, in an age like ours, a meaningless irrelevance.

EPILOGUE

DEMOCRATIC INTELLECTUALISM IN THE TWENTIETH CENTURY

The words "democratic intellect" offer a twentieth-century formulation of an old problem. Does the control of a group (of whatever kind) belong, as of right, to the few (the experts) exclusively, and not at all to the ignorant many? Or are the many entitled to share the control, because the limited knowledge of the many, when it is pooled and critically restated through mutual discussion, provides a lay consensus capable of revealing certain of the limitations of interest in the experts' point of view? Or thirdly it may be held that this consensus knowledge of the many entitles them to have full control, excluding the experts. The middle way of the three is, of course, Walter Elliot's "democratic intellectualism".

The question of the democratic intellect has come alive here in two arguments; one, in the first half of the century, the other in the present half, in regard to the way public education is to select and train the rulers. The earlier arises from the challenge of experimental psychology to the traditional idea that a generalist education centred on philosophy has to precede specialisation. Experiment, it was claimed, had destroyed the generalist thesis by proving that there is no carry-over from one subject to another. Against this, Burnet argued powerfully that the failure of transfer as established by psychologists applies only to rote-learning, not to the kind of learning required of rulers — a learning which depends on comparing experiences of different kinds. (The common sense that has as its basis, as Plato and Aristotle already knew, a comparison of the experiences of sight, hearing, touch, etc., in respect of the same thing.)

The second and later half of the argument does not dispute Burnet's point that philosophy ought to have its traditional role as an overseeing subject. But the revolution in physics, it is contended, has resulted in the creation of a mathematical philosophy, much more accurate than the traditional, which, instead of critically corroborating the common sense of the many, requires it to be set aside as altogether inaccurate, just as the geocentric view was set aside. But these claims of the mathematical philosophers, it is pointed out in the last part of the book, take far too lightly the counter-claims made by Burnet, and subsequently carried further, as to the unshaken position of common sense when considered in its Platonic-Aristotelian sense, as dependent on the comparison of the different senses. Just as the comparison of sight with touch, as Bishop Berkeley and his Scottish followers maintained, makes possible the transcendental knowledge of the body seen as existing externally to, and independent of, the organ of sight, so the comparison — in regard to one's relations to the bodies experienced — between what one learns of them out of one's own direct experience of oneself, and what one learns by "seeing ourselves as others see us" makes possible the understanding of the difficult (because in some respect transempirical) distinctions of common sense between "inner" and "outer", between "the mental" and "the bodily". As J. F. Ferrier neatly put it in speaking of Adam Smith, "Sympathy seems to play the same part in the moral world as touch plays in the physical". (Unpublished course of 1849-50, lecture 63, MS in Edinburgh University Library.)

The mathematical philosophers, thus, have been too quick to set aside as indefensible the claims of classic common sense. But in case they find what I have to say on the subject difficult to understand, I would recommend them to read *Analysis and Dialectic* by J. J. Russell (1923-1975). They will find there not only the well-informed and detailed appreciation of the achievements of mathematical philosophy which is lacking here, but in addition a dialectical critique of the analytical approach which would form a useful starting point for a reconsideration of the ideas of common sense which have been canvassed in the last part of the present book.

NOTES

Chapter 1: DARROCH THE MODERNIST

1   J. F. Ferrier, 'Introduction to the Philosophy of Consciousness', *Blackwood's Edinburgh Magazine* (1838-9), collected in Ferrier's *Lectures and Philosophical Remains*, vol 2 (1866).
2   *Scottish Educational Journal*, 5th Jan 1923.
3   Darroch quoted in A. Hill (ed.), *Second Congress of the Universities of Empire*, London, 1921, p. 113.
4   A. Darroch, *The Place of Psychology in the Training of the Teacher*, pp. 55-65.
5   *The von Hügel-Kemp Smith Letters*, ed. L. F. Barmann, New York, 1982, p. 254.
6   *S.E.J.*, 18th May 1923.
7   Kennedy Stewart, 'The Problem of the Scottish Universities', *Nineteenth Century*, February 1927, pp. 201-207.
8   *Scotsman*, 17th September 1917.
9   Hugh MacDiarmid, *Complete Poems*, ed. M. Grieve and W. R. Aitken, London, 1978, p. 108 ('A Drunk Man Looks at the Thistle').

Chapter 2: BURNET AND THE DEFENCE OF GENERALISM

1   J. Burnet, *Higher Education and the War*, London, 1917, pp. 33-4.
2   *Ibid.*, p. 212.
3   *Ibid.*, p. 165.
4   R. D. Anderson, *Education and Democracy in Victorian Scotland*, Oxford, 1983, p. 291.
5   W. L. Lorimer and A. E. Taylor, 'John Burnet, 1863-1928', *Proceedings of the British Academy*, vol XIV, 1928, pp. 445-467.
6   Burnet, *op. cit.*, p. 213.
7   *Scotsman*, 17th September 1917.
8   J. Burnet, *Essays and Addresses*, London, 1929, p. 125.
9   For example Stewart's Memoir of Adam Smith, section IV, in *The Collected Works of Dugald Stewart*, ed. W. Hamilton, Edinburgh, 1858.
10 For example Reid's *Essays on the Powers of the Human Mind*, essay IV, chapter 1, 'Of Judgement in General'.
11 J. F. Ferrier, *Lectures and Philosophical Remains*, Edinburgh, 1866, especially p. 366.
12 Adam Smith, *A Theory of Moral Sentiments*, part III, chapter 1.
13 Hume, *A Treatise of Human Nature*, ed. Selby-Bigge, pp. 25, 34.
14 Hegel, *Phenomenology of Spirit*, chapter IV.

15 J. Burnet, *Higher Education and the War*, pp. 53 ff., second stage pp. 49-53, first stage pp. 40-48.
16 J. Burnet, *Essays and Addresses*, pp. 225-6.
17 J. Burnet, *Higher Education and the War*, pp. 188-9.
18 Burnet, letters in S.E.D. files: E.D. 26/216. The whole Ordinance 70 controversy is covered in files: E.D. 26/215-217. See letters from Burnet to MacDonald, 22nd September and 23rd November 1919; 12th January 1920.
19 R. D. Anderson, *op. cit.*, pp. 250-1, 282-3.

Chapter 3: WHITTAKER, GIBSON AND THE ORDINANCE 70 CONTROVERSY

1 Whittaker's letter to *The Scotsman* of 5th November 1925 brings the whole correspondence into focus. It is a reply to a leader of the previous day which refers to his earlier letters.
2 Gibson's letter to the S.E.D. is in file E.D. 26/216, dated 22nd Feb 1921.
3 Glasgow University Court report, vol VIII, 20th November 1925, pp. 1202, 1240, 1250.
4 *S.E.J.*, vol X, 7 Jan 1927, pp. 25-6.
5 R. D. Anderson, *op. cit.*, pp. 182-3.
6 Darroch's obituary in the University of Edinburgh Senatus Minutes, vol 4, 1924-1928, p. 7.
7 Gibson, *Proceedings of the E.M.S.*, vol XIV, 1895-6, pp. 148-176, and vol XVII, 1898-9, pp. 9-32.
8 Gibson, articles on the History of Mathematics in Scotland, *Proceedings of the E.M.S.*, vol I (2nd series), 1927-29, pp. 1-18 and 71-93.
9 St Andrews, 1913.
10 D. M. Y. Sommerville, *The Elements of Non-Euclidean Geometry*, London, 1914.
11 John Eaton was lecturer in mathematics at Strathclyde University.

Chapter 4: GRIERSON AND GRIEVE: LITERATURE AND ITS RELATION TO SCIENCE

1 Grierson's reply to Sir Henry Craik's article on university entrance exams, *Scotsman*, 25th October 1921, and also the letter in the *Glasgow Herald*, 5th December 1922; and the S.E.D. files ED 26/1913-16. See also David Daiches' obituary notice of Grierson in *The Proceedings of the British Academy*, 1960, p. 319.
2 Kennedy Stewart, *op. cit.*
3 H. J. C. Grierson, *Rhetoric and English Composition*, Edinburgh, 1944, 2nd ed. revised, for example p. 42.
4 T. Cottrell, 'The scientific textbook as a work of art', in the *Review of English Literature*, vol 3, October 1964.

NOTES

5 *S.E.J.*, vol III, 1920, p. 11.
6 *S.E.J.*, 3rd July 1925 — 4th February 1927.
7 MacDiarmid, *Complete Poems*, p. 203 ('To Circumjack Cencrastus').

Chapter 5: KEMP SMITH AND THE METAPHYSICS OF ORIGINAL SIN

1 This sentence, the last in the book, is omitted in later editions.
2 Duncan MacGillivray's lecture on measurement in education as a science, reviewed in the *S.E.J.*, 1925, vol III, p. 651.
3 See for example A. Bain, *Education as a Science*, London, 1879. For the other side of the argument see S. S. Laurie, *Institutes of Education*, Edinburgh, 1892; 2nd ed. 1899, and *Language and Linguistic Method*, Cambridge, 1890, especially chapter 1.
4 *The Credibility of Divine Existence* (the Collected Papers of Norman Kemp Smith), ed. A. J. D. Porteous, R. D. Maclennan and G. E. Davie, London, 1967.
5 *The von Hügel-Kemp Smith Letters*, p. 88.
6 *Ibid.*, p. 59.
7 *Ibid.*, pp. 26-7.
8 *Ibid.*, p. 263.
9 *Ibid.*, pp. 266-9, 277.
10 Kemp Smith, *The Present Situation in Philosophy*, Inaugural Lecture, Edinburgh University, 16th October 1919. Reprinted as Appendix II of *The von Hügel-Kemp Smith Letters*.
11 *Ibid.*
12 Pringle-Pattison's obituary of A. Campbell Fraser in *Mind*, 1915, esp. pp. 290-2.
13 *The von Hügel-Kemp Smith Letters*, p. 121.

Chapter 6: JOHN ANDERSON AND THE DEWEYITES

1 See John Anderson, *Education and Inquiry*, ed. D. Z. Phillips, Oxford, 1980.
2 J. Dewey, *Democracy and Education*, New York, 1916, p. 144.
3 Anderson, *op. cit.*, p. 136.
4 Dewey, *op. cit.*, p. 341.
5 *Ibid.*, p. 301.
6 *Ibid.*, p. 6.
7 J. Anderson, *Studies in Empirical Philosophy*, Sydney, 1962, pp. 371-2.
8 Anderson, *Education and Inquiry*, p. 104.
9 Dewey, *op. cit.*, p. 394-5.
10 Anderson, *op. cit.*, p. 139.
11 *Ibid.*, pp. 138-9.
12 *Ibid.*, p. 101.
13 Dewey, *op. cit.*, p. 7.

14 *Ibid.*, p. 389.
15 *Ibid.*, p. 300.
16 *Ibid.*, p. 6.
17 J. Burnet, *Greek Philosophy: Thales to Plato*, London, 1914.
18 Anderson, *Studies in Empirical Philosophy*, p. 339.
19 *Ibid.*, p. 338.
20 Dewey, *op. cit.*, p. 85.
21 Anderson, *Education and Inquiry*, pp. 61-2, footnote.
22 Anderson, *Studies in Empirical Philosophy*, pp. 185, 202.
23 Anderson, *Education and Inquiry*, p. 117.
24 *Ibid.*, p. 135.
25 *Ibid.*, pp. 135-6.
26 *Ibid.*, p. 140.
27 *Ibid.*, p. 141.
28 *Ibid.*, p. 109.
29 *Ibid.*, pp. 116-7.
30 T. C. Smout, *A History of the Scottish People 1560-1830*, London and Glasgow, 1969, p. 506.
31 Hume, ed. Green and Grose, *Essays*, vol I, essay XIV.
32 Anderson, *Studies in Empirical Philosophy*, pp. 186-7.
33 *Ibid.*, p. 290.
34 *Ibid.*, p. 86.
35 *Ibid.*, p. 339.
36 *Ibid.*, p. 246.
37 Anderson, *Education and Inquiry*, pp. 101-2.
38 Dewey, *op. cit.*, pp. 219-20.
39 Anderson, *Studies in Empirical Philosophy*, p. 341.
40 Hamilton's edition of Reid, Edinburgh, 1853, p. 878a.
41 N. Kemp Smith, 'The Fruitfulness of the Abstract', in *The Credibility of Divine Existence*.
42 Anderson, *Education and Inquiry*, p. 102.
43 Anderson, *Art and Reality*, Sydney, 1982, p. 74.
44 Dewey, *op. cit.*, p. 7.
45 *Ibid.*, p. 279.
46 *Ibid.*, p. 279.
47 *Ibid.*, p. 282.
48 *Ibid.*, p. 152.
49 *Ibid.*, p. 160.
50 *Ibid.*, p. 144; Anderson, *Education and Inquiry*, p. 141.
51 Anderson, *op. cit.*, p. 106.

Chapter 7: JOHN ANDERSON AND C. M. GRIEVE

1 G. E. Davie, *The Democratic Intellect* (2nd ed., 1964), pp. 316-7, 325; see also Edwin Muir, *Scott and Scotland*, London, 1936; repr. Edinburgh, 1982.

2 See the entry on Masson in *The Dictionary of National Biography*.
3 MacDiarmid, *Complete Poems*, p. 24 ('The Man in the Moon').
4 C. V. Salmon, 'The Central Problem of David Hume's Philosophy', *Jahrbuch für Phänomenologie und Philosophisches Forschung* (1929), p. 299.
5 H. Oxenhorn, *Elemental Things — The Poetry of Hugh MacDiarmid*, Edinburgh, 1984, p. 37.
6 MacDiarmid, *op. cit.*, p. 98 ('Drunk Man').
7 *Ibid.*, p. 162.
8 *Ibid.*, p. 285 ('Cencrastus').
9 *Ibid.*, p. 152 ('Drunk Man').
10 *Ibid.*, p. 163.
11 *Ibid.*, p. 163.
12 *Ibid.*, p. 160.
13 *Ibid.*, p. 160.
14 *Ibid.*, p. 161.
15 *Ibid.*, p. 163.
16 *Ibid.*, p. 47 ('Somersault').
17 *Ibid.*, p. 32 ('The Innumerable Christ').
18 *Ibid.*, p. 107 ('Drunk Man').
19 *Ibid.*, p. 107.
20 *Ibid.*, p. 137.
21 *Ibid.*, p. 156.
22 *Ibid.*, p. 107.
23 *Ibid.*, p. 102.
24 *Ibid.*, p. 112.
25 J. Derrida, trans. D. B. Allison, *The Speech and the Phenomena*, Evanston, 1973.
26 MacDiarmid, *op. cit.*, p. 146.
27 *Ibid.*
28 Oxenhorn, *op. cit.*, p. 90.
29 Dewey, *Democracy and Education*, p. 6.
30 Adam Smith, *A Theory of Moral Sentiments* (ed. Raphael and MacFie), Oxford, 1976, pp. 158-9.
31 Oxenhorn, *op. cit.*, p. 90.
32 MacDiarmid, *op. cit.*, p. 212 ('Cencrastus').
33 N. Kemp Smith, 'The Frtuitfulness of the Abstract', in *The Credibility of Divine Existence*.
34 Anderson, *Studies in Empirical Philosophy*, p. 342.
35 Davie, *op. cit.*, quoted on p. 316.
36 Davie, *op. cit.*, quoted on p. 325.
37 MacDiarmid, *op. cit.*, p. 134 ('Drunk Man').
38 *Ibid.*, p. 94.
39 *Ibid.*, p. 118.
40 *Ibid.*, p. 131.

41 Burnet, *Essays and Addresses*, pp. 236-252.
42 *The Poems of John Davidson*, edited by Andrew Turnbull, Edinburgh, 1973, pp. 293-308.
43 Anderson, *Studies in Empirical Philosophy*, pp. 88-91.
44 *Ibid.*, p. 182.
45 N. Milton, *John Maclean: In the Rapids of Revolution*, London, 1978, pp. 249-250, letter to James Clunie written from Barlinnie Prison, 24 July 1922.
46 All to be found in *Studies in Empirical Philosophy*, p. 485.

Chapter 8: DRUNK MAN OR LUCKY POET?

1 Cf. Hume, *A Treatise of Human Nature*.
2 Anderson, *op. cit.*, pp. 186-7.
3 MacDiarmid, *Complete Poems*, pp. 287-290 ('Cencrastus').
4 *Ibid.*, p. 190.
5 MacDiarmid, *Lucky Poet: A self-study in literature and political ideas*, London, 1943, p. 402.
6 MacDiarmid, *Selected Essays*, London, 1969, p. 70.
7 *Ibid.*, pp. 69, 70.
8 Alfred Korzybski, *Science and Sanity*, New York, 1933, p. 384.
9 Testimonial in Korzybski, *op. cit.*
10 *Ibid.*
11 *Ibid.*
12 J. Passmore, Introduction to Anderson's *Studies in Empirical Philosophy*, p. xvii.
13 MacDiarmid, *Lucky Poet*, p. 347.
14 *Ibid.*, p. 348.
15 *Ibid.*
16 MacDiarmid, *Complete Poems*, p. 189 ('Cencrastus').
17 MacDiarmid, *Lucky Poet*, p. 348.
18 *Ibid.*, p. 343.
19 *Ibid.*, p. 346.
20 Playfair's *Euclid*, 7th ed., ed. Wallace, Edinburgh, 1826, p. 371.
21 Hamilton's edition of Reid, p. 148.
22 MacDiarmid, *op. cit.*, p. 283.
23 MacDiarmid, *Complete Poems*, p. 146 ('Drunk Man').
24 MacDiarmid, *Lucky Poet*, p. 283.
25 MacDiarmid, *Complete Poems*, p. 331 ('Milkwart and Bog Cotton').
26 *Ibid.*, p. 470 ('Lament for Great Music').
27 MacDiarmid, *Lucky Poet*, p. 281.
28 MacDiarmid, *Complete Poems*, p. 190 ('Cencrastus').
29 *Ibid.*, p. 635 ('To the Younger Scottish Writers').
30 *Ibid.*, p. 637.
31 *Ibid.*, p. 423 ('On a Raised Beach').

32   *Ibid.*, p. 424.
33   *Ibid.*, p. 432.

Chapter 9: THE PROBLEMS OF A PRIVILEGED SUBJECT

1   Grieve in *Pictish Review* (1927).
2   MacDiarmid, *Complete Poems*, p. 1252 ('The Dog Pool').
3   See for example, C. H. Waddington, *Behind Appearance*, Edinburgh, 1969.
4   Both in N. Kemp Smith, *The Credibility of Divine Existence*.
5   K. J. W. Craik, *The Nature of Explanation*, Cambridge, 1943, p. 69.
6   *Ibid.*, p. 73.
7   For example, Bower's first contact with Kant's *Critique of Pure Reason* was through Drever's notes of Kemp Smith's lectures.
8   Craik, *op. cit.*, p. 1.
9   A. Macpherson's paper to the Conference on the Nature of University Education, on the quatercentenary of the University of Edinburgh. Published in N. Phillipson (ed.), *Universities, Society and the Future*, Edinburgh, 1984.

Chapter 10: COMMON SENSE AND LOGIC

1   All in Anderson, *Education and Inquiry*.
2   Kemp Smith, *Prolegomena*.
3   G. E. Moore, *Philosophical Studies*, London, 1922, pp. 64-8.
4   In L. Marcil-Lacoste, *Claude Buffier and Thomas Reid*, Montreal, 1982, p. 189.
5   Thomas Brown, *Inquiry into the Relation of Cause and Effect*, and J. F. Ferrier, *Introduction to The Philosophy of Consciousness*.
6   William Dunbar, 'Schir, yet remember . . .', stanza 14.
7   Anderson, *Education and Inquiry* and *Studies in Empirical Philosophy*.

Chapter 11: ANDERSON VERSUS RYLE

1   In Gilbert Ryle, *Critical Essays* (Collected Papers, vol 1), London, 1971.
2   Anderson, *Studies in Empirical Philosophy*, p. 171.
3   Brown, *op. cit.*, p. 113.
4   Anderson, *op. cit.*, p. 161.
5   *Ibid.*, p. 181.
6   Ryle, quoted by Anderson, *Studies in Empirical Philosophy*, p. 181.
7   Anderson, *op. cit.*, p. 185.
8   Anderson, *op. cit.*, p. 185.
9   A. D. Ritchie, *Essays in Philosophy*, London, 1948, pp. 122-3.
10   Anderson, *Studies in Empirical Philosophy*, p. 64.

Chapter 12: SELF-CONSCIOUSNESS AND MUTUAL CONSCIOUSNESS

1   Anderson, *Studies in Empirical Philosophy*, p. 110.
2   *Ibid.*, p. 111.
3   Samuel Alexander, *Space, Time and Deity*, London, 1927, vol II, p. 32.
4   *Ibid.*, p. 32-3.
5   *Ibid.*, p. 25.
6   *Ibid.*, p. 150-1.
7   F. W. J. Schelling, trans. P. Heath, *System of Transcendental Idealism*, Charlottesville, 1978, pp. 71-3.
8   Alexander, *op. cit.*, p. 235.
9   Kemp Smith, *A Commentary to Kant's Critique of Pure Reason*, 2nd ed., London, 1923, p. xliv.
10 Anderson, *Studies in Empirical Philosophy*, p. 94.
11 Bertrand Russell, *An Inquiry into Meaning and Truth*, London, 1940, p. 230.
12 *Ibid.*, p. 147.
13 *Ibid.*, p. 262.
14 Wittgenstein, quoted by Russell, *op. cit.*, p. 268.
15 Wittgenstein, *Tractatus Logico-Philosophicus*, section 5.6331.

Chapter 13: THE OLD LOGIC AND THE NEW

1   Russell, 'The Philosophy of Logical Atomism', in R. C. Marsh (ed.), *Logic and Knowledge*.
2   R. M. Eaton, *General Logic*, London, 1931, p. 169.
3   *Ibid.*
4   Brand Blanshard, 'The Philosophy of Analysis' in *The Proceedings of the British Academy*, 1952. But see also Richard Rorty in P. A. Schillp (ed.), *The Philosophy of Brand Blanshard*, Illinois, 1980.
5   Eaton, *op. cit.*, p. 258.
6   Russell, *op. cit.*, p. 260.
7   Russell, quoted by Eaton, *op. cit.*, p. 264.
8   Eaton, *op. cit.*, pp. 259-61; Russell, *op. cit.*, pp. 199-202.
9   Russell, *op. cit.*, p. 199, 201.

Chapter 14: PLATO AND HEGEL

1   M. B. Foster, *The Political Philosophies of Plato and Hegel*, Oxford, 1935.

Chapter 15: FROM ATOMIC TO MOLECULAR PROPOSITIONS

1   Russell, *Inquiry into Meaning and Truth*, p. 63.
2   *Ibid.*, p. 77.
3   *Ibid.*
4   *Ibid.*, p. 129.

5   Hume, *Treatise*, book I, part I, section VII.
6   Russell, *op. cit.*, pp. 335-6.
7   *Ibid.*, p. 42.
8   *Ibid.*, p. 42.
9   *Ibid.*, p. 82.
10 *Ibid.*, p. 104.
11 *Ibid.*, p. 82.
12 Kemp Smith, *The Credibility of Divine Existence*, p. 299.
13 Russell, 'The Philosophy of Logical Atomism', in Marsh, *op. cit.*, pp. 102-124.
14 Sir William Hamilton, *Discussions on Philosophy and Literature, Education and University Reform*, 2nd ed., London, 1853, p. 707.
15 See the end of the second Dialogue. In A. Campbell Fraser's edition of Berkeley's Works, see vol I, p. 438.

Chapter 16: THE PROBLEM OF CAUSALITY

1   Russell, *An Inquiry into Meaning and Truth*, p. 46.
2   Cf. Alexander, *op. cit.*, pp. 170-176.
3   *Ibid.*, pp. 174-5.
4   Russell, *op. cit.*, p. 98.
5   *Ibid.*, pp. 99, 100.
6   *Ibid.*, p. 101.
7   *Ibid.*, p. 103.
8   Section I, para. 3.
9   Hume, *Treatise*, ed. Selby-Bigge, pp. 37-8, with 65.
10 Bergson, *Time and Free Will*, trans. F. L. Pogson, London, 1910, parts I and II.
11 Kemp Smith, *A Commentary to Kant's Critique of Pure Reason*, 2nd ed., pp. 360-1.
12 *Ibid.*, pp. 366-7.
13 *Ibid.*, pp. 367.
14 Kemp Smith, *op. cit.*, 3rd ed., pp. 444-446.
15 Hume, *Treatise*, pp. 197-198.
16 *Ibid.*, p. 210.
17 Hume, quoted by Brown in his *Inquiry into the Relation of Cause and Effect*, 4th ed., p. 292.
18 *Ibid.*, part IV, section III.
19 For example, Ferrier, *Lectures and Philosophical Remains*, vol II, pp. 326-8, 366.
20 Hume, *op. cit.*, p. 231.
21 *Ibid*, p. 231.
22 *Ibid.*, p. 230.
23 Fraser Cowley, *A Critique of British Empiricism*, London, 1968, pp. 93-105.

24 Hume, *op. cit.*, p. 365.
25 Adam Smith, *A Theory of Moral Sentiments*, part III, chapter 1, paragraph 3.

INDEX

Aberdeen, University of, 28, 31
A Drunk Man Looks at the Thistle,
    see MacDiarmid, Hugh
*Adam Smith as Student and Profes-
    sor* (W. R. Scott), 178
Adamson, Robert, 131-2
Adamson, Rt. Hon. William, 53
Agamemnon, 95
Aguilonius, 187
Alexander, Samuel; his philosophy
    in sharp contrast to Russell's and
    Ryle's, 195, 197, 200, 204;
    superior to Anderson on the
    problem of knowledge of our own
    and others' minds, 209-214, 217;
    source of Anderson's doctrine of
    the categories, 221; and causality,
    224-30, 237, 242-3, 246, 248-9.
Ampère, 260
Analysis and Dialectic, (J. J. Russell),
    173, 180, 263
Anderson, John; defends Greek
    geometry against modern, 36;
    defends the Classical tie-up of
    literature and science, against their
    Romantic separation, 40; Kemp
    Smith's view of original sin and
    Pelagianism, 50; criticises Ashby's
    educational ideas, 61-3; opposes
    Dewey's version of social experi-
    ment as the key to the elimination
    of antagonisms, 63-67; Dewey's
    particularism inferior to Arnold's
    Hellenism, 67-72; remedy for the
    problem of routinisation from the
    philosophical criticism of life, 72-
    77; Burnet, not Dewey, the guide,
    77-85; Dewey destroys the tragic
    sense of life, 85-95; contrast with

C. M. Grieve who moves from a
    Burnet-like classicism to a
    Russell-like modernism, 99-105,
    109-115, 122-3, 125, 130-4, 143,
    149-150,171, 173, 180, 185-6, 188-
    9; versus Russell and Ryle, 191-
    210, 213, 221, 228-230, 240, 242,
    248, 260
Anderson, R. D., 26, 32
Annals of the Five Senses, (Grieve),
    102
Antigone, 95
antisyzygy, 115
Appleby, Sir Humphrey, 163
Appleton, Sir Edward, 101
Aristotle, 22, 77, 85, 133; apple,
    qualities of, 138, 141-144, 150,
    162, 186-188, 194, 251, 258, 260,
    262
Armstrong, 62
Arnold, Matthew, v, 40, 68-70, 73,
    80, 84, 102, 130, 236
Art and Reality, (J. Anderson), 102,
    173
artificial intelligence, 99-100, 168-9,
    179, 217
Arts (faculties and curriculum), 4, 5,
    15, 23, 28-9, 46, 60, 158-9, 164,
    172-3, 176
Ashby, Sir Eric, 62-3, 81-2
Athens, 105; values of, 184; 222
Augustine, 52
Australia(n), 50, 61, 86, 102, 171, 190
Australian Journal of Philosophy,
    230

Bacon, i
Baillie, J. B., 49
Bain, Alexander, 48

McDonald, 166
Macfie, A. L., 177
McGillivray, Duncan, 8, 30, 47
Mackay, John, 34
Mackie, 62
Maclaurin, Colin, 34-5
Maclean, John, 51, 131
MacLean, Sorley, 157
MacMurray, 163-4, 170, 174, 185, 190
Macpherson, Andrew, 173
Mair, John, 133, 174, 179, 180, 189, 195
Malinowski, 148
Mansel, 186
Manual of Psychology, (Stout), 253
Marx, -ist, -ism, 7, 86, 102, 130, 163, 176
Masson, David, 41-45, 103, 114, 122-3
mathematics; position in curriculum, iv, 5, 22, 25, 27-32; a priori and a posteriori approaches to, 33-37, 38, 54, 131-2, 140
Maxwell, James Clerk, 108, 260
Merleau-Ponty, 117, 151, 239
Middle Ages, 20, 64, 83
Mill, J. S., 56, 124, 162, 192, 250
Moore, G. E., 184-6, 188, 213, 229, 246, 260
Muir, Edwin, 146-7, 157

Napier, John, 88
Nature of Explanation, The, (Craik), 169
Neill, A. S., 50, 140
New Age, The, (ed. Orage), 101-2, 104, 134
Newton's law of gravity, 215, 216
Nietzsche, -anism, 49, 111-2, 121
Norway, Norwegian, 92, 104

Ode to Joy, (Schiller), 86
Oppenheimer, 157
Orage, A. R., 101, 134

Ordinance 70, ii, 3, 27-33, 36-38, 40, 46, 49, 54, 57, 60-62, 99, 101, 110, 124, 129, 157, 159
Ordinary Arts Degree, 38, 56, 158-9
original sin, vi, 50-52
Ouspensky, 119-20
Oxenhorn, H., 107-8, 112, 119, 120, 126, 129, 133, 156
Oxford, University of, vi, 4, 9, 12-3, 26, 58, 164, 175-6

Parapsychology, Chair of, 170
Parmenides, 78
Passmore, John, 50, 62
patent law, 15
Paterson, Professor, 55
Peano, 193, 221, 223
Pelagian, -ism, vi, 52, 95, 121, 130, 161
Penny Wheep, (MacDiarmid), 104
Perfectibility of Man, The, (Passmore), 50
Philebus, 75, 154
philosophy, position in the curriculum, iv, 3, 23-4, 32-3, 38, 41, 43, 46-57, 60-1, 157-79
philosophy, 60-1, 137, 147, 151, 167-180
Philosophy and Political Economy, (Bonar), 178
Phenomenology of Perception, (Merleau-Ponty), 117
Phenomenology of the Spirit, (Hegel), 214
physics, iv, 25, 30-1, 79, 132, 138
Pictish Review, 159
Pinkerton, Peter, 34
Plato, 16, 74, 78, 85, 106, 187, 203, 224-228, 233, 245, 260, 262
Playfair, John, 85, 150
Playfair, Lyon, 62
poetry, 79, 83, 93-4, 106, 147
Political Philosophies of Plato and Hegel, The, (Foster), 224
Popper, 143, 191-2, 243

INDEX

Theaetetus, 16, 75, 78, 203-4, 245
thermodynamics, second law of, stated in different ways, 40
Theory of Moral Sentiments, (Adam Smith), 119, 210
Thomson, Arthur, 173
Thomson, Godfrey, 47, 53-4
Thorndike, 6, 14, 16, 18, 48, 57, 77
Thucydides, 15
Time and Free Will, (Bergson), 249
To Circumjack Cencrastus, see MacDiarmid, Hugh
Tractatus Logico-Philosophicus, (Wittgenstein), 217
Trades Union Congress, 53
Traditional Formal Logic, (Sinclair), 161
Treatise of Human Nature, (Hume), 130, 253, 255-257
Trevarthen, Professor, 170
Trocchi, Alexander, 158
Trondheim, University of, 190

Utopia, materialist, 63, 135, 189

Valéry, Paul, 147
Veitch, John, 178
Von Hügel-Kemp Smith Letters, The, (ed. Barmann), 173

Waddington, C. H., 166
Wealth of Nations, The, (Adam Smith), 177
Whitehead, 141-143, 220, 235, 242, 247
Whittaker, E. T., 29-38, 43, 54, 131-2
Wittgenstein, 193, 196, 216-7
Workers' Educational Association (W.E.A.), 51-53

283